Plague of Strangers

URBAN LIFE AND URBAN LANDSCAPE SERIES

Zane L. Miller and Henry D. Shapiro
General Editors

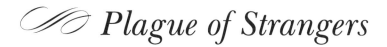

Plague of Strangers

*Social Groups and the Origins of City Services
in Cincinnati, 1819–1870*

Alan I Marcus

Ohio State University Press

Columbus

Library of Congress Cataloging-in-Publication Data

Marcus, Alan I, 1949–
    Plague of strangers : social groups and the origins of city
services in Cincinnati, 1819–1870 / Alan I Marcus.
        p.   cm. — (Urban life and urban landscape series)
    Includes index.
    ISBN 0–8142–0550–X
    1. Urban policy—Ohio—Cincinnati—History—19th century.
    2. Municipal services—Ohio—Cincinnati—History—19th century.
    3. Municipal government—Ohio—Cincinnati—History—19th century.
    4. Human services—Ohio—Cincinnati—History—19th century.
    I. Title.   II. Series.
    HN80.C55M37   1991
    361.2'5'0977178—dc20   91–16750
                                                                          CIP

Printed in the U.S.A.
9 8 7 6 5 4 3 2 1

To Gregory Vance Marcus

for his persistent questioning and
pugnacious spirit

Contents

 *Foreword*

If history is the story of people solving problems, then the historian's first task is to figure out what those problems were. That is difficult enough when the problem solvers of the past don't tell us what they were up to, and we have to go behind their actions to discover the drama in which they were the players. But it is even more difficult when the problem solvers of the past *do* tell us what they were up to. Then we have to go behind their explanations as well as their actions. Their telling was itself a form of problem solving—an attempt to understand the world in which they lived, an effort to establish the legitimacy of their actions as appropriate responses to real problems, and an assertion of the accuracy of their perceptions of their current situation. It was this situation, according to them, that created the problems to begin with. Then especially the historian must be wary. For if the problem solvers of the past were successful in persuading their contemporaries that a problem existed, and ought to be addressed in a particular way, the *history* of their activities will be the story of how they tried to solve that particular problem. Who are we to say that that's not what they were doing?

Because of our commonsense expectations that history will tell us how *then* became *now*, moreover, the activities of the past will appear to us, as it could not have to them, as steps from their time to ours, thus as necessary if not ineluctable stages in the evolution of American

ix

culture and institutions. And the danger is that their actions—in defining problems as well as in trying to solve
them—will lose their character as historical events, the
products of intention and volition and especially of interpretation, and become mere *facts,* unavailable as such
to historical analysis.

This is the difficulty that Alan Marcus confronts so
successfully here, in a volume that is as interesting to me
for what he does as for what he says. He notices first of
all that during the middle decades of the nineteenth
century virtually all American cities experienced a transformation in the style, the structure, and especially the
function of municipal government. At the beginning of
the period, city governments were organized to facilitate
the economic activity of their residents by maintaining
streets, market houses, and a supply of water sufficient
to the needs of local manufactures, or by meeting such
temporary threats to the viability of economic activity as
the occurrence of riot or epidemic disease. At the end of
the period, by contrast, city governments were organized
to protect the cohesiveness of the urban community itself by prohibiting patterns of "inappropriate behavior"
among its own residents—the sale of adulterated foodstuffs, the distribution of impure water to domestic or
commercial users, criminal activity of a variety of kinds,
"unhealthy" activity like eating unripe produce or living
in a tenement house, and finally *inefficient* activity, including the inadequate delivery of public services by in-
competent bureaucrats or corrupt politicians.

This transformation comprises the familiar "municipal revolution" of the mid-nineteenth century, which
yielded "modern" systems of city governance designed
to satisfy "modern" notions about the needs of the urban community, and thus seems to stand at the beginning of urban history as we know it and care about it in
our own time. From our perspective, indeed, the munici-

pal revolution appears as a triumphal achievement in which the "prerevolutionary" structures of city governance were extended and elaborated, despite the political resistance of conservative state legislators from rural regions, in response to real changes in the scale and complexity of the urban situation. It may also be read as a sign of the essential health of American city government throughout its history, the story of a kind of Lamarckian evolution in which the little acorns of the colonial cities grew to mighty oaks by adapting to the harsh climate of contemporary needs instead of enjoying the benign influence of contemporary opportunity.

From the perspective of *the past,* however, the municipal revolution takes quite a different shape. Marcus notices, for example, that the achievements of the mid-century involved no simple accretion of powers or responsibilities to existing agencies of city government but rather the creation of new agencies, sometimes with the same names as the old, including that most fundamental of new agencies, the municipal corporation itself. He notices that contemporaries recognized the newness of these new institutions, explicitly in their arguments based on the need for them and implicitly in their debates about what form they should take and who, in the absence of precedent, should control them—the state, the county, the city, or "the public" through boards of trustees or commissioners.

Marcus also notices that these innovations occurred in much the same way and at about the same time irrespective of the size, location, or age of a city, and irrespective of its particular history or current condition. Explanations of the municipal revolution as a response to real changes in the scale and complexity of urban life, or as the product of a particular city's particular culture or characteristics—both were regular themes in the contemporary debates and have been carried verbatim into the historiography of the American city—are thus brought into question. In Cincinnati, moreover—as good a place for detailed examination as any other—the "contemporary conditions" that the municipal revolution was said to address long antedated their recognition as problems and all attempts to solve them through the instrumentalities of city governance.

So what was going on? Implicit in the mid-nineteenth century transformation of city government, Marcus finds, was a new definition of the city as a social unit. One result was that cities themselves could no longer be viewed as accidental concentrations of diverse individuals pursuing competing, potentially conflicting, economic goals. Instead, as in the parallel (and contemporary) case of the nation and its people, the place and its residents became conflated, so that in the city defined as cohesive community, patterns of conflict or competition appeared to threaten not only the viability but even the reality of each city as community. A second result was that cities had to be differentiated on the one hand from other kinds of corporations, and on the other hand from other kinds of governance units within each state, by being given new kinds of charters, specifying new kinds of powers, for new kinds of purposes. The very existence of the city as community, therefore, came to be seen as the result of intention rather than of accident. But if it was the product of intention, what was it for? Certainly not to serve as the locus of behaviors inimical to its very existence! A third result was, thus, that certain conventional patterns of behavior could no longer be viewed as isolated actions of individuals but became threats to social harmony and social cohesion—to the "health" of the municipal body politic—which the new institutions of city government, including the new boards of health, were explicitly designed to preserve.

In the process of defining new functions for city government and allocating duties to particular agencies, moreover, the municipal revolutionaries of the midcentury were led first to attempt some explanation of what was new about prostitution in the city, or gambling, or catching the cholera, and then to identify and classify those behaviors that seemed inappropriate in a city conceived as a social unit. What they thought was new, Marcus tells us, wasn't prostitution or gambling or catching the cholera per se, but the prevalence within the city of persons who were so ill-adapted to community life as to engage in inappropriate behaviors of these sorts. They were the "strangers" of his title—in-migrants from rural regions in America or abroad, children not yet "cultivated" out of their natural state of savagery, and those so debased or so unethical as to constitute an under-world of criminals; and their presence seemed to constitute a plague as dangerous as the cholera itself.

Nonetheless, it was their behavior that was to be prohibited, not themselves, and this led to the construction of criminal codes, sanitary codes, and so forth, in which the varieties of inappropriate behaviors were classified so that the police would know what they were supposed to do and the street scrapers would know what *they* were supposed to do. It was then only a short step from the classification of inappropriate behaviors into distinct kinds to the classification of persons engaging in such behaviors as distinct groups within the population. By then the city as social unit seemed indeed to be at risk; but it was this in particular that fascinated the writers and social reformers of the later nineteenth century who went adventuring down the street instead of across the deserts and reported with glee on the "deviant" populations inhabiting the cities they themselves chose to call home—the prostitutes and the poets, the politicians,

businessmen, criminals, immigrants, laborers—have I
left anyone out? Pencil in "the professors." Marcus exam-
ines the way these new notions reinforced each other
and yielded that "modern" city in which we live, and
where, for better or worse, we persist in asserting the
value of community even while we celebrate the diversity
and richness of urban life.

Henry D. Shapiro

 Acknowledgments

$O_{ver\ the\ course}$ of a project, you run up debts. Acknowledgments are a way of letting the generous parties know you remember and appreciate their myriad contributions. Zane L. Miller and Henry D. Shapiro have involved themselves with this manuscript from its beginnings as a dissertation and have suffered me for many years. Also at this project's birth were Peter Harsham, Judith Spraul-Schmidt, Robert B. Fairbanks, Ellen Corwin Cangi, Saul T. Benison, and Howard P. Segal. John Duffy, David Katzman, Mark Rose, John Burnham, Mark Foster, and Jon Teaford have read all or part of the manuscript at some point and provided invaluable comments. Present and former colleagues at Iowa State University—Joanne Abel Goldman, Hamilton Cravens, Richard Lowitt, and Robert E. Schofield—have no doubt seen this manuscript in more forms than they would have liked. Nonetheless, they unfailingly managed to put on an enthusiastic front and offer encouragement as well as trenchant remarks. The Vigilantes, an informal group of Iowa State University history faculty, read a chapter and carried on a spirited discussion. Charles Isetts and Barbara Holcomb, formerly of the History of Health Sciences Library and Museum, Health Sciences Library, University of Cincinnati Medical Center, and Frances Forman and Edward Rider of the Cincinnati Historical Society graciously assisted with the inevitable research problems. Others at the aforementioned

repositories as well as the staffs of the Health Sciences
Library, University of Cincinnati Medical Center; Medical History Division, Special Collections Department,
University of Cincinnati Central Library; Hamilton
County Law Library; Cincinnati Public Library; and the
Clerk of Council Office, City of Cincinnati, provided
much help. A special nod should go to then Cincinnati
city councilman David Mann, who I knew only tangen-
tially but whose name I ruthlessly and loudly invoked
whenever city bureaucrats tried to get rid of me by announcing that documents I knew existed had been "destroyed in the 1884 courthouse fire." Special thanks to
Jean, Eunice, Frank, Gregory, Jocelyn, and Heathcliff
Marcus and Marjorie Marcus Schulz, who increase the
joy of writing through their unswerving support and
patience.

 *Introduction*

The role of government in American life has been the subject of intense public scrutiny during the past decade. Not all critics agree, of course, but the thrust of public sentiment is quite evident. We must "get government off our backs." American society is deemed overburdened by governmental regulations and hampered by governmental interference; government has invaded the nation's economic and social life and sapped its vitality. To those who view the contemporary situation in that manner, the remedy is clear. Government needs to be restricted, the functions it usurped returned to the public sector.

Advocates of privatization tend to focus on the national government and argue that governmental intervention is but a recent occurrence. But the regular involvement of government in social and economic questions is much more deeply ingrained in the American fabric than they realize. Its origins do not rest in FDR's New Deal, the Progressive Era, or even the Gilded Age. They do not even lie with the federal government. Regular governmental intercedence was firmly entrenched on a nationwide scale before the national government became interested in centralizing authority to tackle social and economic issues.

Local governments, particularly municipal governments, have been engaged in the business of regulation much longer. As Jon C. Teaford has shown in his impressive *The Municipal Revolution in America: Origins of Modern Urban Government, 1650–1825* (Chicago: University of Chicago Press, 1975), city governments in the colonial period maintained rigid control of economic activities, regulating such things as who could work in a city, the number of citizens employed in various types of enterprises, and the prices of commodities and other goods. And Teaford's study indicates that virtually all colonial cities did so in roughly the same way. The effect of this independent, yet similar, regulation from city to city was to create a sort of regulatory system that spanned the English colonies; there was a set of nationwide economic regulations before there was a nation.

That city governments in the colonial period all functioned with respect to economic matters in a similar manner suggests that their framers clung to a common definition of the role of local government. The absence of persistent debate or even frequent expressions of concern about the propriety or the desirability of that definition implies that it was much more broadly held. Colonials generally seemed to accept and approve of city government's mission. Apparently a consensus had been achieved that city government was responsible for the citizen's economic health.

Teaford finds in the colonial period no similar *de facto* agreement that city government should on a regular basis regulate *social* affairs. His evidence reveals that those responsibilities lay outside city government's purview. Nevertheless, Teaford infers that the crucial juncture stood sometime after about 1825, although he offers virtually no evidence to sustain that claim. Those historians who have traced the evolution of a single aspect of city government, such as the police, have refined Teaford's analysis. They maintain that it was in the mid-nineteenth century that American city government first assumed authority to regulate the social environment. It was during the midcentury years that these regulatory agencies were created and stamped with municipal power.

While single-agency studies aid in the identification process, they also mislead. The extension of municipal influence into the social arena was not an event limited to a single agency or task. It constituted a fundamental reconceptualization of the role of city government. City administration was markedly different in both form and function in 1870 than it had been at the century's start. Characterized by a proliferation of new municipal institutions, laws, and bureaucracies, city governments in 1870 bore more in common with those of the twentieth century than the eighteenth. The provision and regular delivery of a broad range of municipal social services stood at the crux of the matter. From the mid-nineteenth century to the present, city governments have expressly sought to maintain the social environment on a fulltime basis.

Preserving the social environment was a new responsibility for midcentury city governments. It amounted to a matter of intent. For example, early nineteenth century municipally sponsored water for business purposes—massive amounts were needed for different manufacturing processes and for putting out fires in business establishments—was not a social service, while mid-nineteenth century publicly provided water to help prevent disease was. Similarly, an early nineteenth century storm sewer near a business was a commercial service but a home-connected sewer system to carry off wastes and prevent disease constituted a social service. How municipalities came to take on the duty of providing social services, how they developed mechanisms to maintain society, and what instruments they deemed appropriate to the mission are important questions both in terms of the contemporary debate and for American urban history. Historians have been silent on these points; they have not produced a book-length study that provides comprehensive treatment of the origins and development of municipal social services of even a single city. Two works have marked out some important territory, however. Hendrik Hartog's fine legal history *Public Property and Private Power: The Corporation of the City of New York in American Law, 1730–1870* (Chapel Hill: University of North Carolina Press, 1983) covers aspects of midcentury municipal redirection in terms of a rising professional judicial bureaucracy and changing city-state relations. Hartog's work is contrasted with that of Michael Frisch, who takes an internal, presentist perspective. In his *Town into City: Springfield, Massachusetts, and the Meaning of Community, 1840–1880* (Cambridge: Harvard University Press, 1972), Frisch sees antebellum municipal institution building as a natural stage in the shift of the city's social complexion. Introduction of new, different peoples unleashed new social forces, which destroyed Springfield's vaunted cultural homogeneity and moved it down a path toward cultural heterogeneity.

This monograph seeks to go beyond Hartog and Frisch. Its initial focus is on one city, Cincinnati, Ohio. The apparent narrowness of that decision is deliberate. Only by examining in detail a single city can the minutiae of process be considered in the depth sufficient to trace the evolution of municipal action and the rationales for the creation of specific mechanisms.

The process by which Cincinnati city government assumed responsibility for maintaining the social environment was not a simple linear one. Indeed, the municipality offered no social services prior to about 1840. After that date, moreover, the city did not develop one institution after another until it had completed a wide range of social regulatory agencies. Instead, in the 1840s and at its citizens' behest, it erected an entire range in the space of a few short years. Though it initially gained the approval of city inhabitants, that range of new municipal institutions did not remain in favor long. By the mid 1850s and despite the innovations of the 1840s, city residents continually complained that city government had not regulated the social environment. City government did not add to its established institutions, however. Rather, city officials scrapped or modified dramatically their recently developed creations and engaged in a new flurry of institution building and agency formation. What emerged from these activities in the mid 1850s and after was a range of institutions very different from the city's earlier effort.

The events in Cincinnati, then, demonstrate that city government abruptly developed social services and just as suddenly redesigned the agencies or replaced them with new and different ones. Despite its local focus, however, Cincinnati's story has implications for the history of American municipal social services generally. It provides a basis of comparison with other American municipalities. Results of that comparison are striking. It seems that virtually every major American city erected municipal social mechanisms similar to those of Cincinnati at about the same time. As important, these cities apparently overhauled or changed these social engines at a time roughly contemporaneous to Cincinnati and in similar ways. And most significantly, their residents offered similar explanations for the changes.

That cities across America manifested a pattern of municipal activities quite like that of Cincinnati is suggestive. It indicates that neither the growth of municipal responsibility for conducting social relations nor the development of social agencies appropriate for the mission was coterminus with the physical growth and development of cities. Coupled with the fact that citizens in these diverse places provided similar justifications for the origins and development of municipal social services, the similarities of structure and function of municipal governments imply that local demographic and political factors played only a peripheral role in the process. Rather than a mere creature of local circumstances or politics, American city government during the first three-quarters of the nineteenth century apparently also operated within and was the product of a larger framework. No major American city was an island. Each city's inhabitants seemed in some cases to hold common ideas, visions, and social desires. This commonality was reflected in form and function of municipal governments. It meant that midcentury local governments had instituted, in effect, nationwide social regulation.

But this nationwide commonality among cities, their residents, and governments was not regularly acknowledged or identified as such until after the Civil War. Prior to that time, Americans rarely considered the various situations faced by city residents as characteristically urban. These problems and conditions seemed instead the consequence of large and/or dense aggregations of people exhibiting different behaviors. They were crises of American civilization generally, which manifested themselves among concentrated populations, and those sites suffering them were different from other places only because of population concentration or number. That was no small matter, of course, but it did not mark cities as distinctive. Only in the post–Civil War years were cities routinely viewed as peculiar, as fundamentally different from other social environments, an acknowledgment that encouraged city residents to form nationwide mechanisms to confer about, plan, and organize municipal action. In sum, there was in America *de facto* nationwide municipal social regulations several decades before there was an explicit nationwide municipal system.

1 *Serving the American Public*

Few American cities underwent as dramatic a transformation as Cincinnati in the period 1820–1870. In 1820, it stood as a fairly small place, its population resting at roughly 10,000. Four decades later, it was a bustling metropolis, the most populous city in mid-America and the sixth largest in the nation. It was the home of more than 160,000 people. As a tramontane city, Cincinnati was settled much later than most east coast municipalities and as early as 1820 might well be described as a city of immigrants. In that year, native-born Cincinnatians comprised only a handful of the city's residents. Few were even from the state of Ohio. By 1860, however, about half the city's population hailed either from Cincinnati or Ohio.

The city's location and its excellent harborage contributed to its distinctive history. Situated on the Ohio River and at the terminus of the Miami and Erie Canal, it possessed exceptional connections to both New Orleans and New York. And as a consequence, it was intimately tied not only to the east and south, but also to Europe; it accepted extraordinary numbers of European emigres as well as products from foreign ports. Although part of the old Northwest Territory, Cincinnati did not participate in that region's spate of railroad building in the late 1840s and early 1850s and was bypassed by the great eastern trunk lines, which ran well north of the Queen City. The city also had its reverses.

1

By about 1850, it had lost its cherished "Porkopolis" mantle to Chicago, which emerged as the nation's hog slaughtering headquarters, and began to lose ground to New York City in its efforts to become America's book publishing center.

Though Cincinnati was only on the periphery of what would become America's urban industrial heartland, its midcentury citizens were quite familiar with manufacturing. During its reign as the Queen City of the West, a disproportionate number of its residents by mid-nineteenth century standards engaged in some form of this endeavor, often on quite a large scale. It would not be incorrect, perhaps, to suggest that Cincinnati in the mid-nineteenth century experienced a sort of incipient industrialization, which, when coupled with the heavy influx of immigrants and the city's great population growth, foreshadowed the rapid industrialization, urbanization, and immigration that marked late nineteenth century American cities.[1]

All these factors, and others too numerous to mention, combined to make Cincinnati's story unique. The city had its own particular history, different than any other municipality's history. That is, of course, the crux of local history; its practitioners attempt to delineate those forces and social dislocations peculiar to a place and assign them a causative role in later occurrences. But that approach fails for some historical phenomena, one of which is the origin of municipal social services. Though the events of Cincinnati's past were peculiar, its case is not; many American municipalities erected similar governmental institutions and gave them similar powers and tasks at similar times. Put another way, the history of municipal social services suggests that local circumstances were not deterministic but rather provided residents with a focus and rationale for action.

Comparison of Cincinnati with other cities makes that point clear. Virtually every significant American municipality in the early nineteenth century held powers remarkably similar to those of small, western, cosmopolitan Cincinnati and undertook similar duties. Though each city received an individual charter, passed by a special act of the appropriate state legislature, all city governments were very much alike. A city's size, demography, age, political composition, or location did not seem to matter. Nor did the date of the charter's enactment, whether in the century's first decade or in the early years of its fourth. Together these charters indicate the existence in early nineteenth century America of a common and dominant definition of the municipal corporation as a territorial agency within whose boundaries individuals gathered to engage in the pursuit of commerce and manufacturing and whose sole responsibility consisted of providing the opportunity for that pursuit, whether through regulation or by some other means.

Baltimore's first charter, granted by the Maryland legislature in 1796 before the city's remarkable burst of growth, provides a good example. The Monument City's charter, as with those of Cincinnati, defined the boundaries of the city and divided it into wards, mandated the structure of municipal government, and established the manner in which city elections must be conducted. It also incorporated the City of Baltimore, providing city government with all the powers common to corporate bodies in the period and giving it the right to assess private property within the city limits and to collect taxes thereon. The charter then stipulated that the City Council of Baltimore could pass all laws and ordinances necessary to keep the city "in good order," and listed only a few services, all of them designed to protect the

security of the city and therefore the individual's right
and opportunity to participate in commerce and manufacturing. More precisely, the charter permitted council
to prohibit the construction of wooden buildings in
crowded areas, to "provide for the safe storage of gunpowder and naval stores," to elect a constable, to "license
auctions and pawnbrokers," to "restrain and prohibit
gaming," and to "provide for the safekeeping of the
standard of weights." The charter also authorized council to erect and to regulate public pumps, which were
then necessary for market activity, to maintain the port
and the markets, and to survey the terrain of the city, establishing "new streets, lots, lanes and alleys."

The Baltimore charter of 1796 also contained provisions through which the city could deal with emergencies. It directed council to divide the city into fire
districts, to purchase firefighting apparatus, and to
sanction, through the passage of laws governing their
organization, volunteer fire companies. In a similar
manner, it permitted council whenever it deemed necessary "to establish night watches," and "to erect or build
houses of correction, hospitals, or pest houses," either
inside the city or beyond its limits. Finally, the charter
provided for the creation of a board of health commissioners and, "whenever necessary to preserve the health
of the city," for the board to assume power. At those
times, the board's duties included the "prevention and
removal of nuisances" and the establishment of a quarantine "to prevent the introduction of contagious diseases within the city, and within three miles of the
same."[2]

Boston, which received its initial city charter in 1822,
provides another example. A city different in several aspects from Cincinnati or Baltimore, Boston was given
all the privileges and responsibilities common to early
nineteenth century municipal corporations. It was per-

mitted to contract with other parties and to collect taxes and disperse public monies and was required to issue an annual financial statement. The charter also authorized council to lay out and repair streets, to maintain the port, to form a school committee for the direction of the city's common schools, to establish "public buildings" and to pay for their maintenance, and to appoint a city clerk, a register of deeds, and a city treasurer. It furthermore gave council "full and exclusive power to grant licenses to innholders, victuallers, retailers and confectioners," to take from them bonds of surety, and to suspend their privileges, if, in council's judgment, "the order and welfare of said city shall require it."

The Boston charter of 1822 also provided for the appointment of fire wardens, a police warden, and a board of health commissioners. The fire wardens, one selected for each of the city's wards, merely guided the activities during fires of volunteer fire companies and possessed no other duties. The police warden of the City of Boston was charged "to preserve order and decorum" in the municipality and "to repress all riotous, tumultuous and disorderly conduct," and to that end could when necessary enlist others "as may appear necessary to preserve order and decorum, and to prevent the interruption of peace and quiet." The charter also enabled council to set up a board of health, and authorized the board to take action at those times at which "the health, cleanliness, comfort and order of the said city may, in [its] judgment, require."[3]

The municipal charters granted to the cities of Cincinnati, Baltimore, and Boston in the early nineteenth century described and delineated a particular role for municipal government. This role was not limited to these cities, but also found expression in the government of early nineteenth century cities as diverse as Pittsburgh, granted its first municipal charter in 1815,

Louisville (1828), Providence (1831), Rochester, New
York (1834), and Newark, New Jersey (1835).[4]

Not all evidence for the similarity of municipal
governments comes from their charters, however. An investigation of their operations helps bolster the case.
Studies of various cities or branches of government
demonstrate that early nineteenth century American
city governments exercised policing, fire, health, and relief powers only when the city in question was threatened with a catastrophe that seemed to inhibit its
residents' opportunities to pursue commerce and manufacturing. Certainly no contemporary city possessed a
paid standing police force. To be sure, early nineteenth
century Philadelphia, St. Louis, New York, Detroit, Lexington, Boston, Louisville, Milwaukee, Rochester, Pittsburgh, and Washington employed a city marshal or
constable and some deputies, but these men did not constitute a regular police force. The temporary, ad hoc nature of their duties can be seen in the manner that these
officials were paid. Cities rewarded these men with either *per diem* wages for time actually spent in municipal
service or standardized fees for specific acts. Nor did a
night watch comprise a police force. While most of the
aforementioned cities sponsored a night watch for some
part of the early nineteenth century, it was composed of
men moonlighting from their regular daytime jobs.
These watchmen guarded the city's manufacturing and
commercial establishments during the night season—
they did not walk beats—and were paid by the night.[5]

And for police emergencies during the period, such
as riots, municipalities relied on neither marshals nor
watchmen. Instead, cities as different as Detroit, Louisville, Boston, Philadelphia, St. Louis, New York, and
Lexington turned at the onset of a disturbance to standing militias, volunteer paramilitary forces, or citizens'
groups. In effect, city governments deputized these

men for the duration of the crisis, often placing them under the marshals' direction. As soon as cities were once again quiet, the municipalities withdrew their sanction of these forces. City leaders thanked the men for their diligence and sometimes rewarded them for quelling the riot, but no longer considered them municipal employees.[6]

Cities relied upon firefighting mechanisms established according to similar premises. Prior to about 1850, American municipalities often owned firefighting equipment and had designated some individuals to guide firefighting. Frequently identified as fire wardens, these men did not constitute a fulltime fire agency; they neither regularly enforced a city's fire laws nor were responsible alone for extinguishing fires. The actual firefighting was left to volunteer fire companies. Fire wardens only investigated individual complaints about fire nuisances and coordinated the volunteer fire companies' efforts. And as an indication of their ad hoc status, wardens were paid only for days devoted to those tasks. Likewise, volunteer companies received compensation only after fighting blazes and generally not from municipal treasuries. Although they usually used equipment purchased by city governments, companies secured their rewards from grateful property owners, whose establishments had been saved, and from insurance companies. Such was the case in cities as separate and distinctive as Boston, Louisville, St. Louis, Wheeling, Charleston, Philadelphia, Richmond, New Orleans, Washington, Lexington, Utica, and Pittsburgh. This list is far from complete, however. As early as 1811, there were in America forty volunteer fire companies.[7]

The ad hoc, crisis-oriented approach to early nineteenth century municipal problems, manifested so clearly in riot control and firefighting, also extended to poor relief and epidemics. In both cases, municipalities

generally created standing boards to deal with these issues, but empowered these institutions to function only
when catastrophes occurred. Though detailed studies
of poor relief in individual cities are rather slim, it
seems that cities regularly formed boards of overseers to
the poor, but permitted them to act only when city-
menacing crises, such as frigid winters or economic de-
pressions, prohibited large numbers from working. Only
with the threat of massive unemployment and lawlessness—the disruption of normal municipal operations—
did the provision of relief become a subject for city
governments; at all other times it remained the province
of private benevolence.[8]

A much larger body of literature exists on early nineteenth century health boards. In cities as dissimilar as
New Orleans, Pittsburgh, New York, Charlestown, New
Haven, Detroit, Norfolk, Louisville, Wheeling, Milwaukee, Lexington, Newark, Charleston, Baltimore, Chicago, and Boston, these institutions all operated in the
same way. Health boards served to fight epidemics, coming into play only when cities suffered scourges or were
about to do so. Though their members technically remained in office, and although the nuisance laws under
which they operated were still on the books, health
boards were authorized to spend municipal monies and
to exercise their extensive quarantine and cleanup powers only during epidemic emergencies; they could act
only when such epidemics threatened cities' abilities to
provide individual opportunity for the pursuit of commerce and manufacturing.[9]

The provision in cities throughout early nineteenth
century America of police, fire, relief, and health services only during emergencies implies that city location,
age, political or ethnic composition, size, population,
and the like were not factors in determining their municipal governments' form and responsibilities. But while

the similarity of early nineteenth century municipal governments was startling, the persistence of that type of
governance was even more remarkable. Cities underwent marked socioeconomic and demographic changes
during those years, but the thrust of city governments
remained the same. Indeed, the period from the Revolutionary War to about 1840 was hardly static. Cities not
only became more populated, but as early as the 1790s
began to receive in substantial numbers immigrants, not
from Britain and Scotland, but from Germany and
Ireland. Similarly, the emphasis on and the pace of manufacturing quickened dramatically. Cities were clearly
involved; a significant amount of manufacturing took
place there. The pattern began to develop during the
war. Freed from English constraints and prohibitions on
manufacturing, each new state adopted a policy of encouraging home manufactures, not simply for its own
consumption but for export. The resulting chaos and
competition was resolved by the Constitution, which
established a rational trade policy among states. The
Jeffersonian Embargo and the War of 1812 further
fueled the expansion of manufacturing interest, while
subsequent tariff legislation protected nascent and profitable American industries. In short, American governments consciously fostered manufacturing during the
late eighteenth and early nineteenth centuries and city
residents increasingly participated in manufacturing
endeavors.[10]

Despite the dislocation produced by the rise of manufacturing and the confusion resulting from the influx
of hoards of new and different peoples, city governments stayed the same. Their operations engendered little comment, which suggests that city residents approved
of these actions. Not until the late 1830s did citizens
regularly begin to express concern about the state of
their municipalities. And this concern was not directed

initially at city government's functioning, but rather at the character of the urban populus. As several scholars have noted, the complaints were strident, came from virtually every American city, and took on a characteristic form. Those who objected maintained that urban society faced a new menace: groups of individuals unlike previous inhabitants had invaded their cities and could not be trusted to protect themselves or their fellow city dwellers. While the identification of these groups' members differed from city to city—wayward children, Irish, German, Catholics, rural inhabitants, and blacks most frequently were cited—commentators portrayed each offending group similarly: they deemed the group's constituents strangers in two particular ways. First, critics in each place maintained that the group was composed of strangers to American urban life, that these people were unaccustomed to, unfamiliar with, and unprepared for living as part of a social unit in America. Second, these critics claimed that only recently did great numbers of the group appear in the city—they were strangers in the sense of new, unknown arrivals—and argued that the group's persistence threatened the community's welfare. To these men and women, the "new" urbanites constituted a "dangerous class" precisely because of their ignorance of the long-established procedures for American city living: they seemed likely to wreak havoc on themselves and others.[11]

Whether those identified as strangers in each place were actually new to those cities can be debated. Certainly the diversity of cities that virtually simultaneously "discovered" these people implies that in many instances those considered "new" had been lifelong residents of those places. Conversely, the same site diversity makes it impossible to rule out that a place or a few places did indeed experience a deluge of strangers. But that sort of discussion is counterproductive; it ignores the forest for the trees. What was crucial was that Americans in cities across America at about the same time said that their city had been infiltrated by a new group, which behaved unlike previous inhabitants, and acted in accordance with that proposition. It was the *perception* of a city inundated by strangers, not the reality or lack of reality of that situation, that occasioned fear and social action.

The almost simultaneous recognition by city residents across America beginning about 1840 that their municipalities were in the throes of a crisis—a plague of strangers—indicates that the perceived phenomenon did not stem neatly from the peculiarities of the local situation; it was not the simple response to social forces. Cities grew in population, population density, and geographic space differentially. Indeed, the absolute population of American municipalities reflected this trend and so helps further discredit local social forces as the progenitor of a new perception argument. For example, New York City and Philadelphia in 1820 housed roughly as many people as the largest other cities would in 1850. In 1830, these two municipalities were substantially more populous than any of their sister cities two decades later. Similarly, the increase of New York's population by some 80,000 in the period 1820–1830 was unprecedented. Except for Philadelphia and New York again in later decades, no city prior to the Civil War experienced in a single decade such a large population jump.[12]

Nor should differences in the identification of groups from city to city imply that local circumstances were deterministic. The opposite ought to be the case. That citizens of virtually every American city about 1840 defined segments of the population as persistent threats to the public weal suggests that midcentury local situations merely provided foci for the acting out of a more general phenomenon; they served as backdrops. And this perceived midcentury crisis was found in municipalities

throughout America, each of which prided itself on the
uniqueness of its past and present.

Nor should the synchronous nature of this perceived
crisis imply that city residents across the nation were
suddenly overcome by a series of new and similar conditions. Historians have shown that lawlessness and filth
had been partners of American municipalities from
their beginnings. Similarly, epidemic diseases had always
buffeted American cities. Although cholera first reached
the United States in 1832, it was no less fearsome or
deadly than yellow fever or smallpox, two diseases that
had repeatedly struck America in the eighteenth and
early nineteenth centuries. Finally, economic catastrophes had hit America with monotonous regularity.
While the Panic of 1837 was certainly severe, the country's municipalities were not strangers to major depres-
sions. No less than seven, including the massive Panic of
1819, had stung the nation prior to 1837.[13] What made
these established conditions seem so threatening about
1840 did not stem from their newness—despite contemporary laments, they were not in fact new—but from a
new interpretation of their context; they were viewed in
a new way. The key was the new perception of the city as
an *aggregate of groups*. It placed a premium on group behavior, or more simply perhaps, what seemed to make
the group a group. And this act of redefinition converted long-standing conditions and situations that always had characterized American urban society into
society-menacing "problems"; it defined these situations
and conditions as persisting, not occasional—as the consequence of the offending group's inappropriate behavior. This "discovery" not only engendered alarm but also
led to action: identifying these conditions and situations
as problems meant that they demanded resolution. To
do less would undermine the city's vitality.

This perception of a plague of strangers evoked, in
addition to Nativist uprisings, two broad responses. In

line with traditional notions of the separation of public and private spheres, city inhabitants fashioned an extensive benevolent effort, complete with the formation of a slew of new institutions and organizations. Seeking to identify and classify strangers according to the specific causes responsible for their degraded condition, practitioners of benevolence attempted to show strangers the errors of their ways and to teach them the laws of American social living. These "angels of mercy" also decided what type of assistance each stranger required, whether outdoor relief or institutionalization in a particular facility.[14]

Ironically, however, the same perception that led citizens to redouble and extend the benevolent effort also revealed benevolence's inadequacies. And that recognition permitted city residents to examine a new option: municipal government as a source of salvation. Indeed, benevolence lacked the power to compel strangers to act so as to protect themselves and others, and also lacked the resources necessary to maintain the urban environs in the wake of their carelessnesses. Both appeared essential to the public weal and produced among city inhabitants calls to involve city government.

Municipal officials and others heeded these pleas and worked through state legislatures to acquire for their cities the requisite authorities. They were forthcoming; moreover, once in place, these powers revolutionized municipal government. For the first time, American city governments became active, fulltime social service delivery systems. But municipalities did not receive carte blanche from legislatures, nor had they asked for unlimited prerogatives. Their citizens' notions of the singular essence of the plague of strangers both circumscribed the requests and awards; it established the very nature of what services city governments delivered. City governments did not provide a full range of social services but rather only those deemed necessary to resolve the

problem that they had defined. Anything more would
have been at best superfluous, at worst wasteful.

In effect, municipalities beginning in the 1840s received two new important responsibilities. They were to
stop or to prevent strangers from destroying the social
unit and to eliminate the consequences of these strangers' actions, which in a myriad of indistinguishable and
inseparable ways menaced the public interest. Even
more significant, city residents understood that legislatures had granted municipal governments means to
achieve these ends. The legislatures had authorized
cities to levy taxes to install fulltime, paid police forces
and to create mechanisms for the regular removal of
unseemly and potentially dangerous situations and conditions, such as street beggars and filth in the thoroughfares. And cities were quick to act. Boston (1838) was
the first American city to form a police force. New York
(1845), Brooklyn and Philadelphia (1848), Washington,
D.C. (1851), Baltimore (1852), Chicago (1853), St. Louis
(1854), and Milwaukee (1855) followed soon after. All
were quite similar. All worked full time and year round
for the municipalities and all operated under rigorous
and highly differentiated chains of command. But most
members of every force were charged similarly; duties
within police forces were remarkably nonspecialized.[15]
The lack of functional discrimination stemmed from the
presumption that the plague of strangers was multifac-
eted; it would be inefficient and ineffective to pursue
only some ramifications of this plague when each harmful and threatening act was inextricably linked to every
other.

Put another way, midcentury police success depended first and foremost on *identifying strangers.* Only
when these "degraded beings" were known could they be
stopped from unleashing the predictable pattern of hazardous activity inherent in the concept of a plague and

be taught the laws of American social life. That rested as the essence of police responsibility. Each policeman prosecuted that task as he engaged in such seemingly unrelated enterprises as talking to strangers, removing beggars, lighting street lights, investigating nuisances, and the like. Indeed, the plague's complexity required each policeman to undertake a variety of activities that paralleled the plague's many dimensions because early detection stood as the key to a city's protection. A person who committed an apparently minor transgression seemed as dangerous as a more serious offender (though the threat was less immediate) precisely because if left unchecked and unreformed, he would inevitably blossom into a major menace; even the most modest violation of the rules for American social living indicated an unfamiliarity with them in *toto*.

In this view, then, the uncovering of every impropriety signified a police victory. Since situations and conditions that constituted this midcentury crisis were inextricably intertwined, the police by any act of discovery had furthered the public interest generally. For example, breaking up a faro game, arresting the players, and sending them to jail was not merely a stroke against gaming. It was also a triumph over epidemic disease, violent crime, filth, and street begging. The detection of these strangers and their subsequent reformation removed from the city's midst a potential threat to every aspect of the community's welfare. It was not the ending of the game that was crucial, but instead the identification, removal, and reformation of the players. This notion of the proper role of the police encouraged neither functional specialization nor the construction of a "modern" hierarchy of police tasks.

While the police searched out the unaccustomed, unprepared, and unaware, other branches of the new city government moved to mitigate the strangers' nuisances.

In essence, these new agencies regularly removed the
debris of society, whether household and street refuse or
the broken bodies and spirits of those destroyed by their
lack of preparation for mid-nineteenth century American social life. These actions were aimed primarily at
maintaining the status quo. They served to repair damage (damage that in a previous era had been ignored),
not to prevent it. By removing visible signs of the perceived plague of strangers, these new municipal bureaucracies both protected city residents from ignorance's
consequences and provided settings in which benevolence could be effective. Once again, the city of Cincinnati through its boards of the city infirmary and of city
improvements was not alone in providing this social service. The municipal governments of Chicago, Brooklyn,
Baltimore, Boston, Philadelphia, Alexandria, New York,
Rochester, and St. Louis all initiated in the 1840s and
early 1850s programs along these lines.[16]

The suddenness and broad sweep of the mid-
nineteenth century municipal revolution in the purpose
of municipal government, coupled with its radical nature when contrasted with its predecessors, is suggestive.
It not only warns against attempting to ascribe a causative role to the social and political forces operating
within each unique local situation, but it also implies
that American municipalities probably mimicked and
learned from one another. It indicates that as new municipal administrative forms were introduced, American
cities quickly adopted them so as to maintain their station and to improve their citizens' wellbeing. While cities
no doubt engaged in a lively competition and flagrantly
copied each others' practices, it is beside the point. The
spread of the municipal revolution depended on additional factors. It spread not simply because it was possible to redesign city government, but because it was
desirable. Its desirability stemmed from the perception,

articulated by citizens of virtually every major American city, that their cities faced new and similar menaces in these plagues of strangers—a manifestation of the conception of the city as a social unit. To combat the plague as they identified it required in a very particular way the assistance of municipal government; and the new municipal government seemed likely to resolve a problem described in city after city.

A similar argument can be made about the relationship between European cities and their American counterparts. Robert Peel's London police provide an apt example. Institutionalized after years of agitation in 1829, the London police became known quickly to the great number of Europe-touring Americans. These travelers certainly brought their understanding of the police home with them. Yet it remained until 1838 for an American city to erect the nation's first municipal police force and another seven years for the second to be formed. The possibility of creating similar policing bodies in America seemed during that period to lack purpose; it would simply waste money. Only in the late 1830s and throughout the 1840s did the idea of a police gain among American city residents utility and currency. Even then, however, they did not transplant a London-style police in America. Instead, they took the concept of a police and fashioned it into something different. A police force only had applicability in America when it seemed to come directly to bear on the problem that city inhabitants maintained their municipalities were facing.[17]

Conversely, an apparent lack of utility dissuaded American city residents in the period from the late 1830s to the mid 1850s from sanctioning the erection of other, more specialized municipal agencies. The absence of a substantial movement in America to create city institutions devoted exclusively to the fulltime protection of

the public's health stood as a case in point. To be sure,
European precedents for governmental action existed
and were well known in America. The labors of England's Edwin Chadwick stood preeminent. He worked
in the 1830s through the Poor Law Commission to establish the General Health Board and municipal health institutions. Behind this effort rested Chadwick's "sanitary
idea," the notion that disease was preventable and that
disease, living conditions, and poverty were joined.[18]
More important, his pronouncements attracted a handful of advocates in America, most notably the New York
City physician, John Griscom. Although these several
men all failed to drum up support, it was Griscom's lack
of influence in America that was most revealing.

Griscom certainly had many factors in his favor. Operating within a city that might well have laid claim to
having been the most convulsive in midcentury America, he had considerable political clout. Griscom was
born into a wealthy, powerful New York family and his
connections enabled him to secure a patronage post
within city government. He also shined in medical politics. He was instrumental in the establishment of both
the New York Academy of Medicine and the American
Medical Association.

Nor was he shy about expressing his views. As early as
1842, he began to argue the public health cause. He
zealously crusaded in his writings and carried Chadwick's message to both city government and the public.
He also lectured extensively; he missed few occasions to
call for health reform before public or professional gath-
erings. Yet despite Griscom's political standing and his
prodigious efforts as well as the collective experience of
New Yorkers with the social flux of the period, he could
gain among the public virtually no support for his plans.
The situation among his medical colleagues was similar.
Although he employed the New York Academy of Med-

icine as a forum for his pleas, its members remained un-
moved. Griscom gained among his medical brothers
neither disciples nor even converts. In short, Griscom labored in New York virtually alone for over a decade,
pointing out time and again Chadwick's wisdom to unre-
sponsive audiences.[19]

Griscom's inability to generate support for public
health reform did not stem from a lack of energy or influence. Nor was his failure a consequence of the public's disinterest. His difficulties were grounded in the
idea that a health department would not further the
public interest. Although American city residents recognized a connection between poverty, filth, and disease,
they viewed that relationship in terms very different
than Chadwick, Griscom, and a few other Americans;
there was no cause-and-effect linkage. Instead, all these
conditions seemed the consequence of a lack of proper
training. As a result of this understanding, it seemed to
the public that health could not be managed by the
means Griscom offered and had to be approached in another way. Put more straightforwardly, the silence that
greeted Griscom indicated that even among medical
men health preservation was not a separate public issue
before the mid 1850s, but rather an inextricable part of
the amalgam of conditions implicit in the plague of
strangers. The preservation of the public's health neither required nor seemed susceptible to another set of
municipal institutions directed at eliminating the publicly visible manifestations of unpreparedness, unfamiliarity, and unaccustomedness, but could be improved
only by methods designed to cater to the cause of the
plague itself.

In that world, then, health departments were superfluous. The plague could only be controlled through the
identification and reformation of strangers. And the
new city government already was addressing those con-

cerns. The formation of police forces and the creation of municipal asylums, coupled with the renewed benevolent effort, appeared likely to get to the heart of the problem. Nor had the architects of the municipal revolution forgotten about removing potential environmental hazards. The establishment of municipal cleanup operations, whether asylums or street sweeping, served to protect city residents from the noxious influences of others. As a consequence of these safeguards, health boards remained as they had been. In cities as distinct as Milwaukee, St. Louis, Newark, New Orleans, Pittsburgh, Boston, Norfolk, New York, and Rochester, health boards functioned only to beat back epidemic disease, not to prevent it.[20]

Mid-nineteenth century Americans demonstrated no enthusiasm for health departments because these agencies seemed redundant; they would merely duplicate a facet of the efforts of other, broader institutions. That was not the case with fire departments. From the late 1830s, city residents lobbied for their creation. The differences in the public response to these two types of municipal initiatives rested in the prevention–restoration dichotomy. Municipalities engaged in both health preservation and fire prevention, but as part of the attack on the plague of strangers; no new specialized municipal creations aimed solely at those tasks appeared necessary. But stamping out epidemics and putting out fires fitted in a different category, as attempts to restore cities. And while boards of health seemed to function adequately, city inhabitants argued that volunteer fire companies were failures.

As a consequence, the drive to form paid, fulltime municipal fire departments was only an attempt to improve a long-standing emergency-oriented service. Cities established fire departments (they had been purchasing firefighting equipment just as they had been paying for quarantine facilities) to regulate the delivery of a vital service that they had already sanctioned. In that sense, placing firefighting agencies on municipal payrolls did not mark the assumption of new responsibilities by city governments. The desire to regulate these activities more effectively was new, however. Here again, the idea of the plague of strangers figured prominently. Midcentury urbanities in city after city maintained that volunteer companies had fallen into the hands of the unaccustomed, unprepared, or unfamiliar—youths, vagabonds, or immigrants—who had transformed these venerable institutions into vile social clubs. They had become hotbeds of crime, vice, and greed. Their members set fires, fought among themselves, and generally took on the characteristics of gangs or mobs. What was worse, they were not extinguishing blazes as they should.

The clubbiness of volunteer fire companies not only was cited by city residents as justification for municipal fire departments, but it also made establishment of these new institutions difficult; fire departments generally emerged toward the end of the mid-nineteenth century municipal revolution. Indeed, Cincinnati has long claimed to have erected the nation's first city fire department in 1853, and may well be right. The explanation for the delay in creating municipal fire departments was twofold, and stemmed from the fact that volunteer companies comprised an entrenched constituency. Midcentury fire companies were not simply social clubs; they also packed political power. And while firefighting was a time-honored municipal responsibility, long the province of city government, conversion to fulltime, paid fire departments nonetheless required both the state legislatures' authority to levy additional taxes and councils' enabling ordinances. Neither elective body could afford to dismiss volunteer companies from its political calculations. If legislatures and councils managed to put aside these vested political interests, their members often had to contend with threats of gang violence. Such was the case in Cincinnati. J. H. Walker led the agitation against volunteer companies and was rewarded for his crusade with physical harassment, even death threats. The windows of his house were broken and, ironically, the structure was later burned to the ground.

The erection of fire departments usually required both physical and political courage. Proponents found themselves bucking an established interest group that they identified as menacing. That was not the sole difference between fire departments and other new mid-nineteenth century municipal initiatives. Unlike the preventive police, fire departments did not prevent but restore. Coupled with the demand for better regulation of firefighting, that very different mission allowed city residents to organize fire departments functionally. Since prevention of an amalgam of conditions and situations—the plague of strangers—lay outside their purview, fire departments needed only to be structured to accomplish best their special task. That meant a functional division of firemen into hook and ladder men, drivers, pump men, and the like. Fulltime, paid fire departments exhibiting functional specialization were formed in New Orleans and Utica (1855), Rochester (1856), St. Louis (1857), Brooklyn (1858), Richmond (1860), Detroit (1861), Washington (1864), and New York (1865).[21]

Fire departments, then, stood apart from the other aspects of the mid-nineteenth century municipal revolution. But even as proposals to create city firefighting agencies still worked their way through recalcitrant legislatures and uneasy councils, city residents began to express dismay about municipal affairs. As early as the mid 1850s, citizens in virtually every major American city angrily complained about either municipal functioning or city officials. This renewed clamor differed from that of the late 1830s and 1840s in one significant way. While their predecessors blamed city governments' lack of authority for their plight, these later agitators maintained that municipal officials were at fault; these officers failed to demonstrate a commitment to the public weal. It was not the new charges per se that proved enlightening, however, but rather their character. Urbanites damned their city governments for not dealing effectively with crime, vice, filth, pauperism, disease, and the like. These critics did not focus their attention on a class or classes of people whose actions presumably caused these menaces, but instead on the conditions and situations themselves. They argued that it rested upon municipal government to prevent these threats and that that required city officials to devote themselves to eliminating each situation and condition.[22]

This sustained outburst signaled a new phase in American urban history, which can be described in several ways. It certainly seemed to reflect a dramatic shift in emphasis from cause to effect, a tacit acknowledgment that the problem of the plague of strangers was irresolvable and that municipal governments could respond only to the disease's environmental consequences. And if that line of thought was carried to its natural conclusion, the new discourse marked the end of attempts to reform strangers. City residents then sought only to prohibit and punish noxious acts; the new critique signified the introduction of a new chapter in the history of social control.

This interpretation appears not only too drastic, but is also probably without foundation. Efforts to reform strangers seemed to have persisted. Private benevolence continued apace while municipalities created other, new, specialized asylums. More likely the increased attention given to the visible manifestation of improper behavior stemmed from the collapse of the *concept* of the plague of strangers, particularly the notion that the conditions and situations that comprised the plague were amalgamated. Rather than a single indiscretion indicating an inevitable pattern of action embracing crime, vice, street begging, filth, and disease, these questions became disengaged. Each emerged as a distinct and separable public issue, complete with its own clientele of offenders. As a result of this disentanglement, it became possible for the first time to conceive in a meaningful and manageable way of combining both reformation and prevention in an effort to resolve a public problem.[23]

To be sure, the new construct of the mid 1850s and after held much in common with that articulated earlier. City residents continued both to identify dangerous classes and to argue that these people were strangers who lacked the training necessary to protect themselves and others. But mid-1850s social critics differed from their counterparts of previous years by maintaining that the consequences of unfamiliarity, unaccustomedness, and unpreparedness were in each instance potentially limited; the lack of proper training seemed no longer necessarily to predetermine an entire pattern of activity. While teaching and training—reformation—still remained the ultimate objective, manifestations of ignorance took on new meaning. It appeared possible to approach each new public question in isolation; manifestations of ignorance could be categorized and pursued without regard to formerly perceived linkages. Put more briefly, the disintegration of the plague of strangers and its replacement with a series of new, distinct public issues made it conceivable to tackle each new problem independently; it became feasible to erect a special, specific solution for each new public problem. The municipal revolution of the 1840s would give way to the municipal reorganization of subsequent decades.

The frustrations of the mid 1850s and after arose within that framework. Since each new public problem seemed readily distinguishable, each attracted its own notice and developed a core of advocates. In every case, those who expressed concern denounced city fathers for devoting neither sufficient attention nor resources to the particular cause. They gained reinforcements whenever major crises enveloped cities. Whether epidemics, street crime outbreaks, or the like, these events focused public scrutiny on municipal governments and fueled discontent. During those times, the lack of a separate municipal agency designed exclusively to prevent the formation of the situations and conditions that blossomed into a catastrophe was viewed as a further demonstration that municipal officials cared little about the public interest.[24]

Despite these accusations, municipal officials had not turned their backs on their constituencies. Instead, they merely lacked the weapons appropriate to wage the fight. While prevention still served as the means to insure the social unit's wellbeing, the disentanglement of the plague of strangers had made the municipal revolution seem anachronistic. The new city governments of the late 1830s and 1840s had been constructed to cater only to a general, multidimensional, and highly integrated blight. With the emergence in the mid 1850s of discrete public problems, the prevention mechanisms of the earlier period appeared terribly ineffectual. The relative lack of linkages among the new public problems was at the matter's heart. It made the efforts of the earlier prevention devices—a general purpose preventive police and general mop-up operations—seem meager, as if city governments were indifferent. For example, breaking up a faro game in the late 1830s and 1840s had signified a police victory over disease, filth, crime, street begging, and the like. But during the mid 1850s and later, the same act seemed only a stroke against vice. In effect, the articulation of distinct public problems appeared to dilute the police effort. While in the earlier period all police activity seemed to bear on the sole public problem of the plague of strangers, any single act now appeared to deal with only one of many public problems. As a consequence, although the police labored as vigorously as they had in the past, they seemed by comparison inactive, their efforts diminished.

Though there had been no diminution of effort, the police remained at the situation's core. Expansion of police forces seemed mandatory. The fractionalization of the plague not only led to a call for more policemen, but also dictated the form expansion needed to take. Effective prevention required municipal government to create for each discrete public question a coherent body of regulations encompassing every aspect of the question and then to enforce that law energetically and full time. The stipulation that proper enforcement was essential to each question's resolution and that in each instance it constituted a fulltime pursuit was crucial. It implied that each policeman should engage in just one specialized task; to attempt more was to devote less to all. And that proviso was reflected in two main ways. It not only manifested itself in the transformation of municipal police forces into police departments, but it also found expression in the drive to create a police for each public problem; while one police had sufficed previously, citizens in the mid 1850s and after clamored for several policing agencies.

Of these two thrusts, the conversion of police forces into police departments remained less complicated but also less obvious. It seemed an internal municipal matter, requiring neither new state power nor funding. Despite the appearance of free rein, cities generally accomplished the shift to functional specialization—from force to department—within their polices gradually. For example, New York detailed its first policemen in 1852 but continued to refine their particular responsibilities until about 1860. Philadelphia began to make distinctions in police duties in 1854, adopted uniforms with different accouterments in 1856, and passed a misdemeanor code a few years later. Boston created police divisions in 1854, but did not complete the reorganization until 1859. Chicago, on the other hand, moved with surprising rapidity. It formed its first police force in 1853 and transformed that force into a functionally specialized department a scant two years later.[25]

While replacing police forces with departments occurred over some time, creating new policing departments frequently took even longer. Whether filth police, fire police, pauper police, or health police, the reason usually was similar: cities had to seek new authority from state legislatures. Municipalities needed not only to get permission to levy new taxes to pay for these new services, but also to prosecute the services themselves. The case of health police departments (more commonly called simply health departments) stood as a case in point. City governments explicitly had gained power from legislatures to restore municipalities when in the throes of scourges but not the privileges nor manpower that now seemed necessary to prevent epidemic outbreaks. Those powers required additional action by state legislatures.

In contrast to intramunicipal reorganizations of the police, calls for states to provide cities with abilities to create new policing agencies attracted substantial notice. No cause was more conspicuous than health. The emergence of health as a discrete public problem not only led coteries of citizens in each city to adopt the question as their own, but many doctors also championed it. In addition to a sincere desire to protect the public weal, these physicians found in public health an issue that they hoped could serve to cement together a fractionalized medical profession. It could form the basis of medical organization and medical organizations. New medical societies predicated on preserving the public's health would give medical men a bond of union as well as a vehicle from which to demonstrate their commitment to the public's wellbeing. This approach was widespread. Physicians in New York, Chicago, Charleston, Leavenworth, Kansas, and Milwaukee each established a new medical society to focus on the public's health or redirected a standing institution.[26]

The manner in which medical societies tackled the health issue was straightforward. From the onset, they claimed the right to dictate municipal health policy and, as a consequence, to design new municipal health agencies. Without exception, however, these societies failed to achieve their public health goals. Fractionalism within medicine proved too great to overcome, and since the appearance of harmony among doctors took precedence over health, medical societies found themselves incapable of articulating even the most basic health recommendations. They could do little more than call for municipal and state action. The case of the New York Academy of Medicine provided an apt example of the inability of a medical society to mold health policy. As early as 1856, the academy formed a committee to investigate the question of public health. Its efforts resulted only in a resolution urging the legislature to enact a more comprehensive city health law. After drafting the memorial, the committee remained moribund until 1858 when the academy moved to revitalize it by appointing an additional sixteen members. Expansion of the committee did not yield new initiatives, though. While in the early 1860s the academy threw its support behind the New York Sanitary Association, lent its approval to the Citizens' Association of New York, and again requested the passage of more extensive health legislation, its contributions to health policy were nil. The academy had neither taken the lead nor participated nor attempted to participate in the formulation of the municipal health response. It had not shaped the health measures undertaken by the city in the late 1850s and early 1860s. More significantly, it failed even to set an agenda for municipal action.[27]

Medical societies contributed little to the municipal health effort aside from repeatedly bringing the issue before public forums. Other groups, some of which had doctors as members, proved more successful in outlining health reform's particulars. Not all these groups were local, however. In addition to the various city-based citizens' health committees and sanitary organizations, at least one association, the National Quarantine and Sanitary Convention, possessed a national membership. Movement for the convention began in 1856 when Wilson Jewell invited all interested parties to come to Philadelphia to discuss public health matters. Financed by the city of brotherly love, the conclave met in May 1857 and attracted seventy-three delegates representing twenty-six different organizations in nine states. The initial event proceeded successfully, and in the next three years similar assemblies were held in Baltimore, New York, and Boston, the last of which drew 191 participants. At the Boston conclave, the convention's members resolved to meet in Cincinnati the following year, but the onset of hostilities between the states made the group cancel its plans.

During its brief tenure, the National Quarantine and Sanitary Convention grappled extensively with aspects of the public health problem. The consideration of a single health code for cities typified the convention's activities. Members not only discussed the need for municipal regulation of tenements, sewerage, water, and the like, but also worked to hammer out sample sections of the code. The organization was similarly forthright in advocating municipal health departments. It urged legislatures to create within city administrations fulltime, salaried preventative health police dedicated exclusively to the inspection and regulation of the public's health in all its various facets.[28]

While the convention managed to put forth concrete suggestions for health reform, its lack of ties to a single place or political organization diminished its immediate political impact. Political maneuver was essential to the cause; the issue was not so much whether cities ought to prevent disease—the disintegration of the plague of strangers answered that question—but rather how to accomplish that mission. That placed emphasis directly on state legislatures. They were the entities empowered to grant municipalities authority to pursue new tasks and to employ additional personnel; state laws would inevitably define the new municipal health agencies and decide who controlled their operations. As a consequence, legislatures often were faced with several rival claimants for the prize. In some cities, various medical factions competed for control of proposed health departments, while in others lawyers, businessmen, sanitary associations, and the like sought to direct a new municipal health effort.

Sorting through these conflicting propositions and developing a political majority was no easy task for state legislators. The situation was exacerbated, moreover, by city-state tensions. Municipalities themselves were creations of state governments. Yet city governments were demanding complete control of municipal affairs. Conceiving of the city as a self-contained social unit possessing its own problems and concerns, city leaders argued that only city governments could set municipal agendas and priorities and cater to their citizens' needs and desires. This sentiment placed city residents and city governments in direct opposition to state legislatures, most of which were heavily slanted in favor of rural regions. Legislators frequently maintained that cities were swamped with foreign emigres—people who lacked acquaintance with the rules of American urban living—and as a result, could not be trusted to govern themselves. And in an era in which the rights of states were being questioned and in which political parties were beginning to assert themselves, the tendency of state governments was to present municipalities with no new significant authority.[29]

Control of prospective health departments served as a setting to play out conflicts between cities and states. But battles were not limited to not as yet established institutions. Indeed, requests by city governments to expand their powers often backfired. These petitions sometimes led state governments to examine and reassess the municipal/state relationship generally. In most instances, state legislatures concluded that municipal governments needed to be reined in; states sought to regain ascendency over cities. The agency usually selected to dramatize the legislatures' point was the police. Arguably the most important municipal institution aside from councils, mayors, and judges, state legislatures removed police from municipal control by creating boards of police commissioners apart from city governments. While in some cases legislatures justified their actions by reconstructing policing districts to encompass areas greater than city boundaries and, therefore, establishing metropolitan or district polices, that stood as the exception. More frequently, states simply mandated that police boards govern polices and either stipulated separate

elections for commissioners or, more likely, placed appointment power in the hands of state officials, such as
governors. No matter which approach legislatures chose,
the result was similar. City governments lost control of
their police. New York, Baltimore, St. Louis, Kansas
City, Chicago, Detroit, Cleveland, New Orleans, India-
napolis, Omaha, San Francisco, and Milwaukee were
among cities in the late 1850s and early 1860s that suffered the same fate.[30]

Affecting even the police, the intensity and persistence of the fight between cities and states for municipal
control retarded efforts to create new municipal social
services. For example, only one city, Providence, Rhode
Island, managed to erect a health department prior to
the Civil War. The lack of other health departments during this period did not indicate an insensitivity to urban
health problems by either city officials or residents. They
repeatedly complained about the public's health and
urged legislatures to provide cities with the authority
necessary to take action. Despite specific proposals and
overwhelming public sentiment for health departments
and despite the fact that they often expressed concern
for the public's health as well as acknowledged the economic consequences of disease, legislatures refused to
empower cities to establish these institutions. The war
for control of city affairs took precedence.[31]

The ongoing skirmishes placed city governments in
an impossible position. They were defined by city inhabitants as protectors of the public's health, but lacked real
power to do the job. They did not stand idle, however. In
the second half of the 1850s and 1860s, many municipalities tampered with their health boards in an attempt to
add at least some health-maintaining duties to the more
traditional disease-fighting tasks. Though in no case did
results prove completely satisfactory—they could not
form health departments—cities as different as Newark,

New Orleans, Baltimore, New York, Philadelphia, and Richmond all provided additional authority to or reorganized their health boards during those years. For instance, Baltimore in 1856 permitted policemen after spring rains to accompany board members on an inspection of city houses, while in 1861 it divided the city into health districts. New York also used the district approach, also adopted by many southern cities, and appropriated in 1859 an extra $35,000 for its health board to direct a one-time general municipal cleaning. The police were once again involved. Patrolmen served as the board's eyes, alerting it to conditions and situations that especially compromised the public's health.[32]

The police or some other municipal agency was instrumental to what were in fact extralegal health initiatives. But even if no personnel figured in the moves, city governments' ventures into disease prevention still stood as a misapplication of municipal resources. These health-related enterprises expended monies for activities that had not gained legislative sanction, funds that had been designated for other, particular state-approved tasks. While few chose to object directly in public or in court to the municipal usurpation—most citizens who commented criticized city governments for their lack of health efforts—the consequences of misappropriations were nonetheless felt. They manifested themselves in a roundabout fashion, in complaints about the inattention of municipal officials to crime, vice, filth, pauperism, and the like. The use of municipal manpower and finances for health meant simply that cities had less available for their other responsibilities.

There the situation remained. City governments could not pursue effectively the question of health without slighting their legally mandated concerns. Yet there existed significant agitation for health reform. State legislatures were beset by interest groups contending for control of any state-sanctioned municipal health effort. Legislatures themselves were engaged in heated and recurring battles with cities to guide municipal affairs. These several tensions combined to produce impasses for roughly a decade in state after state; the desire for health reform attracted much support and few opponents, but yielded virtually no action. It was not until 1866 that impediments to health department creation were overcome. Cholera was central to that event.

Cholera was a fearsome disease, one that left a trail of devastation in its wake. But the 1866 outbreak was the third major bout with cholera that American cities experienced in thirty-five years. And it was just one of many epidemic diseases that had ravaged the United States during the nineteenth century. What set the 1866 scourge apart from its predecessors was not its severity, but the municipal and state response. That response stemmed directly from the notions of cities as social units and health as a discrete public problem.

As never before, cities prepared for the epidemic. They assiduously cleaned the environs and made extensive quarantine arrangements. Though dramatic, these Herculean efforts pale compared to the municipal campaign when the disease actually arrived. Though granted by states broad latitude to fight disease, city governments quickly exceeded even that authority. Commandeering municipal personnel, equipment, and funds, forcing entry into private dwellings, carrying off individuals to pest houses despite their protests, suspending due process, and the like were not unheard-of tactics for health boards to take in their war against the 1866 scourge.[33] Judges and, ultimately, state legislatures winked at the transgressions. More important, during or soon after the epidemic's conclusion, many legislatures moved to extricate cities from potentially similar situations in the future. Often by legislative fiat, they established departments of health for cities and permitted municipalities to levy taxes for their support. In effect, legislatures ignored the several petitioners for the prize, engaged not in compromise but power politics, and decided the matter themselves.

When viewed in context, the 1866 cholera outbreak had made it politically inexpedient and dangerous to pursue city-state and interest group squabbles without first erecting health departments in some form. Battles did not have to be resolved immediately. They could continue after department formation and could conceivably result in department reorganization. The impromptu cessation of these disputes was reflected in differences in department control. While each new health department operated under a board, there developed no national consensus over who should control the board. Board appointment power in some states went to councils or mayors, in others to legislatures, governors, or judges. In St. Louis and Milwaukee, for example, mayors made appointments. In Chicago the arrangement was quite different: judges of the city's superior court gained the right to select health board members. In New York, the governor alone possessed authority to choose. Nor was there agreement among cities as to board members' qualifications. For instance, at least four of the nine-member health board in New York needed to be physicians, while in Milwaukee the legislative act did not require any board members to be doctors. In St. Louis, medical men were provided by law with three of the five board seats, while in Chicago they could never become a majority; the act limited physicians to but three places on the seven-member board.[34]

Despite the variations in board composition, health departments themselves were quite similar in both form and function. Each was given the task of enforcing the city's health or sanitary code. The departments were composed of salaried inspection and removal forces—health policemen—and granted powers to inspect and remove on a year-round, fulltime basis. More precisely, each health department was headed by a chief executive officer, usually designated the health officer. With the assistance of a clerical staff, the health officer oversaw the department's day-to-day operations and kept track of the paperwork. Under his supervision were several units of inspectors. Each unit was charged with the regulation of a certain facet of the public's health; each was empowered to investigate a different, distinguishable set of health concerns. Meat, milk, market, and sanitary inspectors each had different missions. Though they shared the same objective of safeguarding the public's health, each unit was functionally distinct.[35]

The creation of health departments in the late 1860s in virtually every major American city completed the municipal conversion that had begun about ten years earlier. American cities at this time not only offered a broad range of municipal social services, but had reached that position by traveling remarkably similar paths. Despite uniquely local ethnic tensions, social geographies, economic and political forces, growth patterns, class divisions, physical settings, and the like, city governments formed similar municipal agencies at similar times. Though local circumstances surely contributed to the precise local formulations, the provision of municipal services in city after city does not fit neatly within the rubric of local history.

Nor does it meet the criteria of national history as commonly defined. It neither stemmed from a presidential agenda nor originated as an issue in the national government nor blossomed as the result of a national cataclysm, for example, the Civil War or a nationwide epidemic outbreak. Nonetheless, supplying municipal social services was national in that it occurred nationwide at the same time. Those notions that crystallized in Cincinnati during the late 1830s and in the mid 1850s also emerged in countless other American cities at roughly the same times, and led citizens to adopt strikingly similar courses of action. In effect, the issues that the municipal revolution of the 1840s and early 1850s and the municipal reorganization of the decade after the mid 1850s were to resolve seemed to have been issues of American cities generally, not localities. No matter what peculiarly local social forces were experienced, there existed in municipalities at least with respect to urban situations and conditions an incredible commonality in what city residents identified and when they identified it.

The commonality is surprising because cities possessed no formal mechanisms to trade intelligence or to bind them together. There was no specific national establishment or organization to which cities looked for direction. To be sure, these urban places held a special kinship because each was categorized by the appropriate state legislature as a city, not a village, town, township, or something else. That designation was meaningful in the nineteenth century because it indicated a particular station; it signified that the places had been awarded as much autonomy as state legislatures were willing to grant and that as a consequence, city governments could undertake certain broad classifications of tasks. And city residents clearly knew about other municipalities and their affairs. They frequently traveled and moved among cities, read newspapers, received mail and telegraphic messages, and traded goods. Despite substantial intercommunications among inhabitants of different cities, the entire transmission of information process was essentially haphazard; city dwellers lacked regular channels to discuss and consider city problems with their compatriots in other cities. More to the point, they made no moves to create such conduits.

Most telling, however, is not that city residents probably knew what other inhabitants of cities defined and did. Instead, it is that citizens of virtually every major American municipality discovered those conditions and situations in their environs at about the same time, identified them in similar ways, acted according to those assumptions, and were rewarded by the creation of particular, similar municipal agencies. That leads to two interesting speculations. It appeared either that municipalities were all subjected to the same social forces or that similar ideas about the nature of society were held in cities nationwide and changed roughly at the same time. The first interpretation runs contrary to most current historical scholarship, which emphasizes the uniqueness of intracity dynamics, except on its most gross and least useful level—cities grew, took in immigrants, and increased manufacturing operations. The second interpretation lies outside such scholarship. It depreciates the role of what historians tend to identify as social forces in the generation of ideas about the nature of society and suggests that ideas stand preeminent; they impart particularistic meanings to social circumstances. To carry the argument a step further, it implies that there was something that might be termed "American civilization" in the nineteenth century, that there were ideas shared by an extraordinary number of people and that those ideas determined first what was perceived and then the social realities themselves. Put more simply, ideas of society's nature seemed to have shifted in the late 1830s and again in the mid 1850s. Each time these shifts manifested themselves in the articulation of new city problems, proposals for resolution, and formation of new municipal agencies.

It is the latter possibility that seems particularly intriguing. It suggests the possibility that apparently disparate phenomena were in fact united. Ideas of society's nature are, after all, primarily organizational notions and yield organizational principles, which are revealed in public action. That a large segment of the American populus seems to have held similar notions of social organization at the same time implies that those notions may well have been at work in a wide variety of human endeavors, not just city governments. If that were the case, then a change in those notions would produce a corresponding change in America's institutions.

A redivision, reclassification, and reorganization of society's nature would have had profound implications. Institutional reform would be accorded a high priority. Indeed, new notions of the nature of society would have made institutional reform sensible and, to many, imperative. In essence, change in organizational ideas would make either the organization and function of established institutions seem outmoded or appear viable in a new and different way; institutions or the manner in which they had been considered would become anachronistic. The problem, then, would be to put the institutional structure in line with the new notions. That might produce two characteristic responses. Society might form new institutions in consonance both with the new classification system and the issues revealed by that system, or might bring forth new explanations for established institutions.

Though this argument had been couched in hypothetical terms, there is some evidence to support this interpretation. Several historians have dealt implicitly and in a number of areas with the institutional ramifications of the organizational shift circa 1840. For instance, Stanley Elkins has drawn attention to what he has identified as a midcentury institutional vacuum, to a decline or collapse of institutions designed during the colonial or early national periods. Bruce Sinclair has maintained that a new technical education first emerged in the 1840s, while Ian Tyrrell has detected a significant reorganization in the temperance movement. Others have focused on the new meaning of manifest destiny, the rise of politics and the formation of new political parties, the change in the pursuit of science and the establishment of new scientific institutions, the unfolding of a new economic theory and the development of a nationwide economy, the large-scale introduction of new production techniques (known as the "American System of Manufactures"), the restructuring of American Protestantism, and the emergence of a new type of Judaism, Reform Judaism.[36]

Not all the evidence for this position comes from historians. Both in words and deeds, midcentury contemporaries commented on and pointed to the shift from individual to group. A clear expression of this transformation appeared in the manner in which Americans referred to their country. At the end of the fourth decade, for example, sustained cries for "a distinctly American school of good manners" and a distinctly American literary and artistic corpus—not just national literacy—began to be heard with surprising regularity.[37] While a great variety of people expressed these new views and did so in several ways, few were more articulate than Ralph Waldo Emerson in his plea for an American scholar. Emerson's American scholar constituted a new type of man, a type representative of a particular civilization. Noting that the songs of America "must be sung" and that "we have listened too long to the courtly muses of Europe," Emerson wanted the American scholar to be "Man Thinking," endowed with "self-trust" and aiming "to cheer, to raise, and to guide" other Americans.

Claiming that "our day of dependence, our long appren-
ticeship to the learning of other lands, draws to a close,"
Emerson's scholar was to be a new man serving new
men.[38]

Others focused on more popular areas. The role of
public lectures gained new emphasis. In the 1820s and
1830s, public lectures seemed a means to democratize
knowledge. Abut 1840, however, public lectures, including the new lyceum circuit (on which Emerson himself
held a prominent place) appeared as manifestations not
simply of a democratic political philosophy, but of a particular society. Indeed, in the latter period, lyceums were
referred to as "curiously American inventions," which
acted as "powerful social ligaments, binding together the
vast body of people" who comprised the distinctive
American civilization.[39]

Though the forementioned examples of the change
circa 1840 from individual to group are far from exhaustive, they nonetheless are suggestive. They indicate that
it may be useful to approach mid-nineteenth century
America in a different manner, as a complex system of
thought or ideational constructs. And that approach
opens up the possibility of employing the facts of local
history in a new, exciting way, as a tool with which to
study American history generally. Indeed, if an extraordinary number of Americans held similar notions at the
same time and if those notions manifested themselves in
a variety of institutional initiatives, reform efforts, and
other events, then the central question becomes what
were those notions that made change desirable, even imperative; it focuses attention on the shift in notions. And
that question apparently was not of local circumstances,
but of American civilization generally. The history of the
provision of a broad range of municipal social services
in Cincinnati is in part certainly a history of local dynamics. But it is also something more. It is a history of

the questions of American civilization during the middle period, questions that the municipal revolution and the later municipal reorganization were to solve and questions for which the debates in Cincinnati as an American city were symptomatic. While this book explores the local issues in depth, it also attempts to begin to outline those broader, national concerns.

2 *From Individual to Group*

The town of Cincinnati officially became a city in 1819, an identification that reflected the municipality's explosive growth. During the decade ending in 1820 Cincinnati's population had quadrupled, to nearly 10,000. Never again would the city approach that startling growth rate. Geography no doubt contributed to Cincinnati's unprecedented population surge. Cincinnati's location on the Ohio River and its excellent harbor made it an attractive terminus for those interested in commerce and manufacturing. Even at this early date, the city displayed an exceedingly broad economic base, emerging as the banking center for much of the still-developing Ohio Valley as well as the region's commercial capital. Steamboats anchored in Cincinnati on the average of once a day. They brought with them wares purchased in Philadelphia, Baltimore, New York, Europe, and the Indies to be sold by the city's merchants. Cincinnatians did not restrict themselves to dealing other's products, but also participated extensively in manufacturing. Artisans engaged in the small-scale manufacture of household and farm implements, and others were more ambitious. A copper, brass, and iron foundry; a manufactory of mules, throstles, and cotton gins; a steamboat works; several breweries and distilleries; a manufactory for white and red lead; a chemical works; and saw, cloth, fulling, and flour mills were erected prior to 1820.

43

Cincinnati by 1820 was an exciting, burgeoning western metropolis manifesting a great degree of diversity in its citizens' economic interests. It continued and elaborated on the pre-1820 pattern during the next two decades. In this period, it received public recognition as the "Queen City of the West." By 1830, Cincinnati stood at the center of a sophisticated new transportation network. The Miami, Ohio, and Erie canals, coupled with an improved and extended turnpike system to the south and west, sped the city's goods through the region and facilitated transport of raw materials to the city. Several machine shops, gunpowder and paper mills, foundries, steamboat works, manufactories of steam engines and castings, and a sugar refinery sprung up during the 1820s, as did an important new industry: Cincinnati became the nation's meatpacking center, slaughtering over 40,000 hogs in 1826. That figure increased to an incredible 199,000 hogs just thirteen years later. Other industries dependent on meatpacking also blossomed. Tallow candle, soap, tanning, and chemical manufactories took slaughterhouse refuse and converted it into marketable products. By 1830, the city's population reached almost 25,000, a two-and-one-half-fold increase. It had almost doubled again a decade later.[1]

Thus in the years prior to 1840, Cincinnati experienced phenomenal population growth and economic development. City residents recognized these factors in the late 1810s and sought from the Ohio legislature the authority necessary to keep order in an era of profound change.[2] Their requests resulted in the legislature declaring Cincinnati a "city" in 1819 and providing the city's council with a wide variety of powers. Under the city's earliest municipal charters, Cincinnati could purchase and own property, sue and be sued, and levy taxes on its citizens' property. The legislature also limited the corporation's indebtedness, prohibited it from competing with banks, and required council to publish annually its receipts and expenditures.

In addition to permitting Cincinnati to assume the broad powers implicit in the early nineteenth century corporate device, the charters also specified that council should provide for and regulate its citizens' commercial and manufacturing interests. For example, the legislature empowered council "to erect, establish and regulate the markets and market-places" and to keep them in good repair as places in which the city's inhabitants and others could sell and purchase "articles necessary to sustenance, comfort and convenience." It permitted the municipal corporations "to establish and construct landing places, wharves, docks and basins" and "to fix the rates of landing, wharfage and dockage." It granted council the power "to cause any part of said city to be opened and laid out for a street, lane, alley, market, or market-place or public landing," and to "cause the streets, lanes and alleys to be open and in repair." The legislature also gave the city the authority "to license and regulate all carts, wagons, drays and hackney coaches," and to "grant licenses to tavern keepers, innholders, retailers of spiritous liquors; keepers of ale and porter houses and shops, and all other houses of public entertainment; show men, keepers and managers of theatrical exhibitions, and all other exhibitions for money or other reward; auctioneers for the sale of horses, and other domestic animals, at public auction, in the streets, lanes, alleys and commons of said city." It further stipulated that council could "revoke and suspend such licenses, whenever the good order and welfare of said city may require it."

The city's earliest charters also provided the municipality with several powers meant to restore order. To put out fires, the legislature empowered council "to establish and organize fire companies" and to provide the

companies "with the proper engines and other instruments as shall be necessary." Similarly, it called for the
election in council of a city marshal, gave council the
"power to appoint one or more deputies," and authorized that body "to pass such ordinances as may be necessary for the apprehension and punishment . . . of
persons disturbing the peace of said city." It further empowered council "whenever the public peace of said city
shall require it, to establish a city watch, and organize the
same, under the general superintendence of the City
Marshal." If, during "riots, disturbances and breaches of
the peace," the marshal found himself unable to restore
order, he was permitted to "call to his aid, and command
the assistance of all by-standers and others in the vicinity." To house lawbreakers, council gained the power,
"whenever the public good shall require it," to designate
some area "a city prison and to regulate . . . the internal
government of the same." Likewise, the legislature authorized council to create a health board. It was empowered to invest its board of health "with such powers, and
impose upon it such duties, as shall be necessary to secure said city and the inhabitants thereof, from the evils,
distress and calamities of contagious, malignant and infectious diseases." In addition, council was to provide for
the board's "proper organization, and the election or appointment of the necessary officers thereof," and to
make "such laws, rules and regulations, for the government and support [of the board], as shall be required for
enforcing the most prompt and efficient performance of
its duties, and the lawful exercise of its powers."[3]

It is this last class of powers that proves particularly
fascinating. It implies that from Cincinnati's initial designation as a city, the municipality received authorization to deliver regularly a full range of social services.
To be sure, that ought not to surprise the late twentieth
century mind because city residents were grappling

with the chaos engendered by rapid industrialization, urbanization, and immigration. But an examination of Cincinnati city government's actions prior to 1840 demonstrates that the municipality's early health, police, and fire institutions came into play only during emergencies. At all other times they did nothing. The absence of public objections to this state of affairs is even more startling, as it indicates that city inhabitants approved of city government's policies. Cincinnatians certainly were not shy about speaking out on issues, such as control of the common schools or, in 1829, the lack of enforcement of Ohio's Black Laws. Nor had they remained quiet in the 1810s; in fact, it was public agitation then that had convinced the legislature to present the city with its first municipal charter.[4]

The inescapable conclusion is that Cincinnati's municipal officers employed city government in a manner that satisfied their constituency. That acknowledgment not only leads to a closer reading of the city's earliest charters, but also provides the key to understanding the role, responsibility, and object of Cincinnati's early nineteenth century government. Ironically, it is the very strangeness of these agencies that both forces the admission that they were conceived from notions quite different than later, more modern efforts and helps disclose what those notions were.

Cincinnati's city government actually received from the legislature no social commitment, real or implied; the municipality was neither empowered to offer nor actually offered any social services. By operating only during catastrophes, city government demonstrated that it functioned only to restore the city to its customary state. The health board, marshal and his deputies, watch, and fire companies were neither established to improve the quality of urban life nor did they seek to address that problem. Cincinnati city government prior to about

1840 was not designed to provide social services regularly or occasionally, but to keep the city open or to reopen it swiftly. City government was responsible for creating institutions that aimed to restore order at an emergency's onset so that the privilege of the pursuit of commerce and manufacturing by city residents could continue apace or resume quickly. In that sense, the health board, marshal and his deputies, watch, and fire companies differed little from each other and from city government's more normal tasks. Like such diverse activities as the licensing of carts, the regulation of docks, or the paving of streets, these emergency-oriented institutions gained a place within city administration precisely to provide each citizen the opportunity to engage in commerce and manufacturing; Cincinnati's entire early nineteenth century city government existed only to offer such individual opportunity.

A detailed examination of one of these emergency-based operations makes this clear. The city's health initiatives prior to about 1840 were constructed neither to prevent disease nor to promote health, only to rid the municipality of scourges. Epidemics were catastrophes because all trade with a stricken city ceased immediately. Few chose to journey to a city in the throes of an epidemic and fewer still wanted their city to receive boats, passengers, or cargoes originating from an afflicted port. Indeed, the public's health was never an explicit governmental issue in early nineteenth century Cincinnati, but epidemic disease was because it menaced the city's normal functioning. And city council took the threat quite seriously. It created mechanisms specifically to resist the catastrophe of epidemics.

In its endeavor to comply with its new, formal responsibility "to protect the security and health of the City of Cincinnati," council enacted in the early 1820s numerous ordinances. Much of this legislation sought "to prevent nuisances" and defined what constituted a nuisance broadly. While council classified as nuisances such different activities as racing horses and obstructing sidewalks and thoroughfares, it also passed in this category prohibitions against the creation of noxious substances and noisome conditions. This latter group of ordinances serves as the municipality's health laws.

Council's prompt attention to such substances and conditions indicated that these situations were important to early nineteenth century city residents. That was in fact the case. In an era in which some held to the tenets of the miasmatic theory—that smells arising from animal and vegetable matter engendered disease—the persistence of these environmental nuisances appeared a threat to the city's health. As noxious substances and noisome conditions, council expressly banned the dumping of "the dead carcase [sic] of any animal," or any putrid or rotting meat or fish "in any street, alley, lot or common" within the city, and made it unlawful for anyone "to dig out the earth in any part of the city and leave the excavation open so as to contain water which shall become putrid and offensive."

Nor was that all. Council also made it an offense for "any lot, yard, or cellar" to "contain any stagnant water, filth, or offensive matter of any kind, which is or may become prejudicial to the public health," or to construct a privy lacking "a vault at least ten feet deep." The city's ordinances also specified that "no person shall have, use, or make, or keep in . . . any place whatever . . . any noisome or offensive substance," while making it unlawful "for any butcher or other person, to kill or slaughter" any animal within the city limits except in slaughterhouses, each of which was to "be paved with brick or stone, and the earth below it be made sufficiently solid to prevent its becoming the receptacle of filth and offensive matter." They further mandated that every

slaughtering establishment be equipped with "a tub or
reservoir . . . to receive the blood and offal," and required that the tub or reservoir "be emptied . . . washed
and cleaned at the end of every day." The penalty for
violation of any of these ordinances ranged from five to
fifty dollars for each offense.[5]

The method council chose to enforce the ordinances
was similarly straightforward. It appointed the city marshal and authorized him "or his deputy, or persons appointed under him for the purpose, . . . from time to
time," to "enter into and examine between sunrise and
sunset, any building of any kind, cellar, lot of ground,
vault, or privy which they may know, or be informed,
are foul, damp, or otherwise prejudicial to the public
health." If these men uncovered a violation of the nuisance ordinances, they then could "direct the cleaning,
altering, and amending" of the offensive substance or
condition. And if anyone did "resist or obstruct such officer, or shall neglect or refuse to remove any such nuisance when so directed," the offending party was fined
further "a sum not exceeding twenty dollars."[6]

Though rich in detail and severe in their penalties,
and though the marshal was charged with their enforcement, the noxious substance and noisome condition ordinances bore lightly on city residents. The reason lay in
the fact that individual citizens were expected to report
violations. The marshal neither searched the city for
such violations, nor was he expected to do so. Instead,
he merely responded to or investigated complaints
about specific offenses brought to council or the mayor
by others.[7] And if an epidemic threatened or struck the
city, as with the smallpox outbreaks of 1821 and 1822, or
when a long spell of inclement or hot weather came to
Cincinnati, as was the case during the summer of 1824,
the record shows that council did not radically alter this
procedure. It did, however, provide the marshal with an
assistant to help handle the increased volume of com-

plaints. "Whenever the interests of the city shall require it," council appointed a temporary marshal, whom it designated the health officer and whom it paid *per diem* as a further indication of the temporary nature of the post. And as soon as the epidemic abated or when the weather turned dry or cooler, council relieved the health officer and relied solely on the marshal to respond to nuisance complaints.[8]

For seven years the marshal-health officer system seemed sufficient both during epidemics and in more calm times. But in February 1826, as reports reached Cincinnati of the approach from New Orleans of another attack of smallpox, council moved to fortify its emergency-oriented health efforts.[9] It not only appointed a health officer, but it also established a new governmental institution, Cincinnati's first board of health. Composed of three men who served without pay and with a limited tenure in office of two months, the board was to act as an executive and administrative body. It was to "use whatever means necessary" to "secure the health of the City of Cincinnati." Under the terms of the ordinance creating it, the board was specifically empowered to appoint a physician to inspect persons who sought to enter the city from "any steam boat or keel boat," and to order the wharfmaster to deny entry to the port of all persons "until he, she, or they shall have obtained a certificate signed by the [board's] physician . . . setting forth that he, she, or they is not or are not infected with the Small Pox." The board was also authorized to establish an internal quarantine. It could order "the marshal, his deputy, and the wharfmaster [to] cause to be removed to some suitable place, any person or persons who may be found within the city, infected with Small Pox."[10]

The board during the epidemic of 1826 was charged, then, with establishing and directing the quarantine. Like the earlier noxious substance and noisome condition

ordinances, the thrust of quarantine legislation stemmed
from a prevailing assumption about disease transmission. The impetus rested on the theory of contagion,
which supposed that disease was spread through personal contact or contact with an infected individual's personal property, such as bedding or clothing. But the
health board did not restrict itself to contagion and
quarantines; it also drew on the miasmatic theory. As
part of its effort to secure the city and relying on the
part of the enabling ordinance stating that it could take
"whatever means necessary," the board in practice also
oversaw the marshal's and health officer's activities. Individuals could make complaints directly to the board and
its members would see that either the marshal or health
officer investigated the offending situation as soon as
possible. The board guided, in short, both the new quarantine and old nuisance procedures; it served to consol-
idate the city's disease-fighting force.[11]

Cincinnati's first board of health was short lived. It
was not council's last health pronouncement prior to
1840, however. Council passed additional noxious substance and noisome condition legislation in 1827 and
again in 1839. Neither ordinance changed the manner
in which nuisances were reported or abated. The first
dealt with the dumping of debris on the city's public areas. It levied a fine not to exceed five dollars on any person who cast or lay "any shavings, ashes, mud, dung, or
other filth or annoyance whatsoever, on any pavement,
or in any of the streets, lanes, alleys, or commons of the
city," or who allowed the same to be "thrown down or let
fall from any cart, wagon or other carriage."[12] The second concerned burials, and made it illegal for anyone
during the summer months "to deposit any dead body or
corpse in any public or private vault or tomb within said
city constructed above the surface of the earth." Offenders were subject to a fifty dollar fine. Both of these ordi-

nances, like the body of nuisance legislation already on the books, was enforced by the marshal or health officer only when an individual raised a complaint.[13]

During this same fourteen-year period, council formalized both the post of health officer and the manner in which occupants were appointed to this position. Neither of these refinements, though, signaled a change in the direction of the municipal effort. By April 1826, it had become standard practice for each aspirant to the health officership (during this period the post was also referred to as nuisance officer) to present council with a petition signed by prominent citizens testifying that the candidate in question stood "as a man of integrity and industry and [was] well qualified to discharge the dutys [sic] of that office."[14] Also around this time, council began to spread the responsibilities for responding to complaints about nuisances among several health officers, assigned each authority over a section of the city, and selected them for "one year or until successors were appointed."[15]

These modifications were merely procedural, however, and did not affect the ad hoc nature of the health officer's duties. Indeed, health officers continued to act only when a citizen complained to the authorities about a noxious substance or condition, which he maintained "has become a nuisance" and feared has "become prejudicial to the health of the inhabitants," and sought to have them "interfere [with an individual's property rights] by removing a very serious nuisance" from the city. Like their predecessors, health officers drew pay on a *per diem* basis and, although remaining titular employees of the city, were paid only for the days actually spent investigating complaints or directing the abatement of nuisances.[16]

Also in the same fourteen-year period, council created four different boards of health, which remained, as

did the post of health officer, strikingly similar to the
city's initial effort. The new boards continued to meet
only during or in anticipation of an epidemic, and their
duties, like those of the board of 1826, consisted of developing and implementing plans to combat the disease,
whether it be smallpox or cholera. Only the number of
persons sitting on the various boards changed—at different times four, five, seven, or nine members were ordered—and penalties for violation of the quarantine
were imposed.[17]

The activities of council in 1827 and its board of
health provides a case in point. Council members called
the health board into session after they received notice
that smallpox was "in circulation in different parts of the
adjacent county." Deeming this situation "highly prejudicial to the health of the city," they ordered the board of
health "to report . . . on the public health to Council at
their next meeting." In the meantime, council directed
the board to undertake "whatever measures necessary to
secure the health of the city" and "should it become necessary[,] to publish a list of deaths in the *Cincinnati
Gazette*."[18]

The board began investigating and quickly found
that at least one "person in this city is afflicted with a disease which in the opinion of some of the medical faculty
bears some resemblance to the Small-Pox." The board
refused to wait for council to reconvene, moreover, and
immediately made preparations to fight the disease. In
addition to establishing an external quarantine and for-
warding mortality returns to the newspapers, it also
charged the marshal to secure "a safe and convenient
place without the city and so far from the habitable part
thereof that no danger may be apprehended from the
contagious nature of the disease," where smallpox victims shall be brought and "provided with all the necessities for comfort at the expense of the city." When council

met a few days later, it passed a resolution applauding the board's move and commending it for swift action.[19]

A consideration of the ordinances creating Cincinnati's early nineteenth century boards of health shows that boards formed in the fourteen years after 1826 resembled in method and goal the city's first creation. The ordinance of 1832, council's last pronouncement on the subject prior to the 1840s, serves as an excellent example. Passed to confront Cincinnati's first cholera epidemic, the ordinance established a seven-member board, the members of which held office "for one year or until their successors were appointed." Its members could meet as a board "whenever they may deem it necessary for the security of the city"—which in practice meant during or in anticipation of an epidemic—and "take prompt and efficient measures" to fight the pestilence. During such an epidemic, the board could call upon the city marshal and his deputy to respond to complaints from individual citizens about presumed nuisances. Complaints could be registered with the health board or city council. The marshal or his deputy, the health officer, then investigated and, when necessary, supervised the abatement of the condition that inspired the complaint.[20]

Council also sanctioned this board, as it had the others, to establish both external and internal quarantines. By employing the marshal, his deputy, and the wharfmaster, the board was empowered to secure the municipality from "the introduction of contagious, malignant, dangerous and infectious diseases," and to remove immediately "to some suitable place, any person, or persons, who may be found therein, infected with such disease." Penalties for violation of the quarantine law were to be stiff. Any person who should "knowingly introduce, or aid, or assist in introducing the Small-Pox, yellow fever, or other contagious disease" into the city, or who possessed "any knowledge of any person laboring under such diseases . . . within the city, without forthwith giving notice thereof" to the health board, stood liable to a fine of between one hundred and a thousand dollars.[21]

The board of 1832, then, differed neither organizationally nor substantively from others in this period, and like them too, it neither met nor acted nor had the power to act between epidemics or anticipated disease outbreaks. To be sure, the board did "exist" after the cholera outbreak of 1832 died out, but only in the sense that individuals continued to hold office on the board. Indeed, in subsequent years, city council often moved quickly to fill vacancies on the board when openings appeared, but the board itself met and functioned as a board only when the city seemed threatened by or had actually succumbed to an epidemic. With the disappearance of epidemic conditions, sometimes even when a few cases of the disease persisted, the board also disappeared. Council and the city's inhabitants applauded the efforts of the board and the board gratefully returned to its customary state of inactivity. Its members resumed the fulltime pursuit of their regular occupations, remaining like the militia ready to act instantly at the onset of the next pestilential episode.[22]

The ad hoc nature of both the boards of health and the enforcement of nuisance ordinances in early nineteenth century Cincinnati fit neatly with the notion that city government existed only to allow individuals the opportunity to engage in commerce and manufacturing. So too did the city's law enforcement agencies. From 1819, council employed a city marshal, whose chief daily responsibility was to act as a process server for the city courts. In later years, it occasionally provided him a few temporary assistants—deputy marshals—but made no provision for a police department. A temporary night watch was not formed until 1834, and this night watch, like the marshal and his aides who responded only to complaints of individual citizens, was not a police force in any recognizably "modern" sense. It did not patrol the city or do anything to protect residential areas. Instead, the watchmen were assigned to posts "about the several market places to protect wagons from being robbed." This watch was made permanent in 1837, but its function remained unchanged. Watchmen still hovered near city markets to prevent "burglaries, robberies, and other outrages and disorders" from disrupting any aspect of the city's commercial life.[23]

Neither the marshal and his deputies nor the watch could, of course, quell the riots that occurred in Cincinnati frequently during these years. Nor were they expected to handle such emergencies, the severity of which to contemporaries called for extraordinary measures. On occasions of riot, the security of the city and the protection of life and property became the responsibility of each individual citizen, though in no single case did every citizen of Cincinnati participate in dispersing a mob. Instead, the city marshal during riots either formed and directed deputized bands of city residents or else took control of voluntary paramilitary organizations, such as the Ohio Guard or the Grey Cadets. And occasionally, undeputized individuals, without incurring the wrath of law, pitched in with legitimately deputized riot control forces to battle the mob and restore the city. Upon completion of their task, those individuals received only the gratitude of the city citizenry.

Such was the case with the antiabolitionist riot of 1836. Several public meetings had been held to express concern about Cincinnati gaining a reputation as a site of rabid abolitionism. Led by the city's pro-Whig mayor, Samuel W. Davies, and other prominent citizens, these men objected to the activities of the Ohio Anti-Slavery Society and especially to the publication in Cincinnati of James G. Birney's *The Philanthropist*. In particular, they

maintained that the periodical offended Southern businessmen, discouraged them from purchasing and selling
goods in the Queen City, and therefore hampered the
city's economic growth, and called on Birney to make
their position known. Birney subsequently refused to
cease publication and although civic leaders urged restraint, the younger, more volatile elements in the city
took the matter into their own hands and reconstituted
themselves as a mob. A riot ensued. The mob smashed
the press on which *The Philanthropist* was printed, scattered the type, destroyed the office, and dumped debris
in the river. It then broadened the scope of its attack and
began to roust some blacks as well as other Cincinnati
abolitionists. The marshal and his deputies were powerless to stop the violence, but a citizen's group, headed by
Salmon P. Chase and councilman William M. Corry, a
Democrat, rushed to the marshal's side and helped disperse the mob. As soon as the uproar subsided, council
thanked those who had joined forces with the marshal
during the crisis for their help in returning the city to a
"state of quietness and obedience to laws," and terminated both its sanction of their efforts and their affiliation with government.[24]

Cincinnati's fire agency functioned in the same ad
hoc, emergency-oriented way. The city before 1853 had
no municipally run fire department charged both with
putting out fires and enforcing fire prevention regulations. Beginning in 1825, however, council regularly
appointed fire wardens for each ward and purchased
firefighting equipment, but the responsibility for firefighting remained in the hands of volunteer fire
companies. When a citizen sounded the alarm, several
volunteer companies gathered up their city-supplied
equipment, raced to the scene, and, following the direc-
tions of the appropriate warden, tried to put out the
fire. When the fire was extinguished, members of the

fire companies returned the city's fire equipment and, as did the fire wardens, went back to their regular jobs. This service, like that of the police organizations and the marshal's riot control squads, came free to city government. The fire companies received their rewards either from private contracts, from fire insurance companies, or from the munificence of grateful citizens whose dwellings or establishments they saved.[25]

Like police, fire, and health institutions in the early nineteenth century, the provision of relief in Cincinnati came as an ad hoc response to a situation. Unlike police and fire agencies, however, the responsibility for relief in Cincinnati fell not to municipal government, but to the trustees of the township, for whom the city boards of health provide a good analogue. The trustees, like the health boards, had no staff, and like the boards they responded to pleas for poor relief only during crises; that is, the trustees distributed relief only to individuals plunged into distress by some catastrophe, such as epidemics or extremely cold winters. The system functioned through contracts between the trustees and a physician or a dispensary, a fuel dealer, and a grocer, and it moved on particular cases at the request of any respectable Cincinnatian who knew a distressed person. To obtain relief, individuals requiring aid secured a letter of recommendation to the trustees, indicating that the individual in question permanently resided in the city, needed temporary assistance, and seemed a person of good character and demeanor. Thus armed, the poor person delivered the letter in question to the trustees, who authorized the provision of food, fuel, or medical attention and sent the supplicant to the appropriate place to secure relief.[26]

Described in these terms, the early nineteenth century relief system seemed simple and modest enough, but contemporaries took it seriously, responding to the poverty caused by severe weather or other catastrophes as conditions threatening the security of the city. Since such emergencies put massive numbers of city residents out of work and devastated families, they might if left unattended pile up indebtedness and develop bad habits, thereby extending the poverty created by an emergency beyond that crisis and reducing large numbers of individuals to street begging or engaging in crime. The development and persistence of these disorderly practices, contemporaries agreed, would drain the city's vitality and render it unattractive for commercial activity. Recovering from that stage would further exhaust the public purse, cause entrepreneurs to flee the place for more productive and less expensive settings, and ultimately produce a "dead" city.[27]

The emergency orientation of relief in the early nineteenth century places it comfortably among the city's police, fire, and health agencies. All of these agencies seemed to operate only in response to a critical situation, when the security of the city, not the health or wellbeing of its inhabitants, was threatened. Even the enforcement of the nuisance ordinances, both those dealing with noxious substances and noisome conditions as well as others, demonstrated this orientation; all noxious substances and noisome conditions did not constitute nuisances per se, nor did the racing of horses in the city nor the obstructing of sidewalks and thoroughfares. They became nuisances, and therefore subject to municipal action, only when they menaced the security of the city. It was each citizen's duty to "protect" the security of the city by "preventing" nuisances, by not engaging in those activities likely to become nuisances, and by informing city government of the existence of a situation or condition that threatened the security of the city. And to protect the city and to prevent situations or conditions from constituting nuisances, council dispatched the marshal or his aides to investigate each complaint.

Municipal government in Cincinnati during the early nineteenth century, then, apparently existed to provide for and regulate its citizens' commercial and manufacturing interests and to handle emergencies beyond the control of individuals, with emergencies defined by contemporaries as events or the anticipation of events such as fires, riots, disorders in the city's marketplaces, epidemics, and massive unemployment brought on by some natural disaster. These catastrophes in the world of the early nineteenth century were often recurring rather than extraordinary occurrences, but they acquired catastrophic status because they possessed the potential for disrupting the city's principal *raison d'être* as a place where individuals gathered for commerce and manufacturing.

The notion of crises as destroyers of the city's ability to provide individual opportunity for commerce and manufacturing led Cincinnatians to seek several charter emendations in the early 1830s. Two instances prove particularly illuminating. In 1831, council requested permission from the legislature to construct a bridge across the Ohio River, and a year later petitioned for the authority to purchase a privately owned waterworks. Although both these proposals ultimately were rejected by the state, they nonetheless bolster the proposition that early nineteenth century city governments existed simply to allow individuals to pursue commercial and manufacturing interests.

Extraordinary circumstances dictated Cincinnati's move in both cases. Initially, council considered the bridge matter to protect the city's commercial viability in the face of an outside threat. Since its founding, Cincinnati had competed with Lexington and Louisville for northern Kentucky markets. It managed to do more than hold its own, and by the late 1820s had placed the landlocked Lexington on the defensive. The state of Kentucky acted to save its municipality and, led by its native son, Henry Clay, got the United States Congress to appropriate funds for a road from Maysville to Lexington. President Jackson doomed this plan by vetoing the appropriations bill, however, and Kentucky took a new tack. The state chartered a railroad company that presumably would link Lexington and Louisville. To Cincinnatians, the railroad posed a threat of unprecedented magnitude. Its purpose seemed not merely to restore Lexington, but to make the Ohio city's chief rivals the primary marketplaces for northern Kentucky and, perhaps, southern Ohio and Indiana; it was likely to remove the major portion of Cincinnati's market sphere and cripple that municipality. To counter Kentucky's apparent foray into commercial imperialism, the city council of Cincinnati appealed for improved transportation connections into the area. This would foil its adversary's gambit by positioning Cincinnati within the new commercial network. The Ohio legislature turned council down, however, when Lexington announced that the railroad would not join with Louisville, but instead would run north to Cincinnati. This unanticipated change ended the necessity for the city to ask for exceptional powers.[28]

A similar emergency prompted council's decision to seek ownership of the waterworks. Indeed, it adopted that approach only after the actions of the utility's proprietors menaced the city's commercial life. Several times during the 1820s, the water company failed to fulfill the terms of its contract with the city. Sentiment existed in those periods for a municipal takeover, but the company always managed to stave it off by promising to undertake an expansion of its physical plant. In 1832, council entered the picture. It claimed that the proprietors not only proved incapable of delivering a quantity of water sufficient either to sustain the city's commercial and manufacturing needs or to insure its protection in case of fire, but that they also asked an outrageous price for their valuable commodity. While the company's inability to pump the amount of water necessary was more immediately devastating, the high cost of the local monopoly's water also seemed to affect the security of the city. It threatened to render the city's commercial enterprises uncompetitive with those of surrounding municipalities, which would drive entrepreneurs from Cincinnati and endanger the city's very existence.[29]

Cincinnati received one other charter prior to 1840, the charter of 1834, but it too failed to alter the nature of city government. Instead, the new charter renewed the powers granted the municipality in its earliest charters, and added one responsibility, one right, a single regulating authority, and one service, each of which fell within the spirit of the earlier charter. It transferred the responsibility for the establishment and care of the common schools within the city limits from the state to the municipality, gave Cincinnati the right to use the county prison, authorized council "to regulate . . . the keeping and sale of gunpowder within the city" and, in order to certify that all goods arrived in the city by terms agreed upon by the contracting parties, provided for the appointment of a port warden.[30]

The persistence of the basic form and function of Cincinnati city government between 1819 and about 1840 seems remarkable. The absence of any sort of public expression of dissatisfaction is even more jolting. The apparent acceptance of the notion that city government existed solely to provide individual opportunity to pursue mercantile and manufacturing ventures by early nineteenth century Cincinnatians immediately suggests an extremely homogeneous population; it implies a singlemindedness conceivable only in a society marked by an almost unheard-of uniformity in class, ethnicity, race, and religion. Statistics from this period offer quite a different portrait: Cincinnati by 1820 was a cosmopolitan city. It welcomed a river traffic that brought French, German, Dutch, and Irish immigrants who had originally landed in New Orleans, as well as Pittsburgh's Scotch-Irish. Others traveled overland to Cincinnati, coming from Kentucky, the deep South, central Pennsylvania, and upper New York state. In fact, Cincinnati was so ethnically diverse by about 1820 that a full 20 percent of its population was foreign-born.

The city's ethnic mixture was matched by religious, racial, and economic diversity. By 1820, at least ten different religious congregations had set up shop. The prominent Protestant denominations—Presbyterian, Quaker, Lutheran, Baptist, Methodist, and Episcopal—were firmly entrenched. Catholics were well represented. So too were blacks; as early as 1809, Cincinnati contained enough black residents to sustain a Black Methodist Church. Again, there were great disparities in wealth. Bankers, merchants, manufacturers, shipowners, lawyers, and physicians comprised the city's upper stratum. Its various artisans, clerks, innkeepers, restauranteers, and small businessmen were next in line, while the city's boatmen, laborers, dock hands, and workers constituted a swelling lower order.

Nor did the situation change substantially during the next two decades. Cincinnati continued to be the home of a very heterogeneous population. The expansion of established manufacturing and commercial operations and the introduction of new ones did little to narrow the economic and occupational gulf separating Cincinnati's wealthiest and poorest citizens. Immigrants also persisted in selecting the Queen City as their final port of call. Many steamed up the river from New Orleans, while those who landed at New York reached Cincinnati through the new overland transportation system. As stated earlier, Cincinnati's population in 1830 was almost 25,000, and this figure doubled again in the next decade. Foreign-born residents comprised about 30 percent of the population in 1830 and about 45 percent a decade later. The latter figure is suspect, though, because Charles Cist, the city's census taker in 1840 and again in 1850, apparently counted the children born in America of immigrant parents as well as American-born wives of immigrants as part of the foreign-born population. The percentage of black Cincinnatians also multiplied during the 1820s. Roughly 10 percent of the city's population in 1829 was black. The growth in the number of blacks led to the formation of two new and different black churches, an African Methodist church and a Methodist Episcopal church. Other religious groups also appeared in Cincinnati. A Jewish congregation was formed in 1824 and was soon joined by congregations of Unitarians, Swedenborgians, and Universalists.

A lively urban politics also characterized the post-1819 city. Various coalitions gained control of city council as political alliances were rapidly formed and just as rapidly terminated. Only three mayors presided over the city before 1840, but mayoralty elections were hotly contested, usually swung by a mere few hundred votes. Two of Cincinnati's first three mayors were European immigrants, and all had moved to Cincinnati in adulthood. Their occupations were respectively newspaper editor, lawyer, and textile manufacturer. Cincinnatians took sides on a number of different political questions, especially abolitionism and the contested national election of 1824. Indeed, parties favoring Jackson and John Q. Adams made their presence felt at least through the 1828 election. Whigs and Jacksonian Democrats continued the contest in the next decade.

During the entire period 1819–1840, then, Cincinnati's population exhibited a profound degree of ethnic, religious, racial, political, and economic diversity. To be sure, the city in 1840 had a much larger population than it had twenty years earlier. It also contained a larger percentage of foreign-born residents and had expanded its commercial and manufacturing concerns tremendously. These differences were differences only in scale; the fundamental constitution of the city was staked out by 1820. By that time it already had demonstrated a remarkably cosmopolitan character. It had become a city populated with numerous ethnic, religious, political, racial, and economic groups.

Nor were these diverse peoples isolated from one another. Virtually all labors revolved around the riverfront; because of the primacy of the river trade, all the social strata were pressed into intimate and frequent contact. The city's unique topography also contributed. The populated portion of the city lay in a natural amphitheater, the basin surrounded by hills averaging about 300 feet in height. Only two narrow valleys, one on the west and the other on the northeast, provided entrance to the basin. But the drastic topography was not the sole reason its various peoples lived in close proximity; once again, the river held the key. The city prior to 1827 lacked any type of public transportation; its inhabitants therefore tended to cluster as close as possible to their places of employment, seeking generally to live within a mile or so from their work. Homes further away seemed impractical because it would take residents too long to walk to their jobs. And since the river provided employment for the vast majority of Cincinnatians, virtually all the city's population dwelled in an area much smaller than its roughly five square mile corporate limits. Not until the opening of the Miami Canal in 1827, the introduction of the horsedrawn omnibus in the mid

1830s, and the establishment of the first railroad line in 1841 did a significant portion of the population move away from the waterfront and spread down the western valley.

In practice, almost all of Cincinnati's diverse people lived prior to the mid 1830s jammed in an area of not much more than three square miles. Even in a city as small as Cincinnati in 1820, the population density had already exceeded the amazing figure of 3,000 per square mile. It was even more crowded in 1830 because while the city's population grew to 25,000, its inhabited territory increased only slightly. The dense packing of peoples, coupled with the city's striking heterogeneity, made it impossible as early as 1819 for city residents to avoid intense and persistent interchanges with a wide variety of others not of their cohort, but the situation was even more complex. Except for the port area, there were no residential or business neighborhoods in the 1820s and early 1830s. Coffeehouses, manufactories, shops, and residences stood side by side. Ironically, only in that sense did the city tend toward homogeneity; it lacked land-use specialization.[31]

In early nineteenth century Cincinnati, all the forces by twentieth-century standards seemed in place to plunge the city into social chaos. The proliferation of lower orders might have engendered resentment among them and fear among the elites. In any case, class conflicts regularly could have appeared. Religious, ethnic, and racial tensions might have crystallized and found expression in recurring social strife. With the singular exception of an occasional antiblack riot—there had been sporadic racial antipathy from the mid 1820s—none of these hostilities occurred. The explanation for the lack of social dislocations rested not in the reality of Cincinnati's social situation but in its citizens' perception; social forces emerge as forces only when given that status by ideas. And in early nineteenth century Cincinnati, its residents' ideas were apparently of a very different nature. Cincinnati's diverse peoples acted not as members of rigidly defined socioeconomic, religious, or ethnic cohorts, but as individuals. In that sense, Cincinnati to its early nineteenth century inhabitants did indeed seem homogeneous because as individuals they all were engaged in the same enterprise, each citizen could insure his own fate, wellbeing, and health *provided* that he was granted or offered the key concept of opportunity.[32]

Early nineteenth century commentators repeatedly sounded this theme. The city's leading physician/natural historian, organizer, and entrepreneur par excellence, Daniel Drake, in 1815 stated the case simply. "There is no state in the Union which has not enriched our town with some of its most enterprising or restless citizens; [sic] nor a Kingdom in the West of Europe whose adventurous or desperate exiles are not commingled with us," he reported. Despite the diverse elements in the population, he maintained that all residents were alike because each was characterized by "industry, temperance, morality, and love of gain." Two prominent politician/literateurs, Benjamin Drake (no relation to Daniel) and Edward Deering Mansfield, Daniel Drake's cousin by marriage, agreed with Daniel Drake's assessment but offered more explicit detail. After an exhaustive house-to-house survey of Cincinnati in 1826, Mansfield and Drake boasted that the city was composed of "emigrants from all quarters of the Union, and from different parts of Europe." While the investigators noted great differences in the citizenry's wealth, they argued that Cincinnatians all resided in similarly modest and pleasant circumstances. The city's richest inhabitants avoided all show of luxury, maintained Drake and Mansfield, while its "poorer classes" lived in dwellings marked by the "appearance of comfort and ease." Crime and vice could not gain a foothold in this environment and, as a consequence, "labour receives its reward, and enjoys its security." The reason that Cincinnati stood as such a paragon of civility and virtue stemmed directly from "an entire freedom from political restraint," which left "all at liberty to follow such pursuits as are most agreeable." The presence of individual opportunity "favors the assimilation of all classes to each other, and the adoption of such manners and customs, as are most suitable to our situation." In summary, Drake and Mansfield agreed, opportunity for individual achievement produced "a more rapid amalgamation of manner and feeling, than would be expected among a people so recently collected together, from so many different countries."[33]

It was the city government's job to provide that individual opportunity to pursue commerce and manufacturing, and nothing more. Through the powers specified in its early nineteenth century charters, municipal government undertook a broad range of activities that included the employment of watchmen to guard the marketplaces and ports, the killing of wild and rabid dogs (an unchecked outbreak of rabies constituted an epidemic that like others hampered or terminated commercial operations), and contracting with scavengers to keep the public areas clean and uncluttered.[34] In addition, the municipality received the power to institute a number of temporary, emergency tasks, such as directing city residents to aid the marshal in breaking up a mob. Although some of these agencies, such as health boards or fire wardens, stood ready year round, they were neither to deliver nor did the state create them to deliver social services. These agencies came into play only in time of crisis, a time in which the viability of commerce and manufacturing in the city seemed jeopardized. Then, they swung into action as an integral part of city government, helping to restore order to the threatened or stricken city and enabling its citizens to renew their commercial participation.

The cessation of these emergency practices after the passing of each crisis did not mean that these institutions were ill conceived or that prior to the mid-nineteenth century the Ohio legislature, municipal officials, and city residents were irresponsible. The duties and obligations of these ad hoc bodies as defined in early nineteenth century Cincinnati simply extended only until the city's residents could resume their daily activities. The restoration of that state of affairs served as proof of the efficacy of municipal government, and the efforts of the temporary agencies and personnel no longer seemed necessary. Neither the cessation of the health board's disease-fighting mechanisms at the conclusion of each epidemic nor the absence of municipal institutions designed to provide social services on a full-time, regular basis should be construed to mean that all Cincinnatians in plague-free and peaceful times were either healthy or successful in their pursuit of commerce and manufacturing. Indeed, these two phenomena help uncover the notion that city government's commitment extended not to health and wellbeing, but only to the security of the city. In effect, health and success in early nineteenth century Cincinnati remained the province of each individual.

Though a city government charged only with the task of providing individual opportunity to pursue commerce and manufacturing seemed to work well to early nineteenth century Cincinnatians, the situation about 1840 changed both suddenly and radically. For the next decade and a half, city residents repeatedly grumbled about municipal affairs. In particular, they focused their assaults on the urban environment. Local newspapermen often were in the forefront. Complaining that the municipality "never was so dirty as at the present," one editor claimed, for example, that he could "name fifty streets and alleys whose depths of decayed vegetable and even animal matter sends forth an effluvia which no doubt deters even the scavenger from approaching them." Another journalist identified "alleys and gutters in the most frequently and closely inhabited parts of the city [as] so disgusting and offensive that one has to hold his nostrils in passing," and a third noted that "sink holes and hollows filled with stagnant water are much more common than spots of wholesome grass." He furthermore worried that the hollows, many of which had "been filled up with the scrapings of the alley, and the filth of gutters," contributed to "breeding vermin and spreading disease." And a fourth reporter decried the odor emanating from the city markets, which, he argued, smelled "so bad as to oblige us to shut our front doors." While these unsanitary conditions led "to the great enjoyment of the hogs," who seemed "to occupy more of the public highways than the citizens themselves," they produced "great annoyance" among the city's "more sensitive inhabitants."[35]

Similarly, Cincinnatians during this period claimed that they lived in a time of extensive lawlessness and issued regular and constant complaints to that effect. C. B. Brough, a Democratic city court judge and the editor of the *Cincinnati Daily Enquirer,* argued in 1847, for instance, that "the city was never so infested with criminals of every possible grade, as at the present time." To Brough and many of his fellow citizens, it seemed as if "one cannot walk the streets, after nine o'clock in the evenings, without meeting at every corner, men who are seeking means and opportunity for the commission of crime, women who are lost to all sense of shame, and boys who are much older in villainy than in years." These

Cincinnatians identified "a very strong band of true paupers in this community,—a circle of them extending through the whole city," and likened this circle to a "high-school of vice and crime." There, children were "learning daily lessons of iniquity . . . , and teaching them to the children of happier birth in the great seminary of the street." It was not unusual, it was recounted, "to hear from boys and girls of ten and twelve, and even six and seven, accounts . . . of every evil practice, from simple drunken revelry down to theft and bloodshed."[36]

Horace Bushnell, a city missionary in the 1840s, sounded a similar cry and employed social arithmetic to back up his assertions. "The city," by Bushnell's calculations, "is supplied with one thousand grog-shops," with "an average [of] three attendants" and "at least nine customers." But, he continued, "houses of infamy are more numerous than grog-shops," and he estimated that the city contained over "four thousand women lost to virtue." That was not the extent of the "army [who] prey on the best interests of the community." Bushnell also included in his statistical summary men who frequented prostitutes, labeling them "companions in sin." Together, their numbers exceeded "thirty thousand persons, whose business it is to create pauperism, drunkenness, licentiousness, crime and death."[37]

Contemporary social critics in Cincinnati did not confine themselves to diagnosing and objecting to the state of society, but also attempted to explain why Cincinnati had become afflicted. These efforts did not yield a single, concise explanation for the origins of social disorder. Despite apparent differences, however, the several expositions all were similar in that they placed blame for the troubling situation on the appearance of a specific group of individuals, each member of whom suffered from a deficient or inappropriate preparation for a social existence in America. In that manner, members of all groups identified as culpable were viewed as strangers—strange to American ways—even if they, their parents, and their parents' parents had been Cincinnatians all their lives.

Indeed, it was precisely the identification of *strangers* as a distinct subpopulation that accounted for the perception of these serious social problems. Definition of large population concentrations as social units composed of two main divisions, the members of one of which acted in a manner inimical to the unit's wellbeing, encouraged residents of these concentrations to examine how their fellow inhabitants did in fact act and to scrutinize the physical environment as the place in which improper activity often manifested itself. These observers anticipated finding unseemly conditions or deviations from the idealized pattern of social behavior, any one of which served to confirm the existence of this subpopulation. In this tautological reasoning, each prostitute, disheveled child, or unsightly street was reported—not dismissed as a temporary aberration or an exception—and magnified to constitute an indictment far broader than the individual case merited. It verified that the unit had a crisis of unprecedented proportions within its midst.

This formulation was reflected in the manner in which Cincinnatians from the late 1830s to the early 1850s often referred to these situations and conditions. They termed them "the social evils," by which they meant the evils of collective living in a democratic society where a segment of the collectivity, generally through ignorance, regularly violated behavioral norms and so continually put themselves and their fellows at risk. That understanding spoke to the permanence of the social evils as the price paid for living in behaviorally nonhomogeneous population concentrations—cities—in America.

Again, it must be stressed that the designation *strangers* seemed to describe a "real" portion of the city population, which quite often was *not* synonymous with immigrants. Rather, strangers were all peoples who seemed to act improperly because their pasts were improper; they had not been trained appropriately and, as a consequence, were not prepared to function responsibly within their "new" milieu. Their unfamiliarity with the mode of living demanded as part of a large social unit in democratic society, and their lack of adequate training, made it inevitable that they would engage in its temptations and fall victim to its consequences. They would violate the law, beg on street corners, live in and cause the accumulation of filth, and succumb to disease. More simply, these strangers seemed neither to accept nor fulfill the time-honored responsibilities of individual city residents. They had failed to learn that they had a duty not to create dangerous situations or conditions and to report the existence of hazards when created by others. And their lack of an appropriate American social education spelled disaster for Cincinnati. Strangers were ruining themselves and their "adopted" city.

A number of Cincinnatians tackled the issue of the emergence of strangers head on, characteristically considering it an event of recent origin. One popular Cincinnati explanation centered on migration patterns within the United States, including the movement of portions of the rural population to cities. Arguing that America always contained some who were "uneducated and unreflecting," a writer in the *Cincinnati Daily Gazette* asserted that in the past rural dwellers remained on farms, where, through the orderly routine of farm life, they eventually modified their behavior. Now, this group seemed "to congregate around great centres of commerce," such as Cincinnati, and the writer proposed to resolve the problem of their dangerous actions by having them sent back to the country. C. B. Brough and a correspondent to the *Enquirer,* identified as Los Pobres, put forth alternative explanations. While they recognized that those who produced the social evils could be found throughout America, both argued that the extent of the problem was unique to Cincinnati. Brough claimed that the frequent yellow fever and smallpox epidemics "at the South has thrown upon us all the idle and vicious populations of that region, and our city literally swarms with those who live by crime and vice." Los Pobres, on the other hand, asserted that the indiscriminant generosity of Cincinnatians was at fault. Because Cincinnati's residents bestow alms without judgment, he noted, "we find the adjoining towns and cities shipping their paupers here." If Cincinnatians continued to provide aid to all who sought it, Los Pobres warned, "we might soon expect to see our city turned into a hospital and infirmary for the halt, the maimed, and the blind of the whole Mississippi Valley." To both men, the solution was simple. Cincinnatians could lessen the burden by prohibiting members of uninitiated groups from entering the city's borders.[38]

Others disregarded migration explanations for the origin of the social evils in Cincinnati, and placed blame on the breakdown of the family. Some argued that the social evils stemmed from a parent's intemperance or infidelity, while others attributed their existence to a general decline in parental influence or responsibility. In either case, however, they asserted that the weakening of the family unit constituted an ominous pattern, causing children to reach maturity without receiving the proper moral discipline necessary to insure their success or health. Repeatedly these people focused on the defective childrearing practices caused by the dissolution of the family. For example, John L. Vattier, a distinguished Cincinnati physician, politico, and entrepreneur, denounced the growing custom among women of hiring a wet nurse. Not only was "the submission of infants to the breast of another . . . a perversion of natural affection," but it also deprived children of maternal guidance during their formative years, guidance that would hold them in good stead in America once they reached maturity. And Calvin W. Starbuck, publisher of the *Cincinnati Daily Times,* attributed "many, if not all, the social evils which afflict society" to the failure of mothers to fulfill their "duty in the family circle." Specifically, Starbuck railed against those mothers who neglected childrearing in order to engage in benevolent activity. The neglect, he wrote,

> of the moral education of youth by the female parent, which has pretermitted for the prosecution of vain, fanciful, and visionary schemes of public good, has originated the moral pestilence which now infects our atmosphere; the profanation of the Sabbath day; the neglect of divine worship; the excessive indulgence of sensual appetites, not only drunkenness, but of lust and impunity; and in a word, the notorious, universal, and admitted profligacy and corruption, which stalks unrebuked throughout the land.[39]

A third Cincinnatian expressed similar sentiments, though he did not restrict his analysis to the children of female reformers. He maintained that there were "thousands of young girls [who] are fast becoming women, in this city, destitute of all moral instruction." Not only were these girls only "educated to be destroyed," but their influence would certainly be felt in successive generations. They would become "destroyers in those homes of want and destitution, of intemperance and vice."[40]

Other critics of the family raised different objections. For example, Bushnell absolved mothers, but blamed fathers for the city's plight. Complaining that the fathers' decreasing role in the home accounted for "hundreds and thousands of youths growing up without one particle of moral training," he urged fathers to take a more active part in childrearing and to see that families attended church as a unit each Sunday. The continued failure to heed his advice, Bushnell warned, jeopardized the "social, as well as the moral and religious condition of the city."[41]

Cist agreed in principle with this explanation for strangers, but focused exclusively on the children of prominent men. He argued that their fathers' overwhelming preoccupation with the public weal resulted in familial neglect. As a consequence of this neglect, these children often reached maturity without having experienced a father's firm but loving discipline. And without a father's guiding hand, these young adults frequently became "so far sunk as to glory in their shame, or to become callous under disgrace." Cist provided dramatic examples to bolster his contention. The first was "the daughter of a respectable clergyman" and the "niece of a member of Congress." Lacking during her formative years her father's direction, she became "a public prostitute in this city, whom no remonstrances can rouse, nor recollection shame." The second was the child of "a distinguished son of Pennsylvania," a "grandson of a general officer of the revolution." He had become "a vagabond in our city; now, and not for the first time, on the chain gang, apparently one of the most hopeless of the lost."[42]

Immigration served as another common explanation for the social evils. To proponents of this view, foreign groups seemed to engage most blatantly in inappropriate behavior. Singling out the Germans, who lived in "humblest relation with civilization," and the Irish, who reached civilization's "lowest degradation," a variety of

Cincinnatians suggested that conditions in Europe explained both their flight from the old world and their
plight in the new. James J. Faran, who edited the *Cincinnati Daily Enquirer* after Brough's death in 1849 and later
became the Democratic mayor of the city, contended
that "the whole tendency of political and social events in
Europe is to drive the inhabitants from the poverty, des-
potism and wretchedness there, to the vast fertilities and
free institutions of the new world," to which they could
not easily adjust. Accustomed to living in poverty under
strict, authoritarian regimes, they suddenly encountered
the material abundance and the lack of restraints of
America and found that they lacked the discipline necessary to cope with the bewildering situation.[43]

Taking a similar line, Thomas G. Carroll, physician
to the Orphan's Asylum in Cincinnati, argued that each
immigrant was both weakened by his inability to adjust
to the American climate and "beset with the many temptations unknown to him in his country. The various
kinds of wholesome foods, and above all," Carroll contended, "the facilities for indulgence in strong drink are
prominent among the causes that emigrants fall prey" to
disease. Others, however, concentrated on the crass European traditions and habits that immigrants brought to
America, for although it often was suggested that these
modes of living were suitable to the immigrants' native
lands, they appeared antithetical to Cincinnati. Packing
themselves into tenements, cellars, and abandoned
houses, immigrants wallowed in filth, ignored the potential consequences on health and morals, appeared to en-
joy living in their customary squalor, and seemed to have
an aversion to nature's most salubrious substance, fresh
air. As Carroll commented in the aftermath of a cholera
epidemic, "the foreigner possesses not only filthy habits
in his mode of living, but has a peculiar inclination to
avoid ventilation in his dwelling."[44]

Although contemporary investigations of the social evils suggested that Cincinnati's strangers consciously chose to live in these deplorable conditions and engage in these disgusting habits, many residents of Cincinnati considered it their duty to change the situation. Indeed, to permit entire classifications of people to waste their lives did not speak well of Cincinnatians. Repeatedly in these years, city residents asked: What does it say about us, if we assist, through processes such as tenantage, or condone, by ignoring the situation, the deterioration or even suicide of people in our midst who suffer either from inappropriate or improper training? An unidentified citizen of Cincinnati explicitly expressed that concern when he worried about what type of people we are when we not only allow "foreign emigrants, lately arrived in the country, unaccustomed to our climate, or our mode of living, to crowd themselves into rooms already occupied, . . . [but also when we allow] the owners of the premises or their agents [to] disregard the loathsome condition, as well as the health and comfort of the neighborhood?"[45]

Others hammered at the same theme. For example, J. C. Wright, editor with his brother Louis of the leading Whig paper, the *Cincinnati Daily Gazette,* argued that "preventable death is a thing which ought not to exist . . . in a Christian and Civilized Community." Since strangers seemed incapable of protecting themselves because of ignorance, Wright saw it as the responsibility of his fellow Cincinnatians to enlighten and to educate these unfortunate groups. We "owe it to the cause of common humanity," Wright wrote, "to warn them again and again of the consequences of their imprudence."[46]

Some historians would interpret the previous sentiments as an expression of a pietistic awakening to the problems of midcentury urban life, as a burst of humanitarianism. Advocates of the social control thesis would

find solace in a second thread of the debate.[47] Reformation of members of these groups seemed imperative
not only as a demonstration of benevolence, but also because of their impact on Cincinnati society. Indeed,
"strangers" appeared likely to spawn their noxious habits
throughout the city. Improper and unhealthy influences
on the innocent, the reformed, and the reforming, these
groups, seemingly ever growing, threatened the Queen
City's social fabric. E. D. Mansfield, then editor of the
Daily Cincinnati Chronicle, coeditor of the *Cincinnati Daily
Atlas,* a leading Whig, and still a member of Daniel
Drake's circle, sounded the call to arms in an article decrying the increase in pauperism in the city. We must act
immediately, he asserted, for "if we do not, this class of
population visit back, as they daily do, upon society all its
hardships, with ten-fold interest."[48]

Mansfield did not stand alone in his call to action.
Others worried about the impact on the municipality of
"a certain class of population, whose vices, crimes, and
poverty have made them subjects of disease and early
death," for "in this class, mortality is fearfully great, epidemics are generated and the elements of crime and
pauperism are found." Another Cincinnatian provided
more particular reasons why his fellow citizens must act
now to halt the spread of the social evils. "The man of
property" must endeavor to rid the city of this menace,
he noted, "because his houses and goods are endangered by it; the man of family, rich or poor, because it
threatens with ruin his sons and daughters; the friends
of education, because it is the deadliest foe to knowledge
and labor; the Christian, because it is one of Satan's chief
nets to catch souls with." And one city resident, identified only as Medicus, put the matter more bluntly, pointing out the fact that the city was a place in which
"strangers" interacted with established citizens. "We
must remember," warned Medicus, "that the prince and

the pauper breathe one common air, and that the foul pestilential emanations of the hovel penetrates to the palace and produces its effects there."[49]

In sum, Cincinnatians after about 1840 identified a segment of the city population as inappropriately trained for life in an American social unit. These people all were strangers to American customs. Surprisingly, many commentators offered this assessment even as they acknowledged that members of the pinpointed group had been lifelong residents of American cities; this group of individuals was nonetheless "foreign" because it had failed to learn the rules. The consequences of that apparent ignorance were twofold. Strangers would surely devastate themselves and menace their fellow citizens' lives, activities, and health. The existence of this group posed a continuing threat of unprecedented dimensions. Left unchecked, it regularly would eat at the city's heart. But that was not all. At any moment, the actions of strangers could spark a citywide emergency—epidemic, riot, or the like—of tremendous proportions.

The sudden discovery about 1840 of these strangers and the intensity of the fears unleashed by that discovery are shocking to encounter today. It is even more startling in light of Cincinnati's earlier history. By 1820, the city was already a crowded caldron of diverse ethnic, racial, religious, political, and occupational groups. The diversity of peoples, coupled with the city's land-use patterns, made it virtually impossible for anyone to remain independent of the actions of others; citizens of several races, creeds, and socioeconomic and ethnic groups were repeatedly thrown together. Yet except during crises in which individual opportunity for commerce and manufacturing were hindered, almost no one expressed discontent either about the city's composition (opposition to blacks did surface occasionally) or its government. And between 1820 and about 1840, only the city's

numbers had increased: Cincinnati had become more
heavily and densely populated.

The persistence of the fears first articulated about
1840 for roughly fifteen years is equally disturbing,
While more people poured into Cincinnati during this
period—the city's population topped 115,000 in 1840—
other changes tended to place Cincinnati's diverse peoples in less intimate contact and decrease chances for social confrontations. Indeed, an argument can be made
that Cincinnati's more affluent citizens (presumably
those most threatened by strangers) lived more isolated
and, by extension, safer and more pleasant lives after
1840 than had their counterparts in 1820. In any case,
Cincinnati's "better" citizens in the years after about
1840 had less reason to intermingle with the city's lower
orders.

Several events transformed the cosmopolitan, highly
heterogeneous Cincinnati of 1820 into an increasingly
socially parochial city after 1840. Ironically, the emergence of the railroad as an important factor in the city's
commerce and manufacturing endeavors was one step
towards social parochialism. It facilitated development
of segregated land-use patterns, which gave city sections
a much more homogeneous texture than ever before.
The railroad/commerce and manufacturing connection
deemphasized the river, which had served as the city's
exclusive economic lifeline, and resulted in movement
northward of a substantial part of the city's population.
Beginning in the late 1830s and occasionally during the
next two decades, several entrepreneurs unveiled plans
to construct railroad lines linking Cincinnati to the
north's great cities. None of these projected railroads
was intended to run to the waterfront, but instead to end
operations either on the city's northeast or northwest
fringe, in either case a little less than a mile north of the
river. Though only the northwestern terminal was com-

pleted prior to 1850, opening in 1841, these two prime
locations became sites around which Cincinnatians began to develop their businesses as warehouses, shops,
and some factories moved to take advantage of the railroads' availability or, in the case of the northeast, anticipated availability. As a consequence, the territory both
immediately north of and between either terminal point
and the river took on a commercial and manufacturing
character. And the removal of many commercial and
manufacturing interests from the waterfront eliminated
the constraints that had inhibited population growth at
the city's northernmost points. It permitted Cincinnatians to spill further up the flatlands between the hills
and still remain within walking distance of their jobs.
The new commercial and manufacturing districts took
hold so rapidly and the population pressed outward so
quickly that in the late 1840s the city of Cincinnati was
even annexing land that had stood beyond the city's
northern boundary.

The city's large-scale, foul-smelling industries followed the city's population outward. They settled on the
city's fringe as far as possible from most city residents.
But Cincinnati's fringe and the areas north and south of
the terminal points were not the only sections of the city
to exhibit a degree of land-use specialization. A central
business district crystallized inside the semicircle composed of railroad terminal points and the waterfront.
Coffeehouses, bars, theaters, hotels, banks, insurance
companies, shops, and wholesale and retail stores con-
gregated to and marked the newly defined central business district. So too did religious and governmental
institutions. Each type of concern within this urban core
tended, moreover, to situate itself near other similar establishments; Cincinnati's central business district after
about 1840 contained a banking area, an insurance company enclave, and so forth. And as this district of dis-

tricts took shape, many Queen City inhabitants who had
lived previously in the core sought housing in other
parts of the city. Though no section of the city was entirely homogeneous, the effect of this change in the
downtown land-use pattern was to separate throughout
the city, and on a scale never before approximated, residences from commercial enterprises.

The beginnings of the segregation of commercial
and manufacturing entities seemed likely to alleviate
one potential source of urban unrest. Indeed, the removal of some businesses from residential areas surely
produced a more pleasant living environment. Too, it
was not the only process occurring in the years after
about 1840 that placed Cincinnati's diverse peoples in
less intimate contact. Just as businesses were becoming
isolated from residences and situated near others making or selling similar products, the city's inhabitants were
sorting themselves out into ethnic, religious, racial, and
socioeconomic enclaves. During this period, the lower
west end was identified as the city's Jewish sector, while
blacks gathered in the upper west end. The Irish appeared to take root in the east near the Ohio river bot-
toms (a small group of prominent blacks lived nearby)
and the Germans adopted the area north of the Miami
Canal, a section quickly named "Over the Rhine." The
bulk of the city's native-born Protestants lived closer to
the central business district in a broad arc beneath the
canal and the city's two fashionable residential neighborhoods bordered the core on the east and west.

This dramatic geographic realignment made each
section of Cincinnati more homogeneous, a factor that
ought to have eased ethnic, religious, racial, and socioeconomic tensions. Though no area of the city approached uniformity—no group dominated at densities
approaching 80 percent—and while representatives of
all groups could still be found throughout the city, Cin-

cinnatians after about 1840 lived much more sheltered existences than their counterparts earlier in the century. Increasingly living in neighborhoods more residential in character and inhabited to a greater degree by their own kind, they confronted less frequently other religious, racial, ethnic, and socioeconomic groups. Improvements in mass transport also paved the way for a reduction of potential strains. The availability of inexpensive, rapid transportation—the omnibus, steam commuter railroad, and, finally, the horsedrawn street railway—enabled Cincinnati's prosperous citizens as well as those moderately well-to-do to leave the city, establish residences beyond the hills, and come to the Queen City only for business and pleasure. The siphoning off of these men and women to bedroom suburbs, such as Mount Healthy and Clifton, presented Cincinnati with a population more socioeconomically homogeneous, lessening opportunities for class conflicts.[50]

Despite geographic changes that seemed likely to reduce potential tensions and confrontations, the fact remains that Cincinnatians about 1840 began to complain vociferously and continually about the social evils. Ironically, one explanation for this seemingly contradictory situation rests with the new urban geography. It could be argued that the recurring outbursts of concern stemmed directly from the concentration of specific groups in specific sections of the city; the geographical rearrangement of peoples made groups of individuals exhibiting apparently similar habits more publicly visible and, at the same time, decreased opportunities for individual interaction. In this interpretation, the increased visibility would place a premium on each group's behavioral characteristics, while the absence of repeated firsthand intimate contact would heighten fears; it would accentuate differences among groups and convert those differences into hazards or threats. In that sense,

Cincinnati would have been transformed into a city in which apprehensions and suspicions were generated precisely because its citizens no longer intermingled frequently.

While the explanation may well account for the persistence of objections into the early 1850s, it must be remembered that the process of geographical realignment had only started about 1840. In that earlier year, its barest outlines were not yet discernible, even to a historian viewing the manuscript census in the course of a study done nearly 130 years later. Nor did Cist himself detect any sorting out of peoples while taking and evaluating the 1840 census. He did notice a geographical rearrangement in his 1850 tally, however, and featured that information prominently.[51] That the beginnings of the new urban geography occurred exactly at the same time that Cincinnatians expressed their initial sense of outrage made it unlikely that the former caused the latter. Indeed, the first sustained cries of dissatisfaction emerged in a period when Cincinnatians were still living according to the social geography of 1820. And in the nearly twenty years prior to 1840, that social geography seemed to have engendered little comment; virtually no one, except during emergencies, complained about either the city's social problems or the municipal government.

What was significant, however, and what the nature of the contemporary discourse made clear was that Cincinnatians after about 1840 predicated their efforts on the notion that the city was comprised of groups, not individuals. These "groups" formed the basis for the geographical redistribution of peoples and for the new social and political organizations and clubs. And in the case of municipal affairs, Cincinnatians identified their city as composed of two major divisions, the members of one of which acted in a manner deleterious to its well-

being and the wellbeing of others. Though not addressing the issue of causation, this redefinition of the
composition of the city and by extension of the nature of
urban society fueled both the discovery of the social evils
and the decisions—and they were decisions that trans-
lated into action—to live and associate with those who by
about 1840 seemed to be one's own kind. In effect, it
gave new meaning to long-standing urban conditions as
well as imparting a particular emphasis to new social
situations.

Despite the arguments of social critics, crime, disease, vice, filth, and street begging were not new to mid-
nineteenth century Cincinnati. These conditions not
only existed in the Queen City from its beginnings, but
they also produced a governmental response after 1819
whenever impeding the ability of individuals to participate in commerce and manufacturing. What was new
about 1840, and what produced the regular expression
of concern, was not simply the recognition of the existence of these conditions, but the fact that their existence was seen in a new and different way; it posed a
threat of unprecedented magnitude. And that presumption stemmed from the identification of a new problem,
the presence in Cincinnati of an entire group of people
lacking knowledge of or experience in American social
life. It not only gave meaning to the discovery of the
social evils, but it also transformed the idea of the city
and led to the articulation of the concept of a public
interest.

This "plague of strangers" marked a crucial percep-
tual change, one that made it possible to conceive of an
agent responsible for regulating the interactions among
groups and for maintaining or protecting the public
interest. Indeed, citizens of Cincinnati now seemed
constantly threatened, as if in the midst of a perpetual
crisis, for as part of the social unit known as a city, each

appeared to depend at least in part upon others within the municipality for his wellbeing and health.

Although this plague of strangers seemed a potent menace, Cincinnatians approached the problem with an attitude best described as cautiously optimistic, apparently feeling that they ultimately could bring the situation under control. The reason for their confidence in the face of seeming chaos lay in their assumption that strangers could be taught how to modify their actions and therefore to develop into consummate city residents. And with this view in mind, many set about to provide the training requisite to convert strangers into decent and proper citizens. One branch of this effort revolved around benevolent societies; in the 1840s and early 1850s, Cincinnatians created an incredible number of organizations, each of which was dedicated to the education of urban strangers.[52] Although many involved in benevolent work acknowledged that it gave some indications of success, they also realized even as they participated that it alone did not constitute a permanent solution to the plague of strangers. They did not fault the method, but instead maintained that voluntary associations by themselves could not handle the task; since the influx of strangers seemed likely to continue indefinitely, the problem was simply too massive and too critical to be left to benevolence alone. Louis Wright provided a graphic description of the inability of benevolent efforts alone to provide a lasting cure. Benevolent enterprises, he remarked, "are a sisyphean labor," whose "only certain reward is that which is afforded by the consciousness of having done good work." Those engaged in these activities, Wright continued, "are rolling an immense stone uphill, and must brace their sinews to keep it where they got it. The moment they relax their exertions, it begins to press upon them, and beat them back, and if for an instant they release their hold on it, it begins the descent, and will go down even farther than the point from which they lifted it."[53] To men and women such as Wright, benevolence could never serve as more than an adjunct. While many proved steadfast in their benevolent efforts, they increasingly looked to city government to provide assistance in training the strangers.

$\mathscr{SO}$ 3   *Fighting the Plague*

The social evils were deemed new by city residents, carried to the Queen City by individuals unfamiliar with, unaccustomed to, or unprepared for living as part of a densely populated social unit in a democracy. The decision of Cincinnatians to seek a remedy through the instrumentality of city government for this plague brought to them by strangers sparked a torrent of legislation as well as the creation of new municipal agencies. And as Cincinnatians were embarking upon this new enterprise, the way in which the powers of the municipality might be brought to bear on the problem was by no means obvious. This uncertainty led to extensive experimentation by both Democrats and Whigs. Despite the confusion, however, each attempt to employ city government derived its impetus from a similar proposition; the relationship among city residents seemed to require establishing permanent government-sponsored mechanisms to insure the social unit's constant and regular functioning.

The lack of a clear sense of the best way to involve city government was not the only obstacle city residents faced. They also had to contend with a city charter that outlined a government fitted for a different purpose. Operating under the charter granted by the legislature in 1834, city government found its duties neatly circumscribed, limited to the task of providing individual opportunity for the pursuit of commerce and manufacturing. While municipal officials in the predominantly Whig-controlled city government initially were compelled to work within that confining scheme, they soon stretched the municipal bureaucracy beyond its limits and repeatedly sought additional authority from a recalcitrant legislature. This latter objective struck a resonant chord with the city's prominent citizens. They enthusiastically joined the crusade to secure for the city a governing document that would empower the municipality to form institutions and to enact legislation that seemed likely to fight the plague of strangers.

The governmental campaign to free the municipality of the social evils began quite early, even as the benevolent effort was getting underway. Upset by lawlessness in the city, and citing new dangers arising "from the depredations of incendiaries" and others "committing outrages during the night season," council in 1839 created an adjunct to the marshal and his deputies known as the patrole. The patrole was not a fulltime, paid police force, for under the terms of the 1834 city charter the municipality possessed neither the authority nor the money to create such a body. Instead, the patrole, which acted only during emergencies, consisted entirely of citizens approved by the mayor who wished "voluntarily [to] perform the duties" of "police officers," and who were "vested with the same powers and to the same extent, during the time they are on duty, as other police officers are, for arresting and bringing to justice all offenders to the public peace."[1] Two years later, council sought to strengthen further the night watch by permitting the captain of the watch "to accept the services of any number of volunteer watchmen." Once sanctioned by the captain, these men assumed "all the powers of police officers and watchmen, during the time they may be on duty."[2]

Though restricted by the terms of the charter of
1834, council tried repeatedly in the 1840s to improve
the municipal regulation of newcomers so as to protect
the public interest. In 1842, for example, council decided that the patrole and the volunteer watchmen
failed to provide Cincinnati with the protection its citizens sought. The inadequacy of the voluntary policemen
did not stem from a lack of enthusiasm; volunteers prosecuted their duties with vigor, often fighting among
themselves to make an arrest and therefore increasing
rather than diminishing public disorder. Rather, deeming it "expedient and necessary for the peace and safety
of the city to establish a more effectual police for its protection," council in 1842 organized its volunteers into
companies of "police guards." The new rules set up a
single company of police guards in each ward and stipulated that each company should consist "of not less than
twenty nor more than sixty men." Council also required
that guard members must "be citizens of the United
States and residents of the city, and householders of the
ward in which they may be chosen, and not less than
twenty-one years of age."

These guards, like their immediate predecessors,
were volunteer groups that acted only during emergencies, and the process for forming a company remained
simple. Any twenty men who met the qualifications laid
out in the ordinance of 1842 merely needed to "take an
oath before the mayor of the city to discharge their duties faithfully" and to receive the consent of council to
organize a company. Each guard company was responsible for adding members, and could choose from its own
body a captain and four lieutenants. The captains of the
various companies together selected "a commandant,
who shall be the commander of all the companies" in the
city. In addition, the companies could write "such by-
laws and regulations for their government and action as

may be necessary" for the successful performance of their duties, providing that they enacted nothing "contrary to law." Council retained authority, however, "to dismiss any member or officer for misconduct" and "to dissolve and disband any company for good cause."

The police guards possessed broad law enforcement powers, for they were established to handle disturbances only of sufficient severity to be deemed emergencies. Specifically, council commanded the members of the guards to stand "in readiness, both by day and by night, to protect the city and the inhabitants thereof against injuries by thieves, robbers, and burglars and other persons violating the public peace, and for the suppression of riots, and other disorderly conduct." In short, each member of the guards was "invested, when in actual service, with all the powers and privileges that are conferred by law upon ministerial officers and constables in this state and the marshal of the city of Cincinnati."[3]

Later that same year, council passed another ordinance to protect the public interest, and for the first time provided for the appointment of two men to serve as a day watch. They received the same salary as the night watch—$1.25 per day—and were designated as "police officers" charged with seeing "that the ordinances of the city [were] duly enforced and the peace of the city at all times preserved."[4]

Council in the early 1840s not only tried to strengthen its emergency police services, but also adopted new legislation regulating "Taverns, Coffee Houses and Restaurats [sic]." To be sure, licensing of such establishments was not a new municipal activity, but in 1843 council tightened its grip measurably on these places. To secure a license from council, a potential proprietor now had to present that body with "a recommendation signed by at least twelve respectable householders, residing in the immediate neighborhood of the

house where such Tavern, Coffee House or Restaurat
[sic] is intended to be kept . . . certifying that the peti-
tioner is well qualified" to run an establishment of this
type. A councilman from that ward then investigated
the request for a license, taking "into view the local situation" and "all other circumstances connected with such
application," and reported his findings to council. If
council was "satisfied that the license applied for ought
to be granted," it authorized the city clerk to issue a license for the period of one year.[5]

Similarly, council in the early 1840s banned certain
activities in taverns, coffeehouses, and restaurants, and
provided stiff penalties for violating the new regulations. It stipulated that any proprietor of such a place
who "shall permit or allow any kind of rioting or revel-
ing, drunkenness, lewd or disorderly conduct in his or
her house, or his or her premises," or who kept the business open on the Sabbath, was subject to a fine of not
less than ten nor more than fifty dollars. Upon conviction, council reviewed the offender's application for license, a process often involving the holding of a public
hearing, and could either revoke "the license of such
person," or take "such action thereon as they [sic] may
think proper."

Nor was that all. In the early 1840s council also prohibited both gaming and the serving of liquor to minors
in taverns, coffeehouses, and restaurants. Owners convicted "of playing at or suffering any person or persons,
with his or her consent, to play any game or games, in his
or her house, or his or her premises," had their licenses
automatically suspended for one year and could not
secure another license for a similar period. Similarly,
proprietors who sold or bartered "any wine, cordial,
spirituous liquors, porter, ale, beer, or other fermented
or intoxicating liquors to any person or persons under
the age of 17 years," or who enticed or harbored minors

"in or about his or her house or premises," received a fine of from twenty to one hundred dollars, lost their licenses, and were disqualified from holding another license for one year. Penalties for the sale or barter of liquor without a license were equally harsh, each offense subjecting the violator to a fine of up to one hundred dollars.[6]

Council also attempted to combat the plague of strangers in the early 1840s by passing Sabbatarian legislation. These laws attempted to make Sunday a day for church, reflection, and family, a day on which strangers were prohibited from engaging in many of their "unseemly" activities, but were forced to behave as they "should," and therefore presumably acquire some of the experience they lacked. In 1843, council established penalties of up to twenty dollars for any person "fourteen years or upward" who on the Sabbath was found "sporting, rioting, quarreling, hunting, fishing, shooting, trading, bartering, or selling or buying any goods, wares, or merchandize [sic] or at any common labor." The same ordinance reduced fines on tavern, coffeehouse, or restaurant keepers for violating the Sabbath to twenty dollars for the first offense, but it also made forfeiture of the license mandatory on conviction of a second similar violation. To demonstrate its seriousness to violators of the Sabbath, as well as to others who refused to abide by city laws, council passed in 1844 an ordinance stipulating that convicted offenders delinquent in paying their fines would be removed "to the jail of Hamilton County, until such fines are paid."[7]

Despite the municipal effort in the 1840s to rid the city of the social evils, the situation in Cincinnati seemed to show little improvement. The new ordinances remained virtually unenforceable, for under the charter of 1834 Cincinnati city government was authorized to appoint only the city marshal and his few deputies as

full-time law officers. Only during emergencies, such
as epidemics or riots, did council hold power to add
additional men, whether volunteers or paid, to the law
enforcement effort. Otherwise, violators could be apprehended only by the marshal or his deputies, and since
these men could not canvass the entire city they had to
depend upon complaints registered by citizens. The situation also frustrated law-abiding and responsible persons, who when witnessing a violation of an ordinance
could only inform the marshal and hope that the officer
was unoccupied and could arrest the offender.

The perceived threat of strangers warranted city government's attention, and since council by charter could
deal effectively only with emergency situations it moved
once more during the early 1840s in that direction. In
1844, it abolished the police guards, claiming the organization had proved ineffective, and created a paid emergency force to act under direction of the city marshal.
The ordinance authorized the mayor to designate up to
ten men per ward as "deputy marshals," charging them
to function as city law enforcement officers "whenever,
in the opinion of the Mayor and Marshal of the City, it
shall be necessary to increase the police force of the City,
for the preservation of the public peace, in the case of
riot or otherwise." Between disturbances the deputy
marshals were "to hold themselves in readiness to act at
all times," but they received pay from the city treasury
only for time spent "in actual service," the period in
which they helped quell unlawful activity.[8]

The city's campaign in the 1840s to regulate the actions of those who displayed unacceptable behavior represented but one aspect of the municipal assault. In that
decade council also enacted a different sort of legislation, measures aimed at systematically restoring the
city's sanitary condition, which seemed to council to have
deteriorated because of the actions of strangers. Late in

1844 council stopped distributing contracts itself for street cleaning, an activity it engaged in on an ad hoc basis, and appointed street commissioners to carry out the task.

The street commissioners, who operated year round, awarded contracts ward by ward for cleaning the city's "streets, lanes, alleys, market spaces, and public landings," and supervised the work of contractors. Under penalty of dismissal from office for becoming interested or involved in any city contract, the commissioners dispensed the contracts for street cleaning according to a simple procedure. They accepted sealed bids from the various parties interested in cleaning the city's streets and awarded one-year contracts to the lowest bidder in each ward, requiring surety to insure the faithful performance of the contract. Characteristically, the contracts stipulated that twice each month contractors must "scrape or sweep well each street, lane, alley, and public landing within the limits of his ward, and remove the dirt and rubbish from the same." In addition, the contracts required that on each market day contractors take care to remove all dirt from the market spaces, and provided that "no dirt shall be permitted to remain more than twenty-four hours, on any street, lane, alley, market space, or public landing, after having been swept into ridges or heaps." If a contractor failed to adhere to the provisions of his contract, the commissioners hired others to perform the work at the negligent contractor's expense.[9]

Despite the various efforts of council in the first years of the decade to ban certain unacceptable practices and to police and clean the city more effectively, the plague of strangers seemed not merely to persist, but to proliferate. In late 1844, frustrated members of council complained bitterly about the inability of city government to meet the challenge, arguing that the charter of 1834 unduly restricted city government and urging their fellow councilmen to seek greater powers from the state. According to one distraught councilman, the state had amended the city's charter to provide city government with the authority to deal with unforeseen difficulties in the past, and he persuaded his colleagues to ask the legislature for charter amendments that would enable city government to deal more effectively with what presently seemed an intolerable situation.[10]

That effort paid off, and in February and March of 1845 the legislature enacted three amendments to Cincinnati's charter that permitted the city to do several things. First, they authorized council to reorganize and to expand its paid night watch. Second, they enabled the city to establish a fund for erection of either or both a house of corrections and a house of reformation. Third, they permitted the city during epidemics "to provide for medicine and medical assistance of the Poor" through the use of the township trustees' funds.

Since the municipality had been stricken by smallpox the previous two winters and again during the winter of 1845, council first utilized its new powers by enacting an ordinance "to prevent the spread of small pox [sic] within the city."[11] It authorized the appointment by council "whenever Council shall deem it necessary" of "a suitable number of persons" for no longer than three months "to examine at the residences of all inhabitants of the city," to "ascertain the number of persons who have not been successfully vaccinated and had the genuine vaccine disease," and to offer to vaccinate without charge anyone "in indigent circumstances" not protected from smallpox. Paid by the township trustees, examiners were to keep a register of unvaccinated persons and "give such persons, their parents or guardians, notice to vaccinate within ten days." Following the ten-day grace period, examiners returned to the homes, and upon finding the unvaccinated persons, notified the mayor, who fined them an amount not to exceed five dollars. By this legislation, the city could not compel anyone to get vaccinated, but it could penalize persons for failing to comply with a legislative directive.[12]

The ordinance to prevent the spread of smallpox demonstrated in two main ways city government's acknowledgment of the city as a social unit in which groups interacted. First it placed city government, not the township trustees, in charge of distributing poor relief, in this case gratis vaccination. Secondly, by fining those who refused vaccination, it all but required Cincinnatians to suffer the preventive. This measure, coupled with door-to-door inspections, furthered the public interest because it minimized the disease threat. It not only seemed to benefit newly vaccinated individuals, but also apparently helped to protect the other members of the city from contracting smallpox. In short, the ordinance set city government as responsible both to relieve the poor and to protect the healthy.

Council next adopted an ordinance reorganizing and expanding the night watch, and it proved almost as precedent-shattering as that creating the smallpox examiners. In contrast with past practice, the ordinance prescribed the appointment of paid watchmen for terms of one year and mandated that at least two serve in each ward. It also called for the election of a captain, a first lieutenant, and a second lieutenant of the night watch, gave them authority to call nightly meetings of the force, and permitted the watchmen to roam the streets of the city during "the night season."

The ordinance also marked out new powers and responsibilities for the watch. It authorized the watchmen to enter "any dwelling house or other building" whenever they thought "the lives of the inmates endangered." And it also invested them as police officers "both day

and night" and provided that off-duty watchmen who
made an arrest would receive an extra night's salary. In
effect, it created the city's first police force, but limited
that force's authority and tour of duty to the night
season.[13]

Finally, council took up the issue of erecting a house
of corrections and a house of reformation, which proved
a more thorny question. Council not only had to decide
whether to erect one house or two but also found objec-
tionable several provisions of the state enabling statute.
In particular, the legislature had created a complicated
method of financing the venture and set up a tripartite
division of authority over the structures. The legislation
stipulated that construction of the houses could not begin until at least 100 subscribers, each giving no less than
five dollars nor more than fifty, had contributed to the
building fund. At that point, the city could levy a tax to
raise additional revenue. Subscribers, however, received
more for their money than the creation of a new institution to fight the plague of strangers and public recognition for their benevolence. As a further reward for their
generosity and beneficence, contributors were to enter
into, with city council and the Court of Common Pleas
of Hamilton County, an equal partnership for the control of the houses.[14]

Council preferred to handle the venture some other
way, but a group of impatient citizens insisted on going ahead with the project. Led by Daniel Drake, they
called a public meeting, voted to accept the legislature's
conditions, and established a subscription fund and a
committee of fifteen to interest other citizens in the
enterprise.[15] Within a month, council agreed to cooperate, but did nothing to help the subscribers meet their
quota. Instead, it merely established a mechanism by
which subscribers could be elected to the board of directors of the houses, and created a fund, separate from the

city treasury, in which to keep the money subscribed for the building and support of the houses of reformation and correction.[16]

While Drake and others solicited contributions for the construction of the houses, council moved once more to broaden the powers of the municipality by requesting further amendments to the city's charter. As a first step, council established a committee to investigate possible amendments, while at the same time strengthening its regulation of taverns, coffeehouses, and restaurants by setting up a committee of councilmen who, upon receiving an application for a license, would "make an actual examination of the house" to determine if it were "suitable and necessary." Council also reorganized its street cleaning procedures. Embarrassed by the high cost of contracting for street cleaning by ward, and hamstrung by the city's limited funds for that purpose, council abolished its old system, divided the city into two districts, and hired a contractor for each district to act as street commissioner. These commissioners, however, could not bid for the opportunity to clean the city's streets, for council established a figure it thought both fair and practicable and, as a further inducement, an inducement ironically brought about by the precarious state of the city's finances, stipulated that the municipality need be cleansed just four times a year.[17]

At the same time, pressure continued to mount for the adoption of a new charter as the only really effective means for the city to mitigate perceived social evils. Characteristic spokesmen for this point of view, men like Timothy Walker, a noted Whig attorney, author of the classic "Defence of the Mechanical Philosophy," and president of City Council, and Rufus King, claimed that the city operated under an outdated charter that rendered city government incapable of dealing with the new concerns. To Walker, King, and their allies, who

included a few councilmen and judges as well as nonof-
ficeholders, city government appeared neither inefficient nor inactive, but merely inappropriate for its tasks.
Finally, in 1846, the charter reform forces in Cincinnati
took matters in their own hands. In June of that year
they called a convention of Cincinnati's citizens to redraft the city charter. Convention members established
fourteen committees to look into and report on such
matters as devising a general tax for street cleaning; improving the public schools; setting up fulltime, paid police and fire departments; erecting a city prison and a
house of reformation; improving street lighting as a
means of deterring criminal activity; and reducing the
growing number of paupers in Cincinnati. The convention, which was composed of both Whigs and Democrats, met several times to hear the reports of its
committees, and at the conclusion of these hearings
hammered out a new charter for the government of the
city. This document, participants claimed, would both
solve the problem of the plague of strangers and prove
acceptable to the state legislature.[18]

While the convention waited for the legislature to reconvene in order to submit its proposal for a new city
charter, council late in 1846 passed more ordinances for
the improvement of the urban environment. It enacted a
measure making it "unlawful for any person or persons
owning a cow or cows, to suffer such cow or cows to
stand, lie or feed on any of the sidewalks of the city," and
provided for a fine of not less than three nor more than
five dollars for anyone convicted of the offense. In addition, council passed legislation prohibiting any person
from selling or from offering for sale "any indecent, im-
modest, and lascivious books, pamphlets, papers or pic-
tures" anywhere within the city limits. Violation of this
ordinance carried a fine of fifty dollars and, possibly,
confinement in the county jail, where the prisoner was

to be "fed on bread and water, for any term of time not exceeding ten days, nor less than twenty-four hours."[19]

At about the same time that council passed its obscenity ordinance the state legislature reconvened. Although it took no action on the proposal for a new city charter, it did amend the act empowering Cincinnati to form houses of correction and reformation. The revision made the act more palatable to council by establishing city government as the real power behind the houses. The new law enlarged the city's share in financing the venture, authorized the city to levy a tax for the houses' support, and gave council a clear majority of seats on the board of directors, which as before also contained representatives of the county and the subscribers.[20]

Despite these changes in the state law governing the constitution of the houses, the legislation still required that neither constructing the houses nor levying a tax for that purpose could begin until one hundred subscribers signed up to support the venture. As the campaign to increase the number of contributors floundered, some Cincinnatians demanded that council ignore that part of the law. Mansfield, for example, called for the construction of the houses without further delay. City government, he argued, "needs to create [these] institutions," for although "the poor we shall have always with us . . . they should [not] be left to perish in want, or grow up in vice, or be compelled like wild beasts, to prowl upon society." While he acknowledged that "the family, the school house, and the church" constituted the best places in which to teach proper behavior, Mansfield asserted that these mechanisms, unaided by city government, would certainly fail.[21]

Horace Bushnell agreed. He "hoped that something will be done the ensuing year, effectually, to secure a House of Correction for juvenile offenders" so that "those poor misguided children in Jail," whose only fault was that their "moral training has been wrong," could be housed in more appropriate quarters. As a consequence of their improper training, Bushnell said, these juveniles had turned to crime and ended in jail, where the boys "are wronged, degraded and abused. Their souls are murdered, and most of them bound over to hopeless ruin by the operation of the system." If the city built its house of correction for juvenile offenders, Bushnell insisted, these boys would no longer turn "into desperate criminals," for "the more kindness exhibited towards them, and the more they are treated like men, the greater the hope of their reformation. Punishment alone," he concluded, "has no tendency to reform them; and while all incentives to virtue are removed their condition is almost hopeless."

Bushnell, however, went a step beyond Mansfield. He argued that city government not only needed to begin construction on the house of corrections for juvenile offenders, but that it also had to erect other institutions. He considered the hospital particularly troublesome, for it housed not only the ill and the halt but also many able-bodied poor. "That the poor of the city," he wrote, "should be huddled together in the basement of the Hospital, without regard to character or habits, without incentives to industry or improvement of any kind, is wrong. To make one institution the common receptacle for the sick, blind, lame and insane—to mingle in it all ages, sexes, and possible conditions, certainly is not to secure the greatest amount of moral good or physical comfort." To solve the problem Bushnell proposed that the city sell "one half of the land belonging to the Hospital" and "purchase a farm." There, the city could "erect buildings for the accommodation of all the poor, and their industry properly directed would support them."[22]

Shortly after Bushnell's plea, the city secured the stipulated number of subscribers necessary to start construction on the houses. Council then decided to merge both institutions into a single house of refuge, and in June 1848 passed a property tax for additional funds. Before groundbreaking ceremonies were held for the new house, however, Albert Bushnell, Horace's brother, announced in the summer of 1848 a comprehensive plan to deal with the city's poor, a plan that called for greater involvement by city government.

The creation of a poorhouse figured prominently in Albert Bushnell's plan. But he sought more than a solitary dwelling. Instead, he proposed that city government purchase between one and two hundred acres of farm land at least five miles from the city on which to "erect buildings suitable to the personal wants of the poor." This poorhouse farm, on which "education should be made a prominent feature," would not only "rid our streets from pauperism and crime" but also provide the proper environment in which to teach these strangers how to be proper citizens. Removed from the deleterious influences of the city, and subjected to "a few years of kind instruction from proper instructors," children of the poor, "would become ornaments of society" and their "parents instead of being slaves to whiskey and its awful ravages, would be engaged in honest labor."[23]

Council was intrigued by Bushnell's plan for a poorhouse farm, but understood that city government lacked authority to adopt such a measure. That authority was forthcoming, however, when the legislature reconvened after the first of the year and awarded city government complete control over, as well as financial responsibility for, a poorhouse farm. It permitted council to levy a tax for the purchase and support of the institution and provided for the popular election of a board of directors, designating that one board member should reside in each city ward. The act further stipulated that the board, which it empowered to enter into contracts for the establishment's maintenance, should report to city council "yearly" or "whenever required" on the "state of the institution, with a full and correct account of all their proceedings, contracts, receipts, and disbursements."[24]

To oversee and manage the daily affairs of the poorhouse, the legislature directed the board to appoint a superintendent. In addition to running the house, the superintendent was to "require all persons received into the poor house, to perform such reasonable labor as may be suited to their ages and bodily strength," and to use the profits of this work for the house's daily operations. The legislature also charged the superintendent with notifying the board about the condition of the sick poor—those admitted to the farm "on account of any infirmity or disease"—and to alert the board "whenever such person is so far restored to health and strength as to support himself or herself," at which time the board would discharge the pauper.[25]

Despite passage of this legislation, work on both the house of refuge and the poorhouse went slowly, for about the same time that Bushnell put forth his proposition the city braced itself for an outbreak of cholera. Always a fearsome disease, cholera had last struck Cincinnati in the 1830s, but appeared in the late 1840s to constitute both a graver and a different kind of threat than before. The key to the difference lay in the discovery of the existence of a group of strangers and the corresponding notion of the city as a social unit, which together posited new responsibility on city government for dealing with interactions among its citizens.

The campaign against cholera had begun in the Queen City before the disease reached American shores. Both in tone and in substance, however, the 1849 outpourings differed from those uttered seventeen years earlier. Cincinnatians initiated the offensive when they complained that council by ignoring some sections of the city, which they thought more closely resembled pig sties than places in which people lived, had demonstrated its contempt for the government. Municipal government, they felt, had abdicated its responsibilities. Louis Wright in the fall of 1848 summed up this view neatly. Cincinnati, he wrote, "is now looked upon, and with much truth, as the dirtiest city of its size in the Union. Some of its gutters in the principal streets are so offensive to the eye and nose, as to make a walk along them disgusting. Is there no law requiring the gutters to be cleaned—no officer to see to them?" The problem, he deduced, lay with city officials. "No love of cleanliness," Wright added, "no desire for the health of the people, no fear of cholera . . . , no regard for the wishes of the citizens or of the press, exerts any influence upon the City Council, to take measures to have the city purified."[26]

Council did respond to the threat of cholera, of course, but it did only what it could by charter do. It drafted an additional sanitary nuisance ordinance. The new ordinance provided penalties of up to fifty dollars for any person convicted of "discharging from his house, his factory, or lot, into any street or alley of the city of Cincinnati, any noisome or offensive liquid or substance, prejudicial to the health of the citizens residing on or near such street or alley." Council established a similar fine for "any owner of any vacant or unoccupied lot in said city, who shall suffer or permit any water or other liquid to be and remain on such lot until the same shall become stagnant, offensive, and prejudicial to the health of any citizen of said city." It also made it "unlawful to cast, throw, or leave exposed in any street, lane, alley, lot, common, public ground or watercourse within the city, the dead carcass or offal of any animal, or any putrid or unsound beef, pork, fish, or other putrid or unsound substance," or to "permit any noisome or offensive smoke, steam, or gas, prejudicial to the health of any citizens of said city, to escape or be discharged from any

chimney, or pipe, or other opening, on his lot, or connected with his factory or shop." Violators of these
segments of the new ordinance were liable to a fine of
not more than a hundred dollars.[27]

The cholera threat also inspired council to demonstrate its commitment to the health and wellbeing of the
city's population by changing the manner in which it distributed street cleaning contracts and by reorganizing its
health board. It reinstituted the more expensive system
of contracting for street cleaning, awarding contracts on
a ward-by-ward basis and requiring contractors to scrape
the streets weekly. In reorganizing the health board,
council first asked its present board of health to report
on "what measures can be taken to stop the probable
visit of cholera." Later that month,when the board issued its recommendations, council quickly accepted
them, incorporating the suggestions in an amendment
to the 1832 health ordinance.[28]

Because of the restrictions of the city charter of 1834,
the amendment to the health ordinance provided the
health board with few new powers. Still, it differed from
earlier health legislation in two principal ways. First, it
called the new board the board of public health, which
was the first time that "public" appeared in the title of
the board, a further indication of city government's new
responsibility to protect the health and wellbeing of
city residents. Secondly, the health ordinance explicitly
stated what formerly had been taken for granted. For
example, it expressly directed a sanitary force to serve
under the auspices of the health board by authorizing,
"on the written requisition of the Board of Health or any
member thereof," the city marshal, his deputies, and the
street commissioners, "at all times between sunrise and
sunset, promptly to enter into and examine the condition of any building, cellar, lot of land, enclosure, vault,
privy, or other place" that a member of the board "may

consider to be foul, damp, or otherwise prejudicial to public health." If the suspected area was a nuisance, the force was empowered to remove or abate it "in such a manner as said Board or any member thereof, may direct." The ordinance also stipulated that upon notification by the board, street contractors must "promptly and effectually . . . cause the removal from any street, alley, or other public places in said city, of any filth or impurities, prejudicial to the public health." And more generally, the ordinance "fully empowered" the board "to establish, publish, and enforce all by-laws, rules, and regulations, necessary for requiring the observance, by inhabitants and visitors of said city, of such sanitary regulations and restrictions as shall seem to them best calculated to secure them from such epidemic, infectious, contagious, or malignant diseases, and prevent or check the extension thereof among them."

The ordinance also provided the board with power to do more than to take sanitary precautions. It gave the board the right to select and establish "such extra hospitals . . . as they [sic] may deem proper" for the reception of "any epidemic, infectious, contagious, or malignant disease." The board also received authority to appoint a "clerk, actuary, and health officer," and to set him up in a health office chosen in the central part of the city. The health officer, unlike the board members, received a salary for his efforts, and his job was to gather the particulars on all cases of epidemic disease "coming within the knowledge of the city's practitioners of medicine, keepers of public houses and boarding houses, and officers of steamboats." The board also required "all sextons, or other persons having charge of cemeteries to report" to the health officer, "daily, weekly, or monthly, the names, ages, residences, and diseases, of all persons dying in the city of Cincinnati."[29]

Immediately after passage of the new health ordi-

nance, council and the board began to set in order the
sanitary affairs of the city to ward off the approach of
cholera. One of council's first acts was to provide the
board with almost unlimited authority to draw on the
public purse. Council appropriated a thousand dollars
with which the board members should start the cleanup
of the city, while empowering them to spend "such sums
as may, from time to time, become necessary, for effect-
ing the abatement of nuisances and such other sanitary
measures as they may find essential." As the board
started on its work, council's committee on health initiated hearings on prospective legislation to ban swine
from the municipality and to make it unlawful to toss
garbage in the streets. As a partial solution to the garbage problem, council established the city's first waste
collection system by appointing a scavenger for this purpose and by making council chambers the city's waste
collection office. Under this arrangement, any citizen
who wanted the city to pick up his household waste during the cholera threat need merely deliver to the chambers a note requesting the service and the scavenger
promptly removed the refuse.[30]

Finally, in January 1849, cholera appeared, and the
board moved quickly to exercise its new powers. It appointed a health officer and opened a cholera hospital,
which segregated the victims of the pestilence from their
healthy brethren. During this period, too, the board
through its health officer issued communiques to the
public calling for "a careful attention to temperance,
cleanliness and comfort as the most important means of
preserving health," and published daily mortality returns, claiming that the returns both enhanced "the
security of our citizens" and prevented "exaggerated
statements" from frightening away potential visitors. By
the last week of February, however, the disease had ap-

parently vanished from Cincinnati. The board continued to direct the cleansing of the city, but it closed its cholera hospital, ended its public announcements, and discharged the health officer.[31]

At the beginning of May, however, the disease reappeared. The board immediately reopened the cholera hospital and reappointed the health officer, who resumed his daily bulletins. Council also authorized the board to appoint a day watch, consisting of one man per ward, for the purpose of assisting in the cleaning of the city. Watchmen not only sprinkled the city's streets and spread lime, but they also helped enforce the various legislative directives on health matters. In fact, watchmen proved so zealous in the enforcement of sanitary law that they converted the operation of the Mayor's Court, where fines were levied on those "whose premises are not in the proper order," into a "big business."[32]

During the second bout with cholera, council passed other new measures to improve the city's sanitary condition. It adopted an ordinance compelling owners of soap and grease carts to cover their barrels when riding through the city, and passed a resolution making it "the duty of every citizen to clean his property" daily. In addition, council modified its systems of waste collection and street cleaning. It now required city scavengers and others to pick up from every house at least three times weekly "all house offal" deposited in watertight containers. The new ordinance also required the scavengers at least once a week to go door to door and collect the "stone coal ashes from fire places, stoves, grates, and the sweepings from houses." As to street cleaning, council not only maintained the contracts of the various street scrapers but also authorized councilmen from each ward to appoint an assistant street commissioner for their

ward and appropriated fourteen thousand dollars for
that purpose. The assistant commissioners hired extra
laborers who owned carts, and purchased vast quantities
of lime to insure that the streets were cleaned and disinfected more frequently and more thoroughly. To finance these new services and to pay for the proposed
poorhouse farm, the state legislature authorized council
to enact another special tax on private property within
the city limits.[33]

Despite the unprecedented efforts of the health
board to combat cholera, efforts that now seemed necessary in light of the notions that the city constituted a social unit and that some residents of the city acted in a
manner to damage the public interest, many Cincinnatians remained dissatisfied. They claimed that the city's
sanitary effort was insufficient to deal with the crisis,
that the health board had proved incapable of controlling the epidemic. But these arguments did not find the
board itself at fault. Indeed, neither the design of the
board nor the industry of its members appeared to be
the problem. Instead, critics argued that the board was
placed in an impossible situation, a situation caused by
city government's activities and lack of activity prior to
the onset of the present emergency. Few singled out particular city officials for scorn, however, but blamed the
situation on both the structure and function of municipal government. In particular, Cincinnatians cited city
government's failure to provide a solution to the problem of the plague of strangers as the reason why the pestilence became a cataclysmic event, one with which city
government seemed incapable of dealing.

Critics followed two lines of thought. Some asserted
that municipal government in a variety of ways acted as
a stumbling block to the "transformation" of strangers
and therefore exacerbated an already tense situation.
Mansfield, for one, argued that the unsystematic nature

of city legislation prevented city government from developing a concerted approach to the social evils. In particular, he seized on its failure to provide an environment in which the unaccustomed, unfamiliar, or unprepared readily learned appropriate behavior. To remedy this defect, he urged council to redraft, simplify, and codify its ordinances. "So deficient, so blundering, so utterly confusing are the City Laws," warned Mansfield, that frequently "the lawyers cannot tell what, or how the city has legislated." No wonder, he concluded, "nothing is done." It is "because no one knows what the city has directed to be done!"[34]

Louis Wright, however, raised another and more telling point. He claimed that because of state limitations on the role of city government, it could not dispatch the present epidemic quickly. By this line of reasoning he asserted that during the epidemic it became the duty of all Cincinnatians to help beleaguered city officials. Noting that "with few prominent exceptions" the pestilence struck only "those crowded in large numbers into small and poorly ventilated houses in parts of the city where the least attention is paid to cleanliness, diet, or clothing," and that in these sections stood many houses "filled in the same way, from roof to cellar, accumulating filth, and generating disease," Wright argued that Cincinnatians should assist in abating these conditions. After all, he reasoned, the victims of cholera "are strangers among us—strangers to our language and habits. They know not what to do, nor where to seek relief if they have means, which many of them are destitute of!"[35]

Instead of allowing these degraded beings to perish, Wright proposed that the citizens of Cincinnati take the matter into their own hands. Suggesting that the citizenry operate in conjunction with the health board and council, he recommended that Cincinnati's residents assume unprecedented powers to fight the epidemic. "On such occasions," he reminded his readers, "no one is at liberty to stand aloof," but "every one ought to do what he can do. All agree," he continued, "that the city should be well cleansed. This cannot be done without it being thoroughly examined—all over—in the streets, in the lots, in the houses. This requires time and labor, and if it is to be soon done, many persons must be engaged in the work at the same time. Means should be provided for removing filth, when found, and disinfecting agents purchased for use." Wright recognized, moreover, that "the City Corporation of Cincinnati is too poor" and lacked the authority necessary to undertake such a prodigious task. As a consequence, he urged the city's "citizens to convene in a public meeting, examine into this subject, and secure the efficient action of a suitable number of persons in every ward, in every part of the city. No citizen," he closed, "should be satisfied, in such a state of things, until he knows that all has been done [that] can be done."[36]

In the wake of Wright's proposition, residents of each of the city's wards established associations to care for the sick poor and to aid city government in its efforts to rid the city of the pestilence. The citizens of the first ward acted first, forming themselves into "an Association for the Relief of the Sick . . . to arrest the epidemic in our ward." To this end, the Association, which became a model for residents of other wards, raised money and procured an office "where medicine may be obtained by the poor, free of charge," and "to afford any [additional] relief that may be required." It also banned funeral processions from the ward and asked the health board "to establish numerous depots," their locations posted both in German and English, in which the poor could obtain medicine gratis.

Nor was that all. The Association also formed visiting committees to undertake the systematic cleaning of the ward and to search out individuals who needed aid. It appointed a committee of four persons for each city block in the ward, charging them "to examine immediately into the condition of each house and premises, and to direct the cleansing of the same." If a householder refused to cooperate, the committee was "to order [the cleansing] at the expense of the Association." In addition to inspecting dwellings, the Association also commanded the committee members to note "the conditions of the poor of the ward," and, if necessary, "to supply them with medicine and nurses." To secure the monies necessary to finance these ventures, the Association designated one member from each city block within the ward to act as a fundraiser whose exclusive task consisted of door-to-door solicitation of contributions. The Association capped its anti-cholera campaign by opening a cholera hospital to tend to the ward's sick poor.[37]

The utility of ward-based organizations, such as the first ward association, was not lost on the health board. It quickly sanctioned the ward associations, designating them visiting committees of the board of health, and encouraged residents of every ward to create similar bodies. The board mandated only that the organizations report daily to the health officer "the names of all persons afflicted with cholera or other serious or malignant disease." In this manner, all "who are unable to obtain medical aid" may "be removed to the cholera hospital . . . at the expense of the board." The board, moreover, also brought forth another proposal to help the unfortunates who lacked the knowledge of how to behave in an urban environment, and, therefore, how to protect themselves from disease. It requested in July 1849 that council, for the duration of the epidemic, enact an ordinance making it unlawful to sell at the city's markets "green corn, cabbage, cauliflowers, green peas or beans, rhubarb, radishes, cucumbers, turnips, parsnips, lettuce, or green apples or pears." By prohibiting the sale of these plentiful commodities, board members

reasoned that they could prevent those unacquainted
with the concept of moderation from succumbing to ex-
cesses permitted by the abundances of city life. Although
small quantities of these fruits and vegetables seemed
beneficial, discretion, tempered by moderation, needed
to be exercised in their consumption, for the ingestion of
large amounts of these foods apparently weakened or irri-
tated the stomach and made gluttons liable to disease.[38]

Before council could act on the board's suggestion of
a food ban, the epidemic abated. By the first week of August, the board had withdrawn its support of visiting
committees, stating that they no longer served any purpose, and a week later the board declared the epidemic
ended. Although some cases of the disease still existed in
the city, the board discharged its health officer, closed
the cholera hospital, and resolved to meet again only
when necessary.[39]

With the terrible distraction of the epidemic removed, civic leaders once again focused their attention
on the best methods to free the city of the plague of
strangers and to convert the city's unfamiliar, unaccustomed, or unprepared inhabitants into consummate urbanities. In particular, council continued its efforts to
establish a poorhouse farm, finally in November 1849
selecting and purchasing a suitable plot.[40] Nor was that
all. Early in 1850, the legislature granted council further
authority to combat the social evils and established a new
kind of municipal agency for the City of Cincinnati.
Though cast as an amendment to the act empowering
Cincinnati to erect a poorhouse farm, the Act of 1850
broke new ground, fixing city government as the site for
outdoor relief and creating a fulltime agency to administer assistance systematically. Severing the township
trustees' connection to public aid, the Act put the poorhouse directors in charge of the new effort, stipulating

now that they be three in number and elected by the citizens at large. Unlike the trustees, though, the poorhouse directors were not to rely on recommendations from upstanding citizens, but were authorized to appoint a staff to inquire into the habits of the poor, determine their suitability for assistance, and suggest appropriate measures to aid them. The creation of a staff that worked year round would not only prevent imposition on the public purse, it was argued, but would also insure that each person genuinely in need of aid received it without resorting to the pauperizing practice of street begging. Mandating that directors appoint one overseer to the poor for every ward, the Act directed each overseer to "inquire into the condition and necessities" of the poor residing in his ward, and, if he came upon any person who "ought to be relieved at the public expense," required him to deliver to the directors his recommendations, including "a statement of the name, age, birthplace, length of residence [in the city], previous habits, and present conditions of the person to be relieved." The directors then saw that the poor person was granted provisions, medical treatment, or admission to the poorhouse.[41]

Three days after it amended the poorhouse act, the legislature authorized Cincinnati to form its first full-time police force. To this end, the new Act abolished all distinctions between the night and day watchmen, and specified that the watchmen be elected by the citizenry. Council accepted the new legislation, selected a head for the force, designated him chief of police, and provided him with six lieutenants, who set up regulations for the behavior of force members and established a duty roster. In addition, the chief and his lieutenants divided the city into beats and directed pairs of officers to walk those areas both day and night. Council also took the

opportunity to establish a new pay schedule for the
members of the force, and mandated that none of its
policemen "shall be employed in other business."[42]

While council was organizing its police force, the citizens of Cincinnati were preparing for the state constitutional convention of 1850–1851. During the late 1840s,
many Queen Citians had actively supported the call for
such a convention. They understood that a new state
constitution would not only change the manner in which
the State of Ohio administered its own affairs but, since
the state was the sovereign body from which the municipal corporation derived its powers, it might also give the
city additional weapons with which to pursue the assault
on the social evils.[43] The legislative enactments of 1850
did little to dampen enthusiasm for the convention
and Cincinnatians welcomed its subsequent pronouncements most warmly. Decreeing that Ohio cities and
incorporated villages—municipalities—should be categorized into classes and grades according to population,
the new constitution did away with individual municipal
charters and directed the state legislature to draw up
what was in essence a single statewide municipal code in
which governmental powers were correlated directly to
population size. The convention's directive affirmed the
notion that cities themselves constituted a group of
sorts, which differed both from other corporations (each
group of which, according to the new constitution,
should have its own general laws of incorporation) and
from other local administrative units, such as counties
and townships. But while the constitution acknowledged
a kinship among Ohio municipalities—they were sites of
concentrated populations—it also equated increases in
municipal populations with both increasing population
density and an increasingly bifurcated population.[44]
These two factors seemed deterministic; they changed
the nature of municipal problems and dictated the scope

of municipal authority. Indeed, a bifurcated population in a municipality indicated the presence of a great number of strangers, while a denser population made intense interaction more likely.

During the period in which the convention met, and while the legislature deliberated over the form of the new general municipal law, the Cincinnati City Council used the powers granted in the late 1840s and 1850 to press the war on the plague of strangers. It proceeded with work on the house of refuge, opening its doors late in 1850, and admitted the first inmates to the poorhouse farm in August 1850. The house of refuge, formed for boys under 16 years of age and for girls under 14, stood as "nothing more or less than a School of Reform" in which "the system of discipline, classification, and instruction" functioned "as perfect as possible." Not only did the inmates of this institution, through "solitude and the reforming influences of a quiet and orderly life," have their "hearts exercised and corrected," but they also received training in a trade. In this manner, the adolescents, upon readmission to society, would not revert to their old habits, but would become responsible citizens.[45] Albert Bushnell hailed the opening of the house of refuge and provided a more detailed explanation of its aims. "The youth . . . there," he wrote,

> are 1st, removed from the temptations that have led them astray. 2d, Are compelled to yield obedience to proper rules and regulations; and 3d, Are obliged to employ their time in a useful manner, either in school, or at labor suited to their age and capacity.
>
> These three requisitions are indispensable to reclaim youth of either sex who have once stepped aside from the path of rectitude. To expect a boy or girl, who has commenced a course of crime, however trivial, while spending their time in idleness, subject to no earthly authority, is

preposterous. [sic] As well might we look for the water of
the Ohio to run upstream.

Under [the influences of the house's superintendent]
we may hope that many of these youth will, if continued
there until proper habits are formed, and the principles
instilled in their minds, become useful members of
society.[46]

Similarly, Bushnell and others welcomed the completion of the poorhouse farm. Established near Carthage,
six miles north of the city limits, the poorhouse catered
to the poor, especially those found begging on the city's
streets. Within its portals the poor lived in a strictly regi-
mented environment, engaged in agriculture, learned
the errors of their ways, and in the serene atmosphere
of the countryside reflected on their past indiscretions.
Bushnell, for one, claimed that the poorhouse represented an immense improvement in the manner in
which Cincinnatians dealt with street beggars. Noting
that in the past "organ grinders and other stragglers"
were sent to the county jail, he asked what could have
been "more unwise than to send a man or woman up to
that miserable place," where he or she would associate with persons so degraded that they have become
"thieves, and burglars, and murderers" for "the crime of
having nothing to do and nothing to do it with. What el-
evating and enabling principles," he continued, did
these men and women "there receive, what habits or industry and morality, and what encouragement to hope
for respectability and happiness?"[47]

Pestilential disease also captured the city's attention
in the two-year period between the first session of the
constitutional convention and the passage of the municipal code. During this period epidemics of cholera and
of California, ship, and scarlet fevers struck the munici-

pality, and city government approached these outbreaks in the manner it had responded to epidemics since 1826.[48] It called into session its board of health. The board, as had earlier boards of health, instituted both an internal and external quarantine, and initiated a sanitary cleanup. The board also appointed a health officer to gather and to publish mortality returns, issued guidelines for Cincinnatians to follow to maintain their health, and during the cholera epidemic, established a cholera hospital.[49]

Citizens of Cincinnati once again hailed the efforts of their health board, and on conclusion of the cholera epidemic, proprietors of the Burnet House, the city's grand hotel, demonstrated their appreciation of the board's endeavors by underwriting a vacation for its members to Niagara Falls.[50] Council fared less well, though, and characteristically received blame for the recent epidemic. Indeed, criticism focused on what commentators claimed was council's unwillingness to use its new police and poor relief powers in a manner to protect the health and safety of the municipality's residents. Instead of seeking to regulate the behavior of strangers year round, the effects of which produced crime, vice, and street begging, and sparked pestilential outbreaks, council did little until the situation became intolerable and amenable only to more drastic measures. In effect, critics claimed that city officials created crises through their inaction, crises that city government now had the power and obligation to prevent.

The *Commercial's* Potter, for example, pointed to the unsanitary condition of the city's streets as but one indication of the callousness of municipal officials and of their disregard for city residents' welfare. The filthy state of the city's streets resulted, he argued, from inadequate enforcement of the city's nuisance laws and

council's discontinuation of the practice of hiring scavengers to collect household wastes. Potter further contended that termination of this procedure, in absence of
strict enforcement of the nuisance ordinances by the police, virtually encouraged city inhabitants to toss their
refuse in the streets, a situation that had helped generate the latest epidemic outbreak. Ignoring the fact that
in the past council undertook the collection of kitchen
slop and house offal only when the legislature granted
the municipality the privilege of passing a special tax to
finance this service, Potter checked the city's ordinances
and, upon finding the law requiring the city to provide
waste collection still technically in effect, blasted council
for not furnishing laborers and carts to carry off the
refuse.[51]

Louis Wright approached the situation more pessimistically, To him, too, it seemed that council showed its
contempt for the public interest by neglecting to have
the police strictly enforce the city's sanitary laws prior to
the outbreak. "We have little to hope from public authorities," Wright lamented, because "the general health
and prosperity of the city appear to claim no thought"
from council. The problem, he continued, did not rest
with the city's ordinances. "Many of them [are] good
enough," Wright noted. The fault, according to Wright,
lay in council's failure, especially in the spring and summer months, to insure that the police enforced them.
"What is there," he queried, "to prevent police regulations in Cincinnati, limiting the number of persons to a
room? What is to prevent garbage of houses being carried from the houses by carts, instead of being left to pu-
trify in the streets? What is to prevent the streets from
being swept? What is to prevent the constant supervision
over, and cleaning of alleys and privies?" Council,
Wright observed, passed efficient ordinances governing
most sanitary matters, but until an epidemic actually oc-

curred neglected to "carry them out. The consequence," concluded Wright, "is that we have the most impure city we ever heard complained of."[52]

The attacks on council grew less intense when in May 1852 the state legislature finally completed its initial formulation of the new municipal code. In effect, the new code and the modifications made in it during the next two years reaffirmed the notion that Cincinnati, Ohio's largest city, was a social unit in which groups of individuals differing only in behavior interacted, and that the role of Cincinnati city government was to regulate these interactions in such a way as to encourage homogeneous behavior and thereby to protect the health and wellbeing of all city residents. In addition to restating that the city could create a police force, the new code changed the form of the agency granting poor relief, expanding its duties and powers, and authorized council to establish a fire department and a board of city improvements. These governmental agencies, both old and new, seemed to bear on the plague of strangers and were established to form a comprehensive solution to the problem of its existence and persistence, a problem that had not existed fifteen years earlier.[53]

The state's authorization and the city's subsequent creation of these governmental bodies not only reemphasized the new role of city government as protector of the public interest, but the manner in which the new services were to be employed also reflected the changed way of conceptualizing the city. The organization of the new governmental agencies centralized and systematized the services and insured their delivery on a fulltime, citywide basis. In essence, the mode in which the legislature stipulated that the services should be implemented rested on the assumption that the city itself constituted a whole and that city government needed to function regularly throughout the municipality to regulate the interactions between the city's discordant members.

The board of city improvements, for example, was to become the city's sole agent in charge of restoring order to the municipality's physical environment, and in the face of the existence and proliferation of the unfamiliar, unaccustomed, or unprepared, it had to operate year round. Assuming many duties formerly entrusted to various committees of council, the board stood as the single government agency authorized to distribute building permits, to recommend the awarding of contracts for storm sewer construction and for street paving, cleaning, and repairs, and to insure that private contractors complied with the terms of their contracts. As the only body empowered to permit any of these diverse activities, the board was positioned both to regulate and to coordinate these different, but related, functions of city government.[54]

The new municipal code also reorganized the city's public relief agency, stipulating that the poorhouse directors now constituted the board of the city infirmary. The change was not, however, in name only. The new board not only managed the operations of and retained responsibility for appointing the appropriate superintendents and matrons to run the poorhouse farm, but it also received authorization to govern the affairs of the pest house and the Commercial Hospital—but not to appoint its medical attendants—as well as the new city burying ground. In addition to these tasks, the legislature also permitted the infirmary board to hire a larger and more diverse staff to attend to the outdoor poor. Headed by a clerk, who compiled statistical information and managed the board's finances, the outdoor relief unit of the city infirmary consisted of an overseer to the poor and a grocer for each of the city's sixteen wards, and of two physicians and two apothecaries for each of the city's six poor relief districts. Directed to canvass the entire city, overseers sought to uncover and to classify all cases of pauperism, and to determine what type of relief—institutionalization or outdoor assistance—should be provided. Overseers then reported their conclusions to the clerk who, if institutionalization was deemed inadvisable, ordered either the district physicians or the ward grocer to relieve the suffering. Apothecaries filled whatever prescriptions physicians suggested.[55]

Even the section of the code authorizing Cincinnati to create a municipal fire department seemed to stem from the existence of strangers, though not as a solution to the problem of their discovery but as a manifestation of that discovery. Indeed, in the 1840s, Cincinnatians expressed alarm at what they claimed was a rapid increase in the number of fires in the city and proceeded to explain this increase in several ways. They blamed the increase on the unconscious acts or carelessness of immigrants, on the deliberate acts of youths and vagabonds who grew up innocent of moral training, and on the present method of fighting fires.[56] Of these various explanations, the last proved most telling because it also entailed a criticism of those who fought fires.

Prior to the formulation of the municipal code, Cincinnati relied on volunteer fire companies, each of which strove to reach and extinguish every fire first. In the early nineteenth century, that method engendered little criticism. Midcentury commentators attributed the voluntary companies' previous successes to the fact that citizens, well schooled in the responsibilities of American urban life, manned the firefighting equipment and labored together to extinguish blazes. But they also argued that the situation changed perceptibly after about 1840. Critics maintained that firefighting had become entrusted to a different class of men, untutored strangers; they asserted that as the original fire companies' "older members became less fit for active service," control of firefighting "gradually and silently fell into the hands of boys." Almost immediately, these ignorant boys began to compete for rewards offered by grateful property owners and insurance companies. This competition apparently caused some volunteer companies to set fires simply to pick up the reward. But even if the fire started accidentally, competition between companies could still spell trouble. Disputes raged among fire companies over who reached the scene first and was entitled to the monetary prize. These "fire riots" had become commonplace in the 1840s and often resulted in "violence and even murder." In fact, the city as early as 1841 had established the Cincinnati Fire Association for the purpose of "settling disputes that may arise between one company and another" before they ended in bloodshed.

The riots between fire companies and the increase in the number of fire calls were not the only factors that led Cincinnati to seek the authority to form a municipal fire department. Several citizens also objected to what the voluntary firemen did in firehouses. These city residents complained that the new class of firemen had converted "engine houses" into "places of resort of evenings and on the Sabbath," and that "every species of immorality" went on there. Though not as immediate as riots or arson, the alleged transformation of firehouses into dens of iniquity certainly posed a threat to the public weal and contributed to the dissatisfaction with volunteer fire companies. And when the legislature passed the municipal code, council promptly initiated a formal investigation into the conduct of the volunteer companies and soon replaced them with the city's first fulltime, paid fire department.

The fire department differed in structure and function from other agencies created in the late 1840s and early 1850s. Unlike the rest of the new governmental bodies, the firefighting force was erected for another mission. It owed its establishment not to the battle against the plague of strangers, but to the desire to extinguish fires as expeditiously as possible. And while fires sometimes seemed to result from the actions of strangers, the department nonetheless possessed a single task and was not expected to deal with the problem of unprepared, unfamiliar, or unaccustomed inhabitants. This perception of the department's role permitted city government to design the new institution in a way different from others; each post within the fire department had a special and limited set of duties. Each member, then, performed only one function and, as a further manifestation of unique responsibility, wore a uniform or a badge reflecting his position. More concretely, municipal government was able to divide the members of the fire department by their particular jobs, creating the posts of chief engineer, assistant engineer, lieutenant, and member of a hook and ladder company. The move toward specialization continued within companies, moreover, and each was composed of a captain, foreman, assistant foreman, watchmen, pipemen, firemen, and drivers. Every fireman focused on one and only one aspect of quenching a blaze.[57]

The fire department constituted the last major initiative of the new municipal government of the 1840s and early 1850s. Though the new city administration may appear in retrospect rather limited, it did not seem so to contemporaries. Their apparent satisfaction with the new bureaucracy stemmed from their identification of the problem they faced; the city was swamped with strangers unaccustomed to, unfamiliar with, or unprepared for accepting the responsibilities of midcentury American urban life. The unfamiliarity of these groups' members with rules for proper and successful urban living in a democracy caused them to act at variance with those rules, to engage in a pattern of activity that inevitably led to crime, street begging, vice, filth, and disease. In that sense, then, the plague of strangers comprised a single problem, for the ignorance of these un- or maltutored people resulted in an amalgam of conditions including disease, vice, crime, filth, and street begging. Put another way, these conditions all were the consequence of nonexistent or inappropriate preparation. To resolve this situation seemed a straightforward task. The city could be freed of these inextricably bound conditions merely by making strangers familiar, by providing them with the missing or neglected preparation.

That analysis had spawned Cincinnati's benevolent effort. But the problem had proved a bit more complex in practice. The massive numbers of strangers, coupled with the recognition that their ranks would continually be replenished, seemed to overpower benevolence's capabilities and inspired city residents to seek municipal government's aid. To these men and women, city government now had the twin responsibilities of protecting city inhabitants from the threatening actions of strangers and of maintaining an environment that would encourage benevolence to work its magic.

City government responded quickly to the new challenge. Seeking and receiving additional powers from the state legislature as well as expanding upon its previously granted authority, council in the 1840s and early 1850s produced two broad kinds of legislative enactments. The first prohibited actions not deemed in the public interest, and provided penalties for engaging in activities that menaced the welfare of the city's population. By their very nature, these ordinances were restricted to regulating the interactions of the social unit's inhabitants. Though much more stringent than earlier municipal laws, and though they covered a far broader range of circumstances, what really set this legislation apart was the creation of a fulltime police agency to enforce the dicta on a year-round regular basis. Unlike the early nine-teenth century marshal, the mid-nineteenth century po-lice were not dependent upon individual complaints. Nor did these men receive municipal sanction only dur-ing crises, as did the health officer. Instead, it was their responsibility continuously to traverse the city, uncover all unlawful actions, and arrest perpetrators. Their exis-tence indicated that it had become municipal govern-ment's duty to stop strangers (unlawful activity was perceived as the result of unfamiliarity, unaccustomed-ness, or unpreparedness) from destroying themselves and their fellow citizens.

The second approach sought not to prohibit lawless-ness per se but to repair damages inflicted on the city by strangers. These ordinances set up, for example, mecha-nisms to remove filth from the thoroughfares and to rid the city of street beggars. This category of enactments culminated with the creation of the boards of city im-provements and of the city infirmary. By removing the visible signs of the plague of strangers, these agencies not only protected all city residents from the conse-quences of ignorance, but they also created a "proper" environment, an environment in which teaching through benevolence could take place.

While the acts of the 1840s and early 1850s empow-ered the city to deliver many services for the first time and on a regular basis, they made no change in the man-ner in which the city dealt with epidemic disease. In-deed, none seemed necessary, for city government through its board of health seemed to possess an ade-quate mechanism to handle pestilential outbreaks. Nonetheless, in the nearly decade and a half after 1840, municipal government's responsibility to its citizens' health as well as the problem of health itself had been transformed. Municipal government no longer was responsible only for ridding the municipality of epidemics, but assumed the obligation of mitigating the impact of strangers in Cincinnati year round, assuming that their lack of appropriate preparation for American urban living gave rise to an amalgam of conditions, an unvarying pattern not only of crime, vice, and street begging, but also of unsanitary conditions and disease. City government, in short, was to deal effectively with the manifestations of ignorance—an ignorance that led to inappropriate behavior—and to regulate fulltime the nefarious habits of the ignorant. Put more simply, by mid-nineteenth century definition, unlawfulness was also unhealthful. In essence, then, the problem of health ceased to be an individual concern and became one of the public interest. But it did not require a special remedy because it seemed ameliorable by the general remedies applied to the single problem of the social evils: the police force, the board of the city infirmary, and the board of city improvements. These new governmental agencies seemed to hold the potential to free the city of that amalgam of conditions implicit in the plague of strangers and to protect each city resident from the hazardous actions of others in the city. This perception of the situation made it unnecessary to create new institutions to deal exclusively with health, or to change either the structure or the function of the health board. To do so would have been nonsensical; it would create a duplication of services and merely waste the municipality's limited funds.

4 Coming Apart

In the 1840s and early 1850s, Cincinnatians created new governmental institutions to protect their community year round from the ravages of strangers. These institutions were few in number, but they seemed to fill the bill; in conjunction with ongoing benevolent enterprises, the new city government appeared sufficient to end the chaos precipitated by the discovery of the plague of strangers. Confidence in the effectiveness of the new municipal system was shattered in the mid and late 1850s as complaints about governmental operations abounded. Far more complex than simple dissatisfaction over municipal government's workings, the laments signaled the emergence of new public problems typified by a new public discourse. And these new problems were predicated on notions quite different than the earlier concept of the social evils.

The verbal onslaught began a few years after the legislature passed the municipal code. In this later period, citizens bombarded council and the newspapers with complaints about the state of municipal affairs but often reserved their harshest comments for the city's filthy thoroughfares. Critics of the dirty streets referred to the objects of their scorn in a new way, not simply as manifestations of social decay. Even during healthful, plague-free times, these people identified dirty streets as constituting a specific cause of recurring episodes of pestilential disease, as a permanent threat to health.

And characteristically, blame for the persistence of this health menace fell on municipal government's shoulders, no matter which party held power. "The city allows the streets to be made the receptacles of every species of refuse and dirt," lamented Louis Wright in a typical outburst of the period, a dereliction of duty that ruins the "health, appearance and reputation of the city." Council should remedy its failing by passage of an ordinance "prohibiting the throwing of any refuse into the streets" and by adoption of a method of collecting house offal regularly that provides "for its removal at the city's expense."

Others agreed. For instance, a correspondent to the *Cincinnati Daily Gazette*, who signed his letter "Good Order," expressed similar sentiments more succinctly. Worried abut the "sanitary welfare of the inhabitants" of the city, the writer reminded council and the board of city improvements that "it is the business of government to protect life and health as well as property. All nuisances which destroy life should be abated, whether they be filth in the streets, or drinks at the counter."[1]

Many viewed the prospects for meaningful governmental action more pessimistically. "The streets of Cincinnati," argued James Taylor, who maintained his post as editor of the *Times*, "are dirty, and bid fair always to remain so" because the street contractors and city officials, regardless of party affiliation, acted from self-interest rather than from a sincere commitment to the public health. "If the work is assigned to private contractors," Taylor explained, "they draw the money, make a show of work, and ride over the filthy streets with money jingling in their pockets," and if it "is thrown into the hands of officials, they use it as a political instrument in city elections. They employ men who work little, but electioneer much, and the streets go unclean." By either method, he concluded, we "have had, and we presume will continue to have, dirty streets and filthy alleys."[2]

In the mid 1850s, city officials came under frequent attack, and their ability or desire to restore the city was increasingly questioned. The new municipal agencies of the late 1840s and the early 1850s seemed neither to place the city in good order, protect city residents from the noxious influence of others, nor provide an environment that would facilitate benevolent work. But this time city officials, not the structure of municipal government, bore the brunt of the assault. Many citizens complained that city officials were not meeting their established responsibilities to the public, while others argued that new social realities had produced conditions with which city government refused to deal. In either case, they denounced the municipal fathers for failing to look after the public interest.

Condemnation of municipal officials for their apparent lack of action, a phenomenon new to the mid 1850s, could well have been the product of political partisanship. Frustrated office seekers and party hacks might have sought retribution or political advantage and lambasted those holding elective office and power. To be sure, the decade and a half prior to 1865 was in Cincinnati an era of recurring political instability and contentiousness, marred by several election-day riots. In that fifteen-year period, for example, the mayor's office was held successively by the Whigs, Democrats, Whigs, Democrats, Republicans, Democrats, and Republicans, which merely suggests the dimensions of political turmoil in the Queen City. Not only would such a highly charged political atmosphere likely generate some partisan criticism of office holders, but the repeated electoral reverses might also take their toll. They could prohibit any party from establishing secure control of the municipal bureaucracy and gaining time to implement its programs, a failure that could engender further complaint.

But it was neither the veracity of the objections— they were not true, as city officials acted repeatedly to

eliminate noxious influences—nor their source—they
came from virtually all parts of the political spectrum—
that proves enlightening. Rather, the particulars of the
objections themselves provide the key to understanding
their character. Although the protests suggested that
city officials had failed to fulfill city government's long-
standing obligations or that they had neglected to confront the new social reality, the specifics of the outcries
of the mid 1850s differed strikingly from those of the
previous decade and a half. Indeed, Cincinnatians after
the early 1850s no longer complained about the existence and persistence of the social evils, but about new
and particular problems—the specific and differen-
tiable problems of criminal activity, filth, poverty, and
disease. Unlike the plague of strangers of the earlier period, which resembled a single entity that seemed the
natural and inevitable result of unfamiliarity with, unpreparedness for, or unaccustomedness to the rules of
urban life in democratic America, and, as a consequence
of its essential unity, appeared susceptible to a grand solution, the new problems appeared distinct and distinctive, and each possessed several aspects. Though they all
seemed to bear on the public interest, each facet of each
of these new problems appeared to be caused by a specific type of violation of the rules of American urban life
and remediable only by a solution specifically designed
to blunt the impact of that particular deviation. In essence, then, Cincinnatians in the mid 1850s continued
to differentiate between strangers and established city
dwellers. But within this well-established discourse, a
new subdiscourse began, signalling both the dismissal of
the problem of the social evils and the origin of a series
of new public concerns.

Corresponding to these new public problems was a
general sorting out of strangers into several "dangerous
classes," or subgroups. Since the new problems were dis-

tinct, it followed that their perpetrators also must be different from one another. Cincinnatians continued, for instance, to identify criminals and street beggars as strangers, as individuals unaccustomed to, unprepared for, or unfamiliar with social living in democratic America, but they acknowledged that these two subgroups were not indistinguishable. Each engaged in a particular type of antisocial behavior and each posed a specific, different threat to the social unit.

The assault on municipal officials as inadequate was a product of this framework. City officeholders served as scapegoats, as explanations for a disappointing, menacing, and incompletely understood present. Not recognizing that their notions about the nature of public problems had changed—as manifested by their discourse—Cincinnatians realized only that the methods of the recent past had failed to bring security and resolved that dissonant situation by positing blame squarely in the laps of municipal officials.

City fathers were held culpable for a myriad of circumstances that they did not create. Of these new public issues, the emergence of public health as a distinct public concern, as a series of conditions or situations directly affecting the public interest and requiring municipal government's constant attention if this interest was to be served, proves the most interesting. In effect, city government was most unprepared for this problem; it lacked any agency that might be adapted to come to bear exclusively on it. That was not so with the new problems of criminal activity, filth, and poverty. During the 1840s and early 1850s, the municipality had received permission from the legislature to establish three fulltime, key agencies to fight the social evils. And while these agencies—the police, the board of city improvements, and the board of the city infirmary—were initially provided the particular tasks of arresting lawbreakers and

repairing the city, council possessed the capabilities of
redirecting them. Council itself held the power to refit
and retool them to combat the new distinct public problems of criminal activity, filth, and poverty respectively;
it did not need further authorization from the state legislature to modify these agencies' missions, forms, and
natures.

Council's prerogatives in these areas stemmed from
two factors. First, the legislature originally had granted
these agencies broad and inspecific mandates. Indeed,
they were to challenge a broad and inspecific problem,
the problem of the plague of strangers in its myriad
manifestations. The lack of specificity in the charges
given these agencies provided council great latitude and
flexibility; it placed council as the ultimate arbiter, as the
force controlling these agencies' agendas and establishing their priorities. Second and even more to the point,
the legislature already had permitted council to levy
permanent taxes for these agencies' year-round maintenance. That meant that council was empowered to
employ and pay fulltime, regular personnel. And the
transformation of these agencies' objectives required no
additional staff; the reshuffling would occur internally
and necessitate no extra expenditure.

The problem of public health stood apart from this
thrust. Council was without a mechanism that conceivably could be converted into a meaningful fulltime
health agency. Its board of health certainly could not be
so modified; the legislature specifically had sanctioned
the health board only to fight pestilence, limiting its operations to epidemics or in anticipation of epidemic outbreaks. But authority to redirect the health board was
not council's sole obstacle. It also lacked the means; it
was not empowered to levy a tax for public health purposes. Without a regular, dependable source of funding,
council would be unable to employ the requisite year-

round staff, a staff whose efforts would be entirely devoted to the new public question of public health.

Council's inability to create a public health agency
did not hamper its efforts in other areas. Indeed, council
exercised all its options when confronted with the new
public problems of the mid 1850s and after. In the case
of the distinct problem of criminal activity, for example,
it not only changed its police but also the ordinance governing police action. When authorized in 1850 to create
a fulltime police, council had established a force to battle
the broad, inspecific, and singular problem of the social
evils. And the complex problem the force was to face resulted in council granting it a sweeping mandate; the
police were to uncover and stop all unlawful activity,
with unlawful activity defined as any action that seemed
to threaten the public interest. The comprehensive
nature of the problem led council to create a police
agency characterized by a lack of functional discrimination. Since all policemen received the same charge of
fighting the amalgam of conditions and situations explicit in the concept of the social evils, their duties defied
differentiation; all police efforts bore on the same problem: the unfamiliarity of strangers with the rules of
American social life. Put another way, the legislation that
formed the police paid close attention to the construction of a command hierarchy to insure the police's good
order, but did not apportion responsibilities either
within the force or among its members. Other than the
chief and his lieutenants, all policemen were expected to
perform all police tasks. Indeed, the Act of 1850, which
was reinforced by the new municipal code, placed a premium upon the interchangability of police officers. Except for the highest officials, they all belonged to a single
squad, wore similar uniforms, and carried similar badges.

This type of police apparently had sufficed to combat
the social evils, but in the wake of the emergence of the

distinct problem of criminal activity, it seemed sadly deficient. As a consequence of this assessment, council in
1856 passed a new police ordinance and redesigned its
force. In effect, it created Cincinnati's first police department and directed the agency to attack each of the
facets of the problem of criminal activity. For the first
time, council made a distinction, reflected by the division of the force into squads, between the police's different and distinctive responsibilities. It formed squads of
ward patrolmen, station house keepers, river watchmen,
market watchmen, Miami Canal watchmen, and detec-
tives. Each squad held different ranks, badges, and accouterments to their uniforms and each functioned in a
different capacity. Though they all continued to work
under the direction of the chief and his lieutenants, each
squad dealt with a certain yet separate aspect of criminal
activity.[3]

The drastic reconceptualization of the police into
functionally specialized squads was a reflection of the
crystallization of the new distinct problem of criminal
activity. This crystallization also produced a similar reorganization of the city's criminal laws. In the mid and late
1850s, council for the first time enacted codes of regulations governing specific criminal activity. Comprehensive in nature, each code focused on a facet or facets of
the problem. This systematic gathering of anticrime legislation into codes stood as a new municipal thrust, one
occasioned by the demise of the social evils. To be sure,
council had passed prior to the mid 1850s many measures prohibiting hazardous or violent activities as not
in the public interest. But laws in this earlier period
stemmed from a different assumption; codification
was unnecessary because all municipal regulations ultimately bore on the same problem, the presence in Cincinnati of strangers unfamiliar with, unaccustomed to,
or unprepared for American city life. There was only

this one, true problem and city legislation on that problem, by virtue of its subject's quintessential unity, needed no imposed order. Pre-1855 compilations of city laws, published at the direction of council, further illustrate this oneness. In these volumes, there were no meaningful distinctive categories. The compilations either listed municipal ordinances simply according to date of passage, or placed disease, filth, crime, street begging, vice, and such similar legislation under the general heading of nuisances. Nuisance ordinances were then printed chronologically, not topically. This classification constituted an extremely broad grouping because before the mid 1850s virtually every activity that seemed to menace the public interest was considered a nuisance. No distinction was made within the nuisance classification, for example, between laws prohibiting the dumping of trash on city thoroughfares and those banning gaming. Indeed, no discrimination was conceivable because none existed in the contemporary consciousness.

Council's first attempt to sort out the distinct problem of criminal activity from the plague of strangers surfaced in 1856. In that year, it created the first of several codes regulating facets of this new problem. That work proceeded apace and when council published a compilation of its ordinances a year later, the new code appeared. The process by which council transformed its previously enacted anticrime legislation was straightforward. It began with a search for and a grouping of past laws and sections of laws that now seemed to deal with a particular facet of the problem. When those laws had been collected, council revoked them and instituted in their place a streamlined, comprehensive code of regulations. Following this procedure, council created in 1856 the municipality's first systematic body of law governing the definition of misdemeanors and the regulation of that type of criminal activity; it repealed many ordinances passed during the preceding forty years and replaced them with a single law of some thirty sections. The new code of misdemeanors banned or regulated "prostitution, indecent exhibition of person, indecent behavior, harboring lewd women, dancing and carousals, obscene discourse, selling indecent publications, sporting on Sunday, running horses on the highways," and a series of other similar offenses.[4]

Nor was this Cincinnati's only code regulating such a facet of the new public problem. Council had enacted another in 1855, but this earlier law differed from the misdemeanor code in that it defined what constituted criminal activity only in a particular place; it was restricted to "regulating the markets within the City of Cincinnati." In essence, passage of this code, which followed the collection and repeal of a great variety of ordinances, specified what would become the duties of the police department's new market watchman squad. The market code prohibited or regulated hucksters, the resale of goods, hours of operation, the movement of vehicles, the positioning of dealers and butchers, the posting of placards, and the like, and identified any action not conforming with the law as an illegal act. It also provided stiff penalties for violations. While its provisions were confined to a special place, the market code nonetheless paralleled the code of misdemeanors. The misdemeanor code, which governed completely a certain aspect of criminal activity throughout the city, and the market code represented the municipality's initial formulations of a single comprehensive law to cover at a circumscribed site all facets of a new problem: criminal activity.[5]

Council also established codes to govern the new separate and separable public problems of poverty and filth but included these codes in ordinances regulating the operations of the boards of the city infirmary and of city improvements respectively. Council in that way not only created a distinct body of law aimed at each of those two new specific sets of situations and conditions, but also in the same pieces of legislation outlined the municipality's amelioration programs. Put another way, council redefined and redesigned both the laws and agencies to convert them into particularized solutions to the problems of poverty and filth.[6]

No similar simple alternative presented itself for the new public problem of public health. There existed no fulltime agency to divert nor the authority nor finances to establish a new one. And the question of public health seemed of great moment after about 1855, and to entail a wide range of situations and conditions.

Like the question of dirty streets, housing in the mid 1850s attracted attention as a distinct public health concern, the resolution of which took the form of a war against the tenement. The battle moved on several fronts, but attempts to explain and publicize the cause of the problem dominated the early stages of the fight. In particular, the rapid growth of the city's population stood as the most common explanation of the sudden interest in the tenement as a public issue. The increased demand for housing brought about by the pressure of population, the argument went, spawned a class of price-gouging middlemen who leased single and two-family dwellings from their owners (one paper claimed that most middlemen were recently arrived immigrants) and who, without knowledge of the property owners and without regard for the health of their fellow citizens, milked exorbitant profits from these buildings by converting them into residences for a host of families. The "colonization of the poor" in tenements by unscrupulous middlemen incensed Calvin W. Starbuck, a fervent nativist, who in 1858 became editor of the *Times*. He knew that the "humbler classes are moral in proportion to the degree of comfort by which they are surrounded" and that they "are profitable as employes [sic] in proportion to their health, their cheerfulness and their hope." But if this threat to the public morals did not constitute sufficient reason to indict tenements, Starbuck argued, then tenantage should be condemned because it menaced public health. The public's health is endangered by this practice, he noted, because it creates "fever nests," an intolerable situation because "the fortunes of all classes are so linked together" and these nests seemed likely to spark an epidemic.[7]

Starbuck was not alone in his desire to alert city officials to the tenement house's harmful consequences to the public's health. Others also sought to inform civic leaders of the existence of the tenement problem, to impress upon them their stake in housing reform, and to coerce them to action. The city's newspapers and several benevolent organizations conducted frequent and elaborate housing surveys. Typically, they laid out detailed, ward-by-ward accounts of housing conditions embellished with poignant descriptions of the plight of the poor, their effect on the community's health, and hardheaded analyses of the operation of the tenantage system. Sometimes, moreover, the exposés listed the names of property owners, and most of the studies concluded by inviting owners to investigate what middlemen had done with their property, by calling for a general lowering of rents, and by urging other Cincinnatians to ease the housing shortage through the construction of single-family dwellings. And if entrepreneurs insisted upon putting up multifamily units, housing reformers recommended that building specifications conform closely to the model lodgings of London.[8]

But the mid-nineteenth century housing campaign did not stop with exposés and exhortation. Increasingly after 1860, tenement reformers demanded that council resolve the problem by establishing minimum standards for the construction of housing, by outlawing tenantage, by regulating the maintenance of dwellings, and by instituting a regular system of inspection to make sure landlords complied with the new rules. In essence, participants in the housing crusade claimed that city government possessed responsibility for and was capable of legislating away behavior by either tenement owners or middlemen that injured the health of tenants and endangered the public health.[9]

In addition to being asked to respond to the demands of the housing reformers, council after the mid 1850s had also to contend with those who sought municipal regulation of the "noxious trades," a category that included distilleries, lard manufacturers, soap factories, slaughterhouses, and offal-rendering plants. In Cincinnati, neither the noxious trades nor concern over their effect on the public morals was new. Their identification as a distinct public health issue was, however. As early as the 1820s, Cincinnati had acquired the nickname "Porkopolis," and had also become a center for distilleries. Yet it was not until the 1840s that people publicly began to complain about the stench these businesses created. The new notion of the city as a place in which groups interacted made the smells produced by the noxious trades no longer tolerable. It raised the question of what type of people would permit smells (which seemed not only obnoxious, but devastating to morals) to prevail in the midst of a great population center. In short, the very existence of the noxious trades led Cincinnatians to suggest that proprietors of such trades lacked training in the rules for urban living.[10]

By the mid 1850s, the noxious trades had become a distinct public health problem. Protestors in this period called ward meetings and passed resolutions condemning either specific establishments or the trades in general as menaces to the public health. Describing them as "extremely injurious to the best health of consumers, and detrimental to the best interest of the community at large," the ward groups sent committees to call on proprietors of these unhealthful establishments and to plead with them to eliminate or at least reduce the stench emitted from their factories. They also demanded action from city government, urging council to make it "a penal offense to keep or carry on any such business within the corporate limits," for while everyone would be "disgusted with the savage who will devour the putrid carcasses of animals," these outraged citizens could recognize no difference "between eating such filth and breathing it." Wondering how the city's governmental leaders could "remain indifferent to this matter," members of ward meetings sought to convince council that "such manufactures should be located outside the city," for these establishments "engender disease, and are capable of producing a pestilence."[11]

Like the noxious trades, purity of the water supply entered the public discourse in the late 1850s as a potential health problem. From the moment of the problem's identification, those who worried about it expected city government not only to furnish an adequate supply of water but also to insure and to safeguard its wholesomeness. Joseph McLean, editor of the *Enquirer* after Faran's retirement and as partisan a Democrat as his predecessor, provided a concise statement of this view. "Pure and wholesome water," he wrote, "is a thing so essential to the health and comfort of civilized man, that, in a community like ours, no expenditure should be withholden which is necessary for its procurement."[12]

Although the Ohio River, the source of Cincinnati's water supply, had been polluted by humans dumping sewage and refuse directly into it as early as 1815, concern over the quality of the water first emerged after the mid 1850s, and those who expressed dismay about the water supply claimed that the fouling of the water was a recent occurrence. Four events, each of which, their proponents claimed, caused a new health menace, were posited as explanations for the recent contamination of and the sudden interest in the condition of Cincinnati's drinking water.

One school pointed to the practice of dumping garbage, human waste, and the refuse of noxious establishments into the Ohio River, listed proprietors of noxious trades and immigrants who lived near the river's banks as the chief villains, and demanded that the city government stop those citizens and the owners of offensive manufactures from polluting the city's water.[13] A second group of water critics took a slightly different approach. They conceded that some urban wastes had always found their way into the Ohio, but until recently had dissipated without corrupting the water. Their explanation for the contamination of the water centered on the formation of an eddy current near the water intake pipes. To these critics, dumping refuse into the river itself did not constitute a health hazard. It became a health problem only after the formation of the eddy, for the current pushed the waste toward the intake pipes where it stagnated and then got sucked into the city's water distribution system.[14]

The two other explanations both involved urban growth, but each used it differently. One argued that the boom in urban population had pushed the line of dense settlement upriver to a point above the water intake pipes, a development that made the new suburban population responsible for the problem. The other explanation focused on the construction of buildings during the city's long rainy seasons. These building sites, the argument went, filled up with water, which turned stagnant, and the heavy rains of spring and autumn washed the noxious matter into the river and poisoned the water.[15]

Supporters of all these explanations backed up their theories with chemical analyses of the amount of organic matter in the city's water supply. They also proposed a variety of solutions, ranging from commonsense advice to individuals to boil water before ingesting it to the demand that city government construct a breakfront to disperse the harmful eddy current.[16] But proposals either to construct a new city reservoir or to build a new waterworks farther upstream on the Ohio formed the two most popular solutions to the problem of contaminated water. Backers of the reservoir cited investigations showing that the amount of organic matter in water decreased both as the water settled and in proportion to the time it spent in sunlight. Proponents of the new waterworks dismissed these claims as nonsense, asserting instead that standing water stagnated. They rested their proposal on the theory of the self-purification of running water, which stated that the flow of water dissipated organic matter. For them, moving the waterworks farther upriver and dumping wastes below the intake pipes would insure the salubrity of the water supply.[17]

Like the water supply, the city's milk supply also aroused consternation in the mid 1850s, for it seemed to threaten the public interest by menacing the public health. Indeed, milk reformers frequently raised questions about the purity of milk sold in Cincinnati, particularly milk sold by urban dairymen. Critics of dairymen contended that milk from urban-bred cows consistently ran so low in cream and butterfat that it amounted to little more than white water, and they linked the apparent decline in the quality of milk sold at urban dairies with the rise of distilleries. They claimed that distillers built up or purchased herds of dairy cattle, quartered them near their distilleries, and fed them mash left over from the production of alcohol. And slop-fed cows, critics added, not only produced milk low in nutritional content, but also milk that seemed poisonous. As one Cincinnati medical man succinctly put it, "strychnine whiskey is not more surely fatal than swill milk."[18]

Distillers also were taken to task for selling milk from diseased cows. Although allegedly a common practice, the description of it by Elizabeth Hopkins, a former milkmaid at an urban dairy, struck with sensational force. Hopkins claimed that she had often seen her boss milk cows "less than twenty minutes before their death, and mix this poison with milk from animals he was compelled to chain before they would submit to have their milk taken, so great was the pain to which the process subjected them." Other observers provided additional evidence of the routine nature of milking sick cows, and the newspapers occasionally ran articles decrying the milking of cows with open sores or diseased udders, alluding to the milk of these cows as "thick, feverish, and lumpy, like starch."[19]

Despite expressions to the contrary, however, urban dairies and distilleries were not phenomena peculiar to the late 1850s. As early as 1831 Cincinnati's brewers and distillers built large dairy herds, fed them swill, and sold the milk.[20] What was new, though, was the identification of unwholesome milk as a public health problem.

Nor was that all. Urban dairies themselves seemed to constitute a health problem similar to that posed by the noxious trades. Some Cincinnatians shuddered at the consequences of the "confinement of cows in stalls, from day to day, week to week, in the midst of the horrible miasma that is ever originating in their close and ill-conditioned pens," and wondered how others could support this outrage by patronizing "those dairymen whose establishments are within the corporate limits of the city."[21]

The problems of wholesomeness of the milk supply and of the stench emitted by urban dairies seemed amenable to one of two solutions. Dairies, Cincinnatians suggested, should be moved outside the municipal limits. In this more bucolic environment, cows could feed and roam among "green fields, and by the side of clear running brooks," and then railroads could transport milk "of better quality as to richness and not laden with disease" to the city. Such action would pay an additional dividend by ridding the city of a potent disease threat. But if council refused to enact such legislation, it could at least create a licensing system for dairymen, permitting only "clean" dairies that also eliminated distillery slop from their animals' diet to operate in the city. In either case, however, municipal government was to assume direct responsibility for the regulation of the milk trade.[22]

In a similar manner, the city's citizens in the mid 1850s expressed indignation over the poor quality of the produce, meat, and bread sold at the city's markets. The nature and intensity of feeling over this problem, like that over milk, was new. Prior to this time, the concern voiced about markets revolved around their sanitary condition, not the purity of the goods sold there. While it then seemed appropriate for city government to maintain the "cleanliness and neatness" of "the place where citizens resort in order to purchase daily food," few suggested that government regulate the condition of the meats and produce for sale there.[23]

By the mid 1850s, however, that question too became a burning public health issue. Unlike the past, Cincinnatians contended, when merchants were trustworthy and honest, "adulteration is [now] the rule." Or, as the editor of the *Gazette* put it, many hucksters have "reached such a state of demoralization that the manufacture of adulterated articles of food is regarded as a legitimate [business] practice," a practice he saw as self-perpetuating because "if part resort to [it], the honest dealers cannot sustain themselves, and are forced to do the same"[24]

Although some city residents argued that individuals could help in the fight against adulterated food, they also recognized the need for municipal government to take an active role. They urged their fellow citizens "to refuse to buy that which they know is not genuine" and called on municipal government to set up "a system of seizing and confiscating spurious articles of food," a procedure, they claimed, that would not only "rid the city of most of these frauds" but also "would elevate the morals of the trade."[25]

Some went beyond the issue of adulteration and sought a municipal ban on the sale of green or spoiled produce and rotten meats. By instituting such a prohibition, they reasoned that government could insure that those who lacked familiarity with American abundances would not eat excessive amounts of those substances, sicken themselves, and therefore contribute to a pestilential outbreak. Claiming that immoderate consumption of any of these substances "was detrimental to the public health, and ought to be condemned," those who called for the municipal regulation of green, immature, or rotten food urged council in the public interest to appoint an "Inspector of Markets, whose duty should be to inspect and examine all articles offered for sale, and condemn such as he thinks injurious to the public health."[26]

Housing, noxious trades, and foodstuffs were not the only new public health issues. Prior to the mid 1850s, city government seemed responsible only for the construction of storm and overflow sewers near public areas, such as markets or the riverfront. By this date, however, drainage, too, had become a public health issue. As such, its resolution seemed to require the construction by municipal government of a citywide sewer system rather than scattered sewers to drain particular places. And those making this demand identified two familiar circumstances of allegedly recent origin that created conditions calling for governmental action: urban growth and callous landlords.

Proponents of the urban growth explanation dominated the discussion, and invariably started their case by arguing that the bulk of the city's population no longer lived close to the Ohio River. In those days of more compact settlement, they continued, it was both inexpensive and easy for people to drain their own property. Now with the growth and dispersal of the population, each person could no longer drain his own land, for sewage lines had to be longer and had to cross the property of others. Worse still, the density of the city's population in the mid-nineteenth century made citywide drainage a "necessity," for it would yield "an improvement to the cleanliness in the city" and "protect the health of the community." On those grounds, it seemed imperative for municipal government to construct a citywide system of drainage sewers.[27]

Those who pointed to callous landlords as the cause of the problem reached the same conclusion by a different route. Their analysis paralleled that supporting the municipal regulation of housing, and centered on the inhumanity and selfishness of landlords toward the city's large cellar-dwelling population. They asserted that landlords who failed to keep these loathsome dwellings free of water assisted this segment of Cincinnati's population in its own degradation, produced epidemic conditions, and thereby threatened the health of the entire city.[28]

After the early 1850s, then, Cincinnatians identified a variety of particular circumstances as threatening. They placed responsibility for their correction on municipal government, arguing that these conditions jeopardized not only the health of those engaged in specific activities but also the public health. But municipal government lacked both the institutions and power necessary to attack these new and distinct problems of public health. It could neither design a new agency nor redirect an established entity to serve as a solution to any of the new concerns of improper housing, the noxious trades, the quality of public commodities, drainage, and the like.

Though these barriers prohibited a comprehensive governmental assault on the problem of public health, council managed to find ways to deal with some of its aspects. The municipality developed a twofold approach, patterned closely after its response to the other new distinct problems of filth, poverty, and criminal activity. The formulation of a sanitary code constituted one thrust. To be sure, no legislation barred council from systematizing its previously enacted ordinances and reducing them to a single law. Nor did any edict restrain council from announcing the new code. The difficulty rested in the means of enforcement; council continued to lack a specific public health enforcement mechanism. That dilemma was not in council's power to resolve, of course, and it was forced to go without. It did try to do the next best thing, however. The problem of public health seemed so immediate and the threat so serious that council violated its established agencies. It adapted a portion of these agencies' resources and manpower to suffer as public health enforcement mechanisms. This latter plan of attack not only would produce an unacceptable means to enforce public health dicta, but it also would tend to dilute the municipal onslaught against the problems of criminal activity, poverty, and filth. Despite these glaring shortcomings, council went ahead; it apparently felt it had no other choice.

Council began its public health crusade in 1856 by repealing the numerous ordinances regulating the city's sanitary condition and replacing them with a single

sanitary nuisance law. The new code consisted of four
main parts. Its implementation rested most heavily on
the board of city improvements and marked out new duties for its members.

The first section of the new sanitary code covered
stagnant water, and directed members of the improvement board to report to council the existence of any
"pool of stagnant water, on private property, together
with the name of the owner of the premises on which
such nuisances exist." Council then told the owner "to
fill up or drain the same." If he refused, council ordered
the board of city improvements "to abate the nuisances
and make a return of the cost thereof to the city Auditor,
who shall cause suit to be issued for the amount."

The second section dealt with the removal of sullage.
It prohibited the construction of privies "without vaults
at least twenty feet deep," provided for their cleansing in
the months May through October, and prescribed the
means for removal of wastes. This section stipulated that
during the summer privies could be emptied only "into
closed carts or vessels," that it could be done only at
night, and then only at the direction of a member of the
improvements board. To dispose of the waste, council
authorized the board to secure a suitable spot at the city
landing and to contract with a hopper boat owner, who
would take the sullage into the "middle of the Ohio
River" to be there discharged, making sure that the boat
was "thoroughly washed and cleansed before landing
again." For performing this service, council provided
that the owner "shall receive not more than one dollar"
for every cart of sullage he dumped. In addition, he was
required to dispose "free of charge all carcasses, or other
putrid matter sent to the boat" by the board.

The third part of the code called for the city improvements board to award a contract for the removal of
house offal. It dictated that the board "advertise for pro-

posals for the privilege of collecting the offal" and then "contract with the best bidder for a period not less than one nor more than three years." After the board selected a contractor, it became illegal for any city resident "to cast into, or permit to remain in or upon any part of the premises occupied by him or her, or in or upon any private alley, any kitchen offal, refuse matter or filth of any kind." To make citizens aware of the scavenger's schedule, the board was to post it or leave it on the doorstep "at each and every hotel, tavern, or eating house and dwelling house" within the city. At the appointed times, the scavenger, equipped with "a bell to be rung at the time of call," went "through the city's streets and alleys," and residents, who had been "notified to keep the offal or garbage ready for such scavengers in tight vessels," were supposed to rush to the cart and deposit their filth.

The final section of the ordinance consisted of a collection of rules that failed to fit within the other three categories. This section made it unlawful for any person "to collect or keep any hog or hogs" within the city limits in a manner that might "annoy or offend any neighbor," to allow "cows to stand, lie, or feed on any of the sidewalks," or "to cast any filth or substance whatsoever into sewers or culverts." In addition, this section banned open soap grease carts during the summer, outlawed the dumping of "the dead carcass of offal of any animal, or any putrid or unsound beef, pork, fish, or other putrid or unsound substance," including "any shavings, ashes, mud, or other filth, or annoyance whatsoever," whether intentional or otherwise, on "any street, lane, alley, lot, common, public ground or watercourse within the city," and forbade residents to "make, use, keep, or permit," in "their dwelling-house, shop, store, factory, outhouse, cellar, yard, [or] lot . . . any noisome or offensive liquid, or substance or stagnant water, prejudicial to the health of the citizens or any annoyance to the neighborhood." It

also prohibited the slaughtering of animals in the city
except in places equipped with a tub to receive the animal's blood and in which the floor was "paved with brick
or stone, and the earth below [it] made sufficiently solid
to prevent its becoming the receptacle of filth and offensive matter." Council further stipulated that slaughterhouses must not only "be washed and cleansed" daily,
but also that they "be whitewashed at least once in each
and every [summer] month."

Provisions regulating other noxious trades were also
included in the fourth section of the code. Council made
it unlawful for any person "to discharge from his house,
factory or lot, into any street or alley . . . any noisome
or offensive liquid or substance prejudicial to the health
of the citizens . . . , or suffer or permit any noisome
or offensive smoke, steam, or gas, prejudicial to the
health . . . , to escape or be discharged from any chimney or pipe" on privately owned property. To see that
residents complied with all parts of the code, council
empowered city patrolmen and the improvements board
"from time to time" (which in practice meant when a citizen logged a complaint with the board) to "enter into
and examine, between sunrise and sunset, any building,
cellar, lot of ground, vault or privy, which they may know
or believe to be foul, damp or otherwise prejudicial to
the public health." If their suspicions proved valid, council authorized them "to direct the cleansing, altering, or
amending" of the condition and to provide for "the removal of all nuisances in and about the premises." Violation of any part of the ordinance carried a fine of up to
twenty dollars, with the stipulation, however, that each
day a sanitary hazard existed was to be "considered a distinct offense."[29]

Council did not view the code of 1856 as final, however, but persisted in its efforts to provide the city with a
truly comprehensive and effective nuisance code. In
1857, for example, Cincinnati amended the code to pro-

hibit the mooring within the city limits of any boat receiving "the contents of night-carts, dead animals, or offal." This measure would free city residents from "the evil arising from the generation of miasma," a process, council concluded, that had occurred when hopper boats docked at the public landing. In a similar manner, council strengthened in 1859 the provision regulating slaughterhouses, now mandating that these building possess "a perfectly water-tight floor."[30]

The new sanitary code and its amendments granted city agencies few new powers. Nonetheless, they were part of the second transformation of city government within twenty years. In order to protect the public interest, council now devised means aimed exclusively at maintaining public health. And this led to the formulation of the first body of legislation directed solely at the public health problem. By giving new duties to the members of the improvements board (in the absence of the power to create new municipal agencies) council, in effect, stipulated that the board, in conjunction with those policemen who might be assigned temporarily to them as a sanitary squad, bore the responsibility for defending the public health.[31] Put more simply, the institution of a sanitary nuisance code marked a first step in the reorganization and redirection of city government; it signified that the public's health was a concern separate from other municipal concerns and one that called for its own institutional solutions. Like criminal activity, poverty, and filth, public health was a distinct problem affecting the public interest. And as in the case of those other new problems, it demanded a specific and concrete resolution, one that necessitated a transformation of the nature, organization, and direction of city government.

Despite the comprehensive and rigorous nature of the sanitary code, it alone could not resolve the public health problem, in part because municipal government

lacked the staff necessary to provide for its regular enforcement. Using the members of the improvements
board and city patrolmen to respond to health complaints, though useful, was not an effective means of insuring fulltime compliance with the city's health law.
Both these agencies had other primary duties; the board
sought to maintain and repair the streets or plan new
ones, while patrolmen were to regulate or prohibit criminal activity. The legislature, moreover, granted council
no authority to raise money for the creation of a fulltime
public health staff.[32]

Yet the legislature did help the city tackle its health
problems in other ways. For instance, it provided in
March 1856 for the collection from "all physicians, surgeons, and mid-wives" of records of "births, marriages,
and deaths" throughout the state. The act served as a
means not only to "preserve the name and afford the
means of identifying the connections, and some facts
concerning the personal history of every person who is
born, marries, or dies in the community," but it also
helped to "determine how health, life, and longevity are
affected by age, sex, condition and occupation; by climate, season, and place of residence; and by disease to
which, under any circumstances, man may be subject."
The registration of deaths bore most directly on the
city's health, for it gave municipal government for
the first time information necessary to identify parts of
the city where mortality rates ran high, and the identification of those areas would simplify the task of determining the specific cause of a particular health problem,
often pointing to an immediate remedy.[33]

With some support from the state but largely on its
own, council labored strenuously in the decade after
1855 to protect the public's health. Besides forming a
sanitary nuisance code and applauding the state's work
in establishing the registration law, city government also

created special committees of councilmen and select commissions of concerned citizens and municipal officials to investigate the new health problems and propose possible solutions. And while council often lacked authority to carry out the new solutions, it worked diligently to secure legislative approval and sanction for their implementation. In 1858, for example, council appointed a select committee of the city civil engineer, the board of the city improvements, and council's committee on sewerage to draw up a comprehensive citywide drainage plan. Although the legislature approved the plan and provided the city with the legal authority to begin construction, the city could not do so because it lacked powers of taxation sufficient to undertake a project of this magnitude. In light of this, the city pressed the legislature for a change in the taxation rates, and while waiting for the general assembly to respond, turned its attention to the quality of the city's milk supply, a question that preoccupied council for much of the summer of 1858.[34]

The milk issue rose when a mother claimed her child had died from drinking milk from slop-fed cows, and a councilman immediately proposed that city government prohibit the sale of swill milk. Rather than act rashly, council created a special committee of its members to investigate the feeding of cows that provided milk for the city. The committee suggested that the municipality institute a licensing system for milk dealers and grant licenses only to those sellers who refused to feed their cattle slop feed. For a five-dollar fee, the commission told council, the city could register each dealer's name and address and provide him with a license number to paint on his wagon, a measure that would insure Cincinnati's citizens a pure milk supply. Council as a whole, however, was not certain that slop feed was at fault, and in any case argued that the commission's proposition

was unenforceable. It sent the proposal back to the committee, which amended it to include an annual visit to
each of the city's dairies by council's committee on
health. The amended ordinance also failed to secure the
support necessary for passage and council dropped the
matter.[35]

Almost a year later, the milk issue re-emerged. A city
dairyman, outraged by newspaper allegations about his
lax dairy practices, demanded that city government
investigate the condition of his dairy. The mayor complied with his wishes and appointed a committee of
three citizens, including Taylor of the *Times.* The committee worked swiftly, and a day after its selection, delivered its report, which stated "emphatically [that] we
would not like to use milk from this dairy ourselves, and
we can not recommend the public to do so." When
pushed to act on the case, council refused once more, citing its inability to enforce any new milk legislation.[36]

Although city government failed to resolve the problem of the milk supply, it remained committed to protecting the public's health. To be sure, council's activities
in the public health field declined as the Civil War approached and remained a low priority during its first
years.[37] But even during this great national crisis, the
problem of public health continued to draw some attention from city government, for council early in 1861
finally got the legislature to move on the drainage question. In that year, the general assembly amended the
municipal code, granting cities of the first class the right
to assess private property abutting proposed sewers in
such a manner as to pay for their construction. Even after the passage of this act, however, the plan of council's
select committee of 1858 remained impractical, and
council appointed another committee to devise a
cheaper method to sewer the city. Shortly after the new
committee completed its proposal, the board of city im-

provements took bids, and in early 1864 began to award
contracts to build additional sewers, a program that
would establish Cincinnati's first citywide drainage
system.[38]

As the improvements board took bids on the sewers,
council in 1863 took its initial step to insure the purity of
the water supply, using the now familiar mode of creating special council committees to establish a plan of action to resolve the new problem. Council appointed a
committee of its members to investigate the matter, and
followed its recommendation to construct a "temporary
break-water" above the city's slaughtering establishments "to prevent the eddy which now exists." The measure soon proved inadequate, however, and council
appointed another committee, this time composed of
concerned citizens, "to take into consideration the best
method of obtaining an abundant supply of pure water"
for Cincinnati. After securing legislative authorization,
council implemented the latter committee's suggestions.
It purchased a parcel of land on the Ohio upstream from
the city, far from urban congestion, and built there a
new pumping station and a huge reservoir.[39]

Between the mid 1850s and the mid 1860s, then, city
government tried to protect the city's health in a variety
of ways, but its attempts to clean the city streets represented by far its most concerted effort. Council began its
decade-long crusade on the health problem caused by
filth in the streets by modifying the duties and changing
the procedures of an established municipal agency, the
board of city improvements. Eventually though, its institutional tampering yielded the creation of a new governmental body, the street cleaning department, formed
specifically to protect the public health by keeping the
public thoroughfares free of refuse.

Founded in the early 1850s with general responsibility for ordering the city's physical environment, the

board of city improvements by mandate of the council
had begun in the mid 1850s to divide that broad assign-
ment into separate tasks and distinct problems. With respect to the health problem of filthy streets, council
directed the board in various ways "to systematize the
system of street-cleaning." It called on the improvements board to issue contracts for street cleaning to the
lowest bidder, to vary the length of the contracts from
one to three years, to ask the city police to check on
the workings of the contractors, to insist that contractors
post surety bonds, to experiment with street sweeping
machines, and to assign street cleaning contracts first
by ward, then by districts, and ultimately citywide. In
fact, council in the name of efficiency even allowed the
board to distribute contracts to the politically faithful,
asserting that linking party to public service insured
greater responsiveness and accountability, and, as a consequence, increased effectiveness on the part of the
contractors.[40]

Despite the diversity of these new approaches to
street cleaning, citizens continued to complain about the
filthy condition of the city streets. The situation finally
came to a head in 1864 when council created a select
committee to investigate the conduct of street cleaners.
Much to the surprise of many Cincinnatians, who looked
upon the contractors as "public leeches," the committee
found the cleaners blameless. Investigators attributed
the contractors' poor performance to the rising cost of
labor and materials, and recommended that council either release the cleaners from their contracts or boost
their pay by 40 percent. Council concurred with its committee's assessment and gave the contractors a 33⅓ percent increase over the life of the contracts.[41]

At first, city residents seemed to be willing to go
along with council. Indeed, criticism of street cleaning
dropped sharply after the investigation. Within a few

months, however, intense outrage surfaced once again. To many, the streets seemed as filthy and the street cleaning effort as lackadaisical as ever. Critics now demanded that council rescind the increases and either compel the contractors to do their work or relinquish their surety.[42]

Stung by the constant abuse, all three contractors resigned. They asserted their innocence, and laid the blame for the dirty streets on an uncooperative public and on city government itself. Citing the repeated tearing up of the streets for constructing storm sewers, for laying gas and water lines, and for erecting buildings, the contractors explained the municipal government, by encouraging these activities, prevented them from fulfilling their contracts. They came down especially hard on the temporary city ordinance permitting builders to store their unused lumber and stone on the thoroughfares and allowing them to dump building refuse, including plaster, onto the streets. They argued that municipal government by condoning these actions had violated the contracts and placed them in an impossible position. They stood either liable to heavy fines and the forfeiture of their bonds or, if forced to comply with the terms of their contracts, face to face with bankruptcy.[43]

Council took a hard line in considering their request to get someone else to do the job. It passed a resolution revoking the 33⅓ percent increase and commanding the improvements board either to see that the contractors complied fully and totally with specifications in their contracts or to initiate legal proceedings against them. The board disagreed with council, however, and as soon as board members received written confirmation of the resignations they voted unanimously to nullify the contracts, subject to council's approval.[44]

With council and the board of city improvements at loggerheads, Mayor L. A. Harris stepped in to breach the potential impasse. As president *ex officio* of the improvements board, he rehashed for council the reasons for the contractors' inability to fulfill the terms of their contracts. He also explained the board's position by stressing the urgency of the situation, claiming that the city's health depended on prompt action. Instead of pursuing a vindicative course because of "circumstances beyond [the contractors'] control" or for "an error in judgment," he urged council to cancel the contracts and to implement an entirely new system of street cleaning. Noting the legislature's recent passage of a new tax law provided the city with more money for street cleaning, he recommended that council permit the improvements board itself "to purchase horses and carts and employ laborers" to rid the city streets of accumulated filth, reasoning that these expenditures would in the long run save the city money because government could put the city's streets in good order more economically than independent contractors.[45]

Council adopted Harris's proposal, and within two weeks the board had hired 104 men and bought 90 carts.[46] Council, however, turned street cleaning over to the board only as a temporary, stopgap measure. Worried about centralizing too much power in the board's hands, and deciding that public works and street cleaning were separate problems, council early in 1866 severed the connection between the board and the cleaning of the city's streets. It created instead an entirely new board to oversee street scraping and empowered the new body, the board of supervisors of street cleaning, to form a street cleaning department.[47] Dividing the city into five districts relatively equal in population, the new board employed over 200 men on a regular, fulltime, paid basis. The board did not run the day-to-day operations of the department, however, but ceded that responsibility to the department's executive officer, the superintendent of streets. Charged with maintaining discipline among department employees, a force consisting of stable keepers, maintenance men, and cartmen, the superintendent's duties included making sure that cartmen met their schedules and hiring a clerk to control the department's finances.[48]

Under the new board, the actual practice of street cleaning as well as its management resembled a garbage collection operation. In addition to scraping muck off roadways each afternoon, cartmen equipped their carts with bells and on at least three mornings each week went door to door collecting the kitchen slop and house offal. Ringing their bells to signal their approach, cartmen gathered wastes from each household. This procedure, the street cleaning department's superintendent claimed, deterred city residents from dumping trash onto the streets.[49]

While the formation of a street cleaning department served only to resolve the problem of filth in the streets, it was part of a larger pattern of municipal action. In the years after the mid 1850s, as the problem of the social evils was replaced by public perception of distinct and separate municipal concerns or series of concerns, city government was called on to provide an effective solution to each new problem or series of problems. In an attempt to protect the public interest in the matter of health, municipal government created a sanitary nuisance code; formed special council committees and commissions of citizens and municipal officials to consider the water supply, the quality of milk, and drainage; started the construction of a new waterworks and reservoir; and began laying storm sewers on a systematic, citywide basis. During this period, it also attempted to modify both the structure and function of the health board, transforming it from a body that acted only during anticipated or actual outbreaks of pestilence into a new type of institution, one that would work fulltime to provide solutions to the issues affecting the public's health.

This endeavor did not proceed either smoothly or rapidly. It was marred by two recurring disputes: one pitting the city against the state for primacy in Cincinnati's affairs, the other among several groups of physicians competing for dominance in the Queen City and for control of the city's medical institutions. Neither found a speedy resolution and both hindered the city's efforts to form its new health agency.

5 Medical Complications

In the last half of the 1850s, a large group of Cincinnati medical men turned their attention to public health. Their concern coincided with that of many city residents, who clamored for governmental action. But unlike most of their nonmedical contemporaries, these physicians sought to direct any new governmental health effort. The argument offered to support their position was neither diffuse nor complex: Doctors long had treated disease, and its prevention as well as community health maintenance stood squarely as a medical question. Public health fell clearly within the profession's traditional social role.

These doctors did more than talk. In March 1857 they established an organization, the Academy of Medicine of Cincinnati, to investigate public health concerns and to become the city's public health authority. Open to all like-minded physicians, the academy was to advise both government and the public on health matters; the society became the first organization in Cincinnati to claim that its policy rested on disease prevention and health maintenance. As a complete sanitary organization, the academy would pursue, according to Reuben D. Mussey, the venerable Nestor of Cincinnati medicine and the society's first president, "the investigation and discussion of such subjects as vital statistics, public and private hygiene, adulterations of food, progress in medicine and surgery, the conditions of the atmosphere in relation to epidemics, original observations of disease, [and] encouragement of medical scholarship."[1]

The first paper presented to the new society, Cornelius G. Comegys's treatise, "On the Adulteration of Food," reinforced Mussey's statements and in that sense comprised a most appropriate keynote address. Checking sixteen samples of milk, each procured from a different milk dealer, Comegys, a specialist in the diseases of women and children, found at least six samples totally unfit for human consumption. Describing the sale of adulterated foodstuffs as a common occurrence, and one that extended far beyond the milk supply, he argued that it was "the duty of our city government to appoint competent persons to investigate the subject." To this end, he proposed that academy members formally convey their dismay to council, and offered a resolution for the society's consideration.[2]

In the resolution, Comegys argued that municipal government should act, and what he wanted was the creation of "a permanent commission, clothed with full power to investigate thoroughly the nature and extent of the adulterations of the chief articles used as food and beverages by the people of Cincinnati." Since the society felt "that hygiene is one of the most important departments of medical science," and since it possessed "no [official] authority or means to investigate the matter," it called on government to take up the problem. The resolution, in short, merely reaffirmed the position that the academy had already taken with respect to its role on the public health question. It accepted as fact the previously expressed contention that the academy comprised the only sanitary authority in the city, and it implied that government should sanction that role by adopting ordinances or by taking other steps suggested by the academy.[3]

The sentiments expressed in Comegys's resolution were by no means unique. Nine of the first sixteen papers presented at the academy dealt with public health concerns. They covered such diverse subjects as the evils of tobacco, the prevention and treatment of sunstroke, strychnine whiskey as a cause of delirium tremens, vaccine disease, and another essay on the adulteration of milk. All of these came under the scrutiny of the academy's members as part of their effort to demonstrate the indispensability of its members to the health of the city residents.[4]

City government apparently took notice of the academy's efforts. Less than a year after the society's formation, council reorganized its health board, the first change in the health ordinance since 1849. Though much like earlier boards of health, the board of 1858 differed from its predecessors in a few important particulars. It could, for example, establish a quarantine station farther down the Ohio River from the city than before, and it could increase penalties for violation of the quarantine. But what really set it apart from earlier health boards was that it stood as city government's first attempt to solve the new problem of public health through its agencies. Council made the new health board a perpetual institution, requiring it to meet not merely during or in anticipation of an epidemic, but at least once every three months. The new legislation also divided the city into four health districts, entrusting each to the care of three resident members of the board, one of whom had to be a "practicing physician" and serve the district as "Health Commissioner."

Responsibilities of the health commissioners, though few, were central to the new board's efforts. They included establishment of an office in each district and regular collection, not just during epidemics, of mortality returns. This was done by requiring that sextons and undertakers deliver to the health commissioner's office a burial certificate before they received permission to bury a body or remove it from the city. Each certificate

listed the "name, age, sex, color and disease of which
said person died, date of death; also whether married or
single, the residence and occupation (if any) of the deceased." The commissioners then compiled the reports,
and, once a month, gave council a summary.[5]

The fulltime registry of mortality statistics became
the means to provide city government with the necessary early indication of an epidemic's approach. Record-
ing all deaths would help to isolate particular health
problems and aid in pointing out specific plague spots; it
also would alert the board and council to any sharp increase in the number of deaths in Cincinnati and their
cause. As a means to warn city government during the
first stages of a disease outbreak, mortality statistics
seemed a way to get around the absence of a section in
the muncipal code permitting cities, except during epidemics, to create sanitary inspection and enforcement
agencies. Though city government was unable to prevent disease by hiring inspection and enforcement
forces, it certainly appeared capable of devising a
method to keep itself informed as to the present state of
the city's health and, if deemed necessary, to provide a
quick counterattack.[6]

The board of 1858 also broke with previous practice
in other ways. The ordinance sanctioning the board, for
example, required that four board members must be
physicians, a requirement that established one group,
physicians, as an integral part of city government's
health program. To be sure, council had elected medical
men to posts on earlier health boards, but the board of
1858 was the first to restrict the allocation of positions to
those individuals of a specific group. And implementation of this section of the ordinance also signaled a victory for members of the Academy of Medicine. While
the wording of the ordinance gave no particular group
of physicians preference, council appointed only acad-

emy members to the health commissioners' posts during
the board's existence.[7] Whether council was moved because of the arguments or show of unity and openness
on the academy's part, or because some of the organization's members also served as councilmen, city government by its actions clearly recognized the academy as an
important adjunct to the public health efforts.

Finally, the new board's creation also signaled a
change in the nature of health protection by municipal
government, for the board operated not only during epidemics, but year round. Although the new board lacked
authority to enforce sanitary measures except during
pestilential episodes, both its permanence and its regularly scheduled meetings demonstrated city government's commitment to assume continuing responsibility
for public health through sick and healthy seasons. By
changing the health board into a year-round institution,
council prepared the municipality to launch a swift assault at the first indication of the onset of disease.

In Cincinnati, however, the new powers granted the
health board of 1858 did not spare it heavy criticism. In
fact, within six months of its organization, a movement
surfaced in council to abolish the board and to form another structured along different lines. Antagonists of the
board claimed that it was not a board at all, but rather a
series of boards, each of which oversaw a single district.
Arguing that a health commissioner for each district led
to fragmentation not only of policy but also in collection
of mortality returns, critics proposed that the city repeal
the ordinance creating the board and establish instead
"a central Board of Health." The suggested board,
headed by a health officer, would "more effectually con-
sult for the public protection" and would specify "the
means by which this desideratum may be obtained."[8]

Although the move in council to reform the board
lacked sufficient support to topple it, the effort indi-

cated existence of dissatisfaction with the board of 1858. The board's sectional orientation, however, was not the only bone of contention. Many Cincinnatians disliked the board's practice of providing council but not the press with mortality returns. To some Cincinnatians, this procedure seemed a dreadful mistake. Withholding this important information from the newspapers kept citizens in the dark about the city's health, and since returns contained a great deal of information on how the deceased had lived, their suppression destroyed their educational utility. Faran, as he did so often, neatly expressed this latter concern. He favored publication of mortality returns because "health is generally the consequence of morality, and all that tends to impress this fact on the public mind should be supported."[9]

Perhaps the most strenuous objections to the board rested not on its performance, but on its inability to perform. Some Cincinnatians criticized the board and by extension city government for reacting to rather than preventing outbreaks of disease. In effect, they attacked the board for being a health board, not a health department, and they did so in no uncertain terms. "The city has not had a properly organized and efficient Health Department," thundered Starbuck. "In fact," he continued, "except during the prevalence of epidemics, no attention whatever is given by municipal government to [public health] matters." Instead of a viable disease prevention system, concluded Starbuck, Cincinnati had only a board of health, "composed of respectable gentlemen, who received little or no compensation, and have been delegated with no power, who meet semi-occasionally, do nothing and adjourn."[10]

City council, of course, could not on its own respond very effectively to many complaints raised by the critics of the board of 1858. Until the state legislature authorized the city to create a fulltime, paid inspection force and gave the municipality the right to regulate certain activities, such as noxious trades or food adulteration— powers apparently necessary to solve the new public health problems—council stood powerless to produce the desired reforms. Despite its impotence, however, council remained committed to municipal government's responsibility to assume the lead in the urban health effort, although it did so without the assistance of the academy. Indeed, when council next tampered with the health board, the Academy of Medicine no longer ranked as a factor in establishing municipal health policy.

Despite the academy's apparent success in influencing council concerning the structure of the health board of 1858, that move, rather than a first step, marked the apex of the academy's ability to affect municipal health legislation. To be sure, its policies remained the same, for it persisted in its attempt to provide a forum for its members to address public health issues. During the next several years, in fact, the academy considered such diverse topics as the proliferation of the criminal act of abortion, the distinction between vaccina and variola, the mode of transmission of puerperal fever, remedies for diphtheria, and the classification and treatment of an outbreak of skin disease among children.[11] But on none of these subjects did the academy adopt a single policy to influence or guide council as it tried to improve municipal mechanisms for defending the public health.

The source of divisiveness in the academy on these issues lay in the very nature of the organization. It was to serve as an umbrella organization, to disguise and reduce factional jealousies among its members. Desire for the appearance of harmony prohibited the society from offering a single coherent set of recommendations for municipal action. Perhaps the academy's most sustained efforts to guide municipal policy on public health questions focused on the frequent diarrhea and dysentery outbreaks among Cincinnatians, and its treatment of this issue demonstrated its incapacity to be helpful. The problem first came to the academy's attention late in 1863 when its members noted a sharp upturn in the number of diarrhea and dysentery cases, and the society devoted an entire session to its consideration. At the meeting, however, academy members could not agree on what caused the siege of diarrhea and dysentery cases.

One segment of the academy argued that the condition of the Ohio River produced the disease. Pointing to the filth pouring into the river upstream from the city, proponents of this explanation blamed both city inhabitants and proprietors of the noxious trades for causing the epidemic outbreak. Others, however, claimed that the epidemic did not originate in the water supply, but stemmed from "a change in diet." Their observations, they declared, led them to believe that Cincinnatians were consuming excessive amounts of unsalted pork, which in combination with the lingering effects of the recent diphtheria and scarletina outbreaks, caused an epidemic of gastrointestinal illness. Unable as a committee of the whole to reach agreement, the academy appointed a committee of three to investigate the epidemic and to report its findings to the society.[12]

A month later, the committee delivered its report. Carefully delineating the demographics of the outbreak, the committee stated to the academy that the epidemic spread "to all parts of the city, affecting all classes, ages, and sexes." Symptoms of the disease varied, however. They ranged from "a simple diarrhea with a tendency to dysentery," to more severe attacks characterized by "unusual prostration and obstinacy to treatment." Physicians in the city found "relieving the mucous membrane of the bowel by gentle laxatives"— mercurials, opiates, and astringents—the most efficacious mode of treatment.

As for the cause of the outbreak, the committee reminded the society of the prevalence within the past year of typhoid fever, erysipelas, measles, scarletina, diphtheria, jaundice, and skin disease. Claiming that those diseases also comprised "inflammations of the mucuous membranes," the committee suggested that all came from the same source, the water supply. Citing the result of a recent chemical analysis revealing that over fifty percent of the city's water really consisted of organic matter, the committee hypothesized that "such impurity is likely to develop severe and extensive diarrhea, in systems already made susceptible by what are commonly considered atmospheric causes of disease."

In an attempt to ascertain the outbreak's atmospheric causes, the committee checked the meterological records for the past two years. It discovered nothing unusual. Then the committee contacted physicians in neighboring villages, who reported no diarrheal disease in their localities. From this information, the committee determined that in Cincinnati "the well-known negligence in proper street cleaning and sewerage" predisposed city residents to the recent diseases. When predisposed persons drank the contaminated city water, their mucuous membranes became inflamed and the symptoms of that class of disease expressed themselves.[13]

The academy took no action on its committee's report, however, and when several months later a similar outbreak occurred, some of the academy's members, frustrated by the society's inaction during the past epidemic, sent a letter to the newspapers. The letter linked existence of the typhoid-like epidemic to formation of an eddy current near the waterworks, and urged council to construct a seawall directing the current and its accompanying noxious matter away from the water intake pipes.[14]

Soon after the letter appeared in the city's dailies, those physicians, who believed the outbreak a consequence of changes in diet, pressed for an opportunity to present their case. They called on the academy to investigate the situation. The academy soon accepted the challenge and established a new committee to look into the latest disease outbreak.[15]

The academy stacked the new committee heavily in favor of advocates of the water-borne explanation, and its determinations reflected that bias and proved more clear cut than its predecessors. The committee attributed the disease to the eddy current, and to substantiate its case, the committee produced an historical study correlating quantity of animals slaughtered in Cincinnati with appearance of intestinal disease among its citizens. The study demonstrated that the city's population seemed to suffer more frequently from diarrhea and dysentery during peak slaughtering months.[16]

Still, the academy could not act. In fact, it made no public announcement of its research on the problem. This was because the split among its members over the cause of the disease would render presumptuous any public statement pretending to express the wisdom of the city's sanitary authority. Such a statement would also expose the rift to the public and undermine public confidence in the organization. While members might band together and make statements or recommendations outside the academy, any public pronouncement claiming to represent a consensus of the divided society certainly would destroy the appearance of harmony and *esprit de corps* its fellows sought to cultivate.

Despite the organization's failure to articulate a cogent set of health policies, many of its members looked on its treatment of the health issue as a successful venture. The simple act of bringing the topic before the academy seemed advantageous. By making public health inquiries and discussions the chief pursuit of the society, the academy's leaders not only interested their brethren in the issue, but also demonstrated the organization's concern to municipal government and the public. Even though it could offer no policy recommendation save municipal action of some kind, the academy's members had done their part to mark public health as a distinctly medical subject. Ironically, the society was able to rally for a new municipal health policy, but was proscribed from elaborating the new program.

In much the same way, the academy proved incapable of mediating any other dispute among its members. And the fear of disharmony that stopped the organization from announcing a set of health policies was acute and realistic; academy members had engaged in numerous contests prior to the organization's formation. These contests were neither genteel nor dignified because the stakes were high: domination of Cincinnati medicine stood as the ultimate goal. Three factions of physicians participated in these recurring battles and each claimed a local medical college as its political base. The Medical College of Ohio contingent was perhaps the most well entrenched. The faction revolved around the city's oldest medical college and presently had control of the state-owned but city-located Commercial Hospital. The Miami Medical College faction was the next in line. Based at the faltering Miami Medical College, which had opened in 1852, it included many of Cincinnati's up-and-coming medical men. The least influential group called the Cincinnati College of Medicine and Surgery its home. Led by the college's proprieter, Alvah H. Baker, it had neither the other factions' power nor members. Nonetheless, its opportunity for mischief was considerable because Baker's substantial bankroll financed its every move.

Although domination of Cincinnati medicine was the final objective of the factional feuds, the Commercial Hospital usually was the immediate prize. It seemed the best means to insure that end because control of the state-supported institution would raise a faction to the first rank. The college's faculty and advocates would gain appointment power over paying hospital posts and the right to set hospital medical policy. The faction would swell in numbers as nonaligned doctors rushed for the chance to secure hospital privileges. The college-hospital connection would also attract students to the college because clinical facilities seemed an important factor in midcentury medical education. That, in turn, would boost the faction's standing, guarantee the college's advancement, and enable its faculty to increase its earnings.

While rewards for control of the hospital were substantial, criteria for selecting one faction over the others were obscure. The faction's compositions were remarkably similar and each offered a similar rationale. Each possessed some of the city's most respected and prestigeous physicians and each claimed to deserve to lead medical Cincinnati. Each faction argued that it reflected the best of Cincinnati medicine; that is, its members supremely demonstrated their concern for the public weal, were in tune with the latest scientific techniques, and conducted their affairs admirably. In that sense, the factions resembled the mid-nineteenth century Democratic, Whig, and Republican parties, each of whom maintained that the public interest would be best served if it controlled governmental operations. But unlike the parties who seemed to espouse different programs, the medical factions all had essentially the same program. There was no simple method to judge the medical factions' conflicting leadership claims. While success of political parties depended upon election results, physicians had no such mechanism.

This lack of an adjudication mechanism, coupled with the paucity of issues, made it virtually impossible to decide which faction merited the post, which produced considerable posturing and political infighting, and helps explain today why control of the Commercial Hospital appeared so crucial. The academy could offer no assistance in this endeavor because it was powerless to arbitrate its members' disputes. As a consequence, internecine battles continued to rage. But while the hospital remained the primary focus, the health board increasingly assumed importance. Indeed, organization of the hospital and health board would determine which faction would control those institutions and through them dominate Cincinnati medicine. These "medical complications" would influence municipal health policy.

This was not the only contest that helped shape municipal policy. As physician factions were fighting, city council waged war with the state for municipal control. Imbued with a sense of the city as social unit, councilmen and others demanded preeminence over the health board and hospital. They argued specifically that the health of the city's citizens was a city problem, that the health board and hospital were city agencies, and that city agencies ought to come under city government's complete control.

State government's reluctance to cede authority to the city stemmed from the perception that strangers constituted a substantial percentage of Cincinnati's population. These men and women were unaware of, unprepared for, and unaccustomed to living in a democracy and so could not be trusted to elect men who would guide city institutions in the best interests of the citizens generally. That the Queen City was comprised of a fair number of Democrats while the state legislature was predominantly rural Republican made city-state tensions appear a simple partisan political issue. It was not. On the question of the city managing its own affairs, Cincinnati-based Democrats and Republicans overwhelmingly agreed that it was a municipal right. But they frequently contended about who in the city ought to exercise oversight and control. That was the true crux of the matter.

The debate between the city and the state, while intense, unleashed few pryotechnics. This was not the case with the factional disputes. They resumed within a few months of the academy's formation and demonstrated the new society's impotence. The next episode in the battle for control began as the Miami and Ohio factions struck a deal and entered into an uneasy truce. In the "best interests of medical education in the West and to insure the gentlemen engaged in teaching a proper pecuniary reward for this labor," the Medical College of Ohio absorbed the struggling Miami Medical College and appointed the professors of the now defunct Miami school to the chairs of obstetrics and the diseases of women and children, descriptive anatomy, chemistry, and the institutes of medicine.[17] About a year later, members of the Miami faction moved to solidify their position within the Medical College of Ohio, demanding and receiving clinical professorships at the Commercial Hospital. They did not acquire these posts at the Ohio faction's expense, however, for the college's trustees, citing the increase in students brought about by consolidation, merely doubled the number of hospital positions. In this manner, the two factions possessed an equal opportunity to engage in clinical instruction.[18]

Now sharing clinical privileges with the Ohioans, the Miamians changed their stance on the hospital question. At a meeting of the school's faculty, the Miamians proposed that it "look into securing a more permanent connection between the Hospital and the Ohio Medical College." Hoping to acquire the right not only to head the medical department "in perpetuity," but also to run all the hospital's affairs, the Ohioans joined with their new colleagues, readily agreeing to their suggestion.

The faculty as a whole then dispatched a delegation of Miami men to Columbus to urge the legislature to modify the hospital's charter.[19]

The Miamians' initiative was bound to cause trouble. The charter under which the hospital then operated made a clear distinction between its medical affairs and day-to-day operations. While the charter placed primacy in hospital medical matters in the hands of the Ohio college, it specifically reserved all other authority for Cincinnati's board of the city infirmary. And when the legislature rejected the Miami-inspired request, it was the infirmary board's turn to act. Immediately following the Medical College of Ohio's failure to seize control of the hospital's administration, the board of the city infirmary launched an assault on the relationship between the school and the hospital. It delivered a special report to council on the condition of the institution that described the structure, already labeled "a disgrace to the city" by Dorothea Dix, as dilapidated and recommended the construction of a new edifice.

The infirmary board's report also laid out charges unrelated to the hospital's physical plant. The institution suffered, the board complained, because its charter tied it exclusively to the Medical College of Ohio; in the name of providing more efficacious medical treatment, the college often interfered with the infirmary board's supervision of the daily operations of the hospital. This, in effect, gave the faculty *de facto* control over the hospital, leaving the infirmary board in the intolerable position of governing the hospital by law, but unable to make decisions concerning its management. To correct this defect in the hospital's administration the board proposed that council petition the legislature to give the city infirmary the right to appoint medical attendants.[20]

Council agreed with the infirmary board's grievance, and vowed not to support the building of a new hospital facility until the legislature ceded total control of the

institution to the city through the infirmary board. Indeed, council not only called the standing arrangement
inefficient, but also described the linkage between the
Ohio college and the hospital as an idea whose time had
passed. In the early nineteenth century, the argument
went, Cincinnati was but a small municipality and the
college's monopoly insured competent medical attention for sick boatmen and strangers stranded in the city.
Now the city had grown, and many physicians vied for
the privilege of manning hospital posts. The city's best
interest would be served if it could choose the most
distinguished practitioners to care for the hospital's
patients.

By the same logic the city should also decide who
could practice at its hospital. Sustained financially by citizens of Cincinnati, the hospital now provided medical
care not to the citizens of Ohio, but only for the city's sick
poor. This view of the hospital made it an institution in
and of the city, a role that ultimately rested on the notion that the city was a social unit and should have full
control of agencies that dealt with health matters. The
Times' James Taylor neatly summed up council's sentiments. "The Commercial Hospital," he wrote,

> is an institution of the city, sustained at the expense of the
> city, and the control of it should be entirely in the city. Ev-
> ery citizen is interested in claiming that we shall have con-
> trol of our institutions. We control our infirmary, our
> house of refuge and other city property, and why not our
> own hospital?[21]

Coinciding with council's development of a new hospital view, Baker's faction submitted a petition to council
supporting the infirmary board's contention and backing council's plan. His faction also joined in the attack on
the Ohio college in other ways, for Baker sought to dis-

rupt the merger of the Miami and Ohio colleges. For that purpose, he converted the Cincinnati College of Medicine and Surgery into a free school in an effort to attract students from the Ohio college. In his petition to council, and underlying his decision to convert his college into a free school, rested the claim that the relationship between the Ohio college and the hospital placed his school at a competitive disadvantage. Since 1854 his students could attend lectures at the hospital, Baker acknowledged, but only after purchasing tickets from the infirmary board and then only to study under professors of the Ohio college. This situation set up a two-tiered system of clinical instruction, insulting the Cincinnati College faculty and hampering its drive for students.

The procedure of having his students study clinical medicine under professors of the Medical College of Ohio, Baker continued, implied that members of the Ohio faculty represented the best of Cincinnati medicine. According to Baker, this view created an unfortunate situation, for it not only damaged the reputation of city doctors, but also made Cincinnati a second-rate center for the study of medicine. For Baker, the hospital afforded local medical colleges an excellent place to engage in clinical medicine. Its control by what he deemed mediocre physicians limited the city's drawing power as a medical center, however, and prohibited many medical men from developing national reputations as clinical teachers.[22]

Despite the backing of Baker's faction, the legislature paid no heed to council's wishes. Supporters of the Ohio faction, their position reinforced by the Miami college merger, built up support among both Republican and American party legislators, who argued successfully that the municipality should not be given the right to govern all of its affairs. As a result, the relationship between the college and hospital remained as it had been, with the old charter intact and the college in charge of the hospital.[23]

After the legislature reaffirmed its authority over the hospital in early 1859, the Ohio and Miami factions launched a counterattack on Baker's faction and the infirmary board. First, they notified the city infirmary that they were terminating the agreement by which it sold hospital tickets to area medical students and used the revenue to support hospital operations. Initially, the infirmary balked at the Ohio faculty's decision to abrogate the agreement. Then, it finally promised to comply, but failed to keep that promise. In response, a member of the Ohio faculty, acting as a representative of the college, filed suit against the directors of the city infirmary in superior court to block the sale of hospital tickets.[24]

The judge upheld the Ohio college, ordering the infirmary directors to stop selling hospital tickets. Once more the board agreed to stop the practice, and once more it broke the agreement. Within a few months it began again to offer hospital tickets to students of Baker's college, at which point the Ohio faculty dropped its efforts to quash the practice.[25]

About six months after the judicial decision, however, the Miami faction split with the Medical College of Ohio, which changed the situation radically. The decision to end the truce between Miamians and Ohioans stemmed ostensibly from a dispute over the qualifications and performance of one faculty member. The Miami faction resigned from the Medical College of Ohio faculty, one Miamian noted, because a member of the Ohio faction who served on the faculty suffered "from certain infirmaties [sic] of temper and judgment" that made it impossible for the Miamians "to maintain their professional connection with him."[26]

Trustees of the Ohio college quickly accepted the resignations and appointed Marmaduke Wright to reorganize the faculty. Wright's appointment infuriated the Miamians, who saw him as the very antithesis of a medical gentleman and as an anathema to medicine. They asserted, moreover, that he gained the new position not because of his exemplary conduct or scientific attainments, but "by playing the part of a brawling politician in the Know-Nothing party." In this role, Wright frequently made his opposition to his fellow physicians' actions "the burden of a political stump-speech," damaging their public reputation.[27]

But Wright's interference in the Ohio Medical Society's decision to adopt the American Medical Association's code of ethics most rankled the Miamians. In addition to speaking out publicly against the code, Wright used skillful parliamentary maneuvers first to delay action on the code and, once the state society accepted it, to get it overturned.[28] With the despicable Wright at the helm of the Ohio college, the Miamians prepared for war, their first step being to open a summer school of medicine and to prepare preliminary plans to reopen the Miami Medical College.[29]

The Ohio college retaliated by filing another suit against the infirmary directors in superior court. Like the earlier suit, it sought to bar the city infirmary board from selling hospital tickets. But it also requested that the infirmary directors be made to pay for medical attendants supplied by the Ohio college—resident physicians, apothecaries, and house surgeons—but not its clinical lecturers. This move was calculated to boost college enrollments, for it had in the past filled these posts with unpaid second-year students and recent graduates.[30]

After a brief deliberation, the court ruled in favor of the Ohio college, yet once more the board of the city infirmary failed to honor the judicial decision. This time, however, Wright obtained a judgment against the infirmary board for noncompliance and had its members arrested. Properly chastized, the infirmary directors agreed to obey the court's decree.[31]

Although finally forced to abide by the court's judgment, the infirmary board did what it could to disrupt the Ohio college's plan. It stopped the sale of hospital tickets, but it also tried to restrict the Ohio faction's ability to appoint its many students to the hospital staff. The board claimed that the hospital's charter placed exact limitations on the number of hospital attendants. This charter, in fact, provided for only two resident physicians and one apothecary or house surgeon, and specified that these three posts should be filled by the Ohio faculty, not its students. Enforcement of that charter provision would doom the Ohio college's scheme to offer these positions as inducements to enroll in the college.[32]

Bolstered by the charter, the infirmary board then took the offensive. It argued that any single failure by the Ohio faculty to fulfill its obligations to the hospital constituted an abrogation of the charter. The board next insisted upon a written declaration of the college's intent and, if it chose to maintain its relationship with the hospital, a written commitment to assume the prescribed duties. With reluctance, Wright sent the necessary letters and the Ohio college accepted its new tasks, including the appointment of faculty members rather than students or recent graduates as resident physicians and apothecary-house surgeon.[33]

The battle had not ended, however, for students at Baker's college joined the fray. Cessation of the sale of hospital tickets had left them without access to the hospital. Unable to obtain clinical experience—deemed a prerequisite in the mid-nineteenth century to successful medical practice—students of the Cincinnati College of Medicine and Surgery petitioned council for the privilege of entering the hospital and attending the clinical lectures.[34]

Council referred their petition to a special committee, charging its members to fully investigate the matter. In a letter to the committee, Wright defended the Ohio college's position. "Because one College is deficient in instruction," he noted, why "should another college be called upon to make up the deficiency?" This seemed particularly maddening to Wright because Baker's college as "a free college" threatened "to annihilate the Medical College of Ohio." Besides, continued Wright, admission to the hospital of students from the Cincinnati College of Medicine and Surgery might spark physical violence. If council mixed "the students of 'Baker's School' with those of the Ohio Medical College," he warned, it would ruin any "probability of peace in the hospital." In closing, he reminded the committee that whatever the various arguments on either side of the question, the whole matter boiled down to a battle for control of the medical community. It was, he observed, a contest between "the ins and the outs."[35]

A few weeks later, the special committee recommended council sever the connection between the Ohio college and the Commercial Hospital. The committee, its chairman told council, reached its decision on two basic grounds. First, it seemed proper for the city to possess complete authority over its hospital. As the situation now stood, he reminded his fellow councilmen, "the City of Cincinnati had to assume the responsibility of the management of the hospital, is compelled to furnish all supplies and pay all its expenses." This seemed unfair, for while the city's inhabitants bore all the financial burden, the municipality held "no control over the most important part of the whole institution, namely, its medical department."

The second basis for the decision rested on the notion that while "it is undoubtable the duty of the Legislative authorities to encourage institutions of learning, so also is it their duty to encourage all alike." In this case, the legislature failed to provide the city's other medical schools with the same privileges it bestowed on the Medical College of Ohio. Reminding his colleagues that when the legislature chartered the hospital the Ohio Medical College was the only medical school in Cincinnati, the committee's chairman noted that during the past forty years "other schools have grown up." At present, he continued, these medical schools are "filled with students striving to acquire the knowledge sufficient to alleviate the suffering of mankind, and to them the experience acquired by Hospital practice is as essential as to the students of the Ohio College."

To correct these deficiencies, the committee proposed that council send the city solicitor to Columbus to petition the legislature "to grant the City of Cincinnati full and exclusive control of the Commercial Hospital."[36] Council overwhelmingly adopted that recommendation and simultaneously reaffirmed its opposition to construction of a new hospital so long as the Ohio college controlled the institution's medical department. And to demonstrate the seriousness of its intent, council required the solicitor not merely to forward the petition requesting that control of the hospital be given to the board of the city infirmary, but also "to attend the meetings of the legislature, and press the subject before the body."[37]

Meanwhile, the Miami faction joined the movement to separate the Ohio college and the hospital. It called a general meeting of the medical community for that purpose, but with Baker's faction already in league with the infirmary board, and with the Ohio faction fighting to maintain its relationship to the hospital, few of the members saw any reason to attend. As a consequence, Miami men constituted the vast majority of those who attended the meeting, and they moved quickly and smoothly.

They first resolved that the college-hospital union "is a monopoly grievous to the regular medical profession" because it impeded "one of the most important objects of all modern hospitals—the giving of the best and most efficient clinical instruction." The assembly then declared that the college's control of the hospital "is preventing and will prevent the erection of a new building" and therefore deprived the city of the opportunity to become "the first point in the West for clinical advantages."[38]

To end the college's stranglehold on the hospital, the meeting elected five physicians, including Murphy and Mendenhall, to go to Columbus and "join the City Solicitor in urging the separation of the two institutions." The Miamians did not want control of the hospital to be vested in the city infirmary, however. Threatened by what they claimed was a grab for power by Baker's faction and the infirmary board—a board which contained no physicians, but guided most of the city's relief efforts—members of the Miami faction proposed that the legislature create a new five-person board to govern hospital affairs. To be composed of three men appointed by the superior court of Cincinnati and two by the major, the new board would both place the hospital in city hands and "take the management of the hospital out of politics and prevent any corruption."[39]

A few months after the physicians' conclave, the legislature modified the hospital's charter. As if to symbolize transfer to the city, it changed the hospital's name to the Commercial Hospital of Cincinnati. But the legislature neither placed the infirmary board in control of the hospital nor gave council the appointment power. Instead, it formed a new seven-person board of trustees to oversee all hospital affairs, including selection of its medical staff. And it stipulated that the new board members should be appointed in various ways. Each

appointed member served for a term of five years. Two
members were to be chosen by the superior court justices, and the legislature empowered the governor to select one trustee and authorized the justices of the court
of common pleas of Hamilton County to pick two others.
In addition, it granted places *ex officio* to the mayor and
to the senior member in point of service of the infirmary
board.[40]

Although the legislature's organization of the new
board prevented the Democratically controlled council
from making appointments to the new board, the issues
involved were more complex than party politics. Arguments in the legislature focused on who represented the
interests of Cincinnati's citizens. Separating the hospital
from the legislative branch of municipal government,
while allowing popularly elected city officials to control a
majority of seats on the hospital board, provided Cincinnati with authority to govern its own hospital. But *how*
the city should govern its hospital—that is, by which
Cincinnatians—not *whether* it should, was the real issue.
By excluding council and by diffusing the appointment
power, the legislature intended to decrease the likeli-
hood of the hospital being run by self-interested men or
those out solely for personal gain. By placing responsibility for the new board in the hands of Cincinnatians
who would presumably safeguard the community's interests, and by bolstering their number with men from
outside the municipality, the legislature sought to insure
that the hospital would be governed in a proper
manner.[41]

As it turned out, this new arrangement gave the Miami faction *de facto* control of the hospital. While the Miamians themselves received appointment to three places
on the hospital board, they needed only to secure the
support of one lay board member to assume authority.
For over ten years they found it easy to drum up an ad-

ditional vote on crucial issues, for several board members generally backed the faction's contentions.[42]

Creation of a new hospital board in 1861 did not end fighting among council, the infirmary board, and the Miami faction. Later that year, council repealed the troubled health ordinance of 1858 and established a new "central Board of Health." It was composed of council's three-person committee on health, three trustees of the city infirmary, and "a physician in good repute" who also served the city as its fulltime, paid health officer for a period of three years. The board was charged with meeting at least monthly, and possessed all the powers of the previous health board, but did not divide the city into health districts. The board differed sharply from the board of 1858, moreover, in that the ordinance creating it assigned several new duties to the health officer.[43]

The new ordinance required the health officer to report monthly to council on "the general sanitary condition of the city," and "in case of epidemics" to suggest to that body "hygenic measures for the prevention and suppression of the menacing disease." In addition, the health officer was authorized to set up an office in city hall, hire an assistant, and to schedule regular office hours. Establishment of an office and regular hours, it was argued, would both facilitate collection of mortality returns and make it easier for citizens to bring their grievances to the health officer or his assistant. The health officer was expected to visit the site that engendered each complaint and to investigate its present state. If he thought it a nuisance, he could demand that the owner abate the noxious substance or condition, and if necessary call on the city police to correct the situation at the owner's expense. And if the noisome condition recurred, the health officer could use his powers of persuasion; he could name the offender in his monthly report to council and in the newspapers, actions designed to force the owner to cooperate.[44]

To many, the new health board seemed to represent a great improvement in the manner in which municipal government managed the new problems of the public health. It looked ominous to the Miamians, however, for council selected the faction's old foe, Marmaduke Wright, as the board's seventh member and health officer. And after the next council election, the results of which gave Republicans control of council, members of the Miami faction and their supporters initiated a drive to unseat Wright. They succeeded, and council cashiered Wright by abolishing the health board, refusing in the process to pay Wright his salary for his unfulfilled term of office.[45]

Explanations for council's sudden action varied. Some justified it by stressing Wright's bad character, while others said merely that the city had more pressing needs on which to spend its limited funds. Those who centered their fire on Wright stated that the new board had proven ineffectual because Wright refused to devote his full time to his position, that he no longer stood in good repute among his medical colleagues, or that he personally antagonized prominent councilmen. Those who questioned the standing of a board of health among the city's priorities stressed that "protection from confederate treachery" constituted a more immediate problem and required the city to concentrate its monies in that direction.

Wright's supporters offered a different reason for council's abrupt decision. They asserted that Wright had discovered that council, in direct violation of city ordinances and without regard to the community's health, had allowed street contractors to dump refuse within the city limits, not far from the heart of the city, and in the heavily populated West End. To prevent Wright from making these disclosures, the argument went, council terminated the health board the very day of the night he planned to expose the pernicious arrangement and to call the perpetrators to task.[46]

Wright himself made these same charges in his final report to council, which came in the form of an address and received full coverage in many of the city's dailies.[47] But Wright did not stop there. He barricaded himself in the health office, refusing to leave until the city police forcibly removed him from the premises. In response to his eviction, Wright obtained a writ of mandamus against the city, claiming that it could not terminate his appointment as health officer without paying him full compensation.[48] That moved the scene to the courtroom, where Wright argued that the ordinance creating the board and his acceptance of the health officership constituted a contract. If that were the case, he contended, the city could not abrogate the pact unless it paid his salary over the term of his appointment. The city solicitor, who handled the case for council, disagreed. He said the city received authority from the state legislature to enact a health ordinance, and that authority implicitly included the right to rescind the ordinance, thereby nullifying any obligation assumed by the board under the ordinance.[49]

After a brief deliberation, the judge ruled in favor of the city. Murphy in the *Lancet and Observer* celebrated the actions of council and the judge less for their legal acuity than for the judgment these actions expressed about Wright's character. "As much as the city needs the services of a well-educated and competent health officer," Murphy wrote, "we do not imagine it will suffer much from the repeal of the late ordinance, and the abolition of the office of Health Officer." This was because the officer in question was not "a competent person whose advice, suggestions and reports" would "be of

some service to the city."[50] Wright's sons took these remarks as character assassination, and in revenge pum-
meled with their canes the clubfooted and arthritic
Murphy, who charged them with assault and had them
arrested.[51]

Shortly after the violent termination of the 1861
fight over the health board, council again took up the
issue. In November 1861, Democrats put forth a proposal that the Republicans found unacceptable. Before
council's Republicans could put forth their own alternative proposal, however, intensification of the Civil War
deflected attention from health questions. Indeed, during the war years few Cincinnatians complained that
municipal government was ignoring the city's health,
and public clamor over health matters dropped off
markedly. The war distracted doctors, too, and led to a
cessation of medical disputes. Many physicians left the
city to man field hospitals while others kept busy staff-
ing temporary hospitals in the Queen City.[52] By 1865,
however, Cincinnatians began once more to agitate for a
new health board, and quarreling among factions resumed. This round of the fight began when Wright and
the Ohio faculty requested permission from the college
trustees to spend their own funds in an attempt to reac-
quire through the courts exclusive control of the Commercial Hospital. Specifically, they hoped to secure a
writ compelling the hospital's trustees to hire only Medical College of Ohio members. This action was appropriate, they claimed, because the hospital act of 1861, which
turned the hospital over to the Miamians, violated the
hospital's charter, and because the hospital board used
its authority to place the Ohio college at a disadvantage.
The Miamians, Wright and his colleagues contended,
not only employed physicians from other colleges to lecture at the hospital but also excluded members of the
Medical College of Ohio from attending any of the hospital's patients.[53]

While Wright and his faculty awaited the decision of
the Ohio Medical College's trustees, council's committee
on health began to consider creation of another health
board because a cholera epidemic was at that moment
devastating Russia and seemed headed for Cincinnati.
The committee acted cautiously, for it felt that in the
past council had failed to anticipate the approach of disease and as a result had often adopted "measures both
inoperative and foolish." By acting early and judiciously,
the committee hoped to assist council in adopting a
health ordinance that would "tend to modify if not entirely shield and protect this community from the ravages of disease and death."[54]

The Committee's initial presentation suggested a
board of health composed of the seven trustees of the
Commercial Hospital and council's four-member committee on health, an arrangement that would have given
control of the board to the Miamians. On the floor of
council, however, the board's composition was enlarged
by addition of the council president and a councilman
selected at large. To the Miami faction and its many supporters, the amendment posed a grave threat. By providing the legislative branch of city government with the
majority of board seats, it seemed likely to tip the board's
balance to the opponents of their faction.[55]

The Miamians tried to defeat the amendment, but
they faced a formidable coalition composed of the Democratic minority on council, a few Republican council
members who thought council should control all local
governmental institutions, and supporters of the infirmary board, Baker's college, and the Ohio faction. Their
efforts to push the amendment fell a single vote short.
And council, fearful of a deadlock that might prevent
creation of a board of health, voted to refer the health
ordinance to a special committee.[56]

Two months later, this special committee issued its
report. It recommended that council follow the first

committee's proposal and establish a board of health made up of the hospital trustees and council's health committee. This recommendation also ran into some opposition, but council nonetheless passed the health ordinance, giving in effect the Miami faction control over the new health board.[57]

In many respects, the health board of 1865 resembled closely the boards of health created in 1858 and 1861. In fact, the powers granted the new board as well as its rules for organization deviated from those of the board of 1861 in only three, albeit important, ways. First, during epidemics or in anticipation of an epidemic, the ordinance empowered the board to create a body of physicians similar to those of the outdoor relief department of the city infirmary. Detailed by ward, the new city physicians would not only furnish "medical treatment and care to the indigent sick of the city" but also examine "into all nuisances, sources of filth and causes of sickness" at the site of each visit. And city physicians, though receiving their salaries from the infirmary board and their medicine from its apothecaries, would report their findings "weekly or oftener to the Health Officer."[58]

The second innovative feature of the 1865 board was to increase the responsibilities and expand the authority of the health officer. As before, he could look into or direct the city police to investigate a reported nuisance or pestilential substance on private property. But unlike previous health officers, the new official, who was appointed by the board, now held the power during the threat of an epidemic first to obtain a judgment against a sanitary offender, which could include a fine of no more than fifty dollars, and then to abate the noxious substance or condition "at the expense of the person upon whose premises such nuisances, causes of sickness, and sources of filth may be found to exist."[59]

This provision, which shifted the cost of keeping private property in good sanitary condition from the city to the property owner, allowed city government to use its limited funds more efficiently. Indeed, it prevented dissipation of municipal revenues on cleaning private property and on long legal battles usually necessary to force property owners to repay the costs. In effect, the new policy enabled the board to seek out and to cause the removal of more substances, substances that in the past seemed too costly to remove, and permitted the board to devote a greater proportion of its funds to cleaning up and maintaining public property.

The new ordinance also provided the health officer with greater powers to deal with the noxious trades. It authorized him whenever he deemed it imperative for the health of the city to declare "any business, trade, or profession carried on in the city . . . detrimental to the public health and cause an action to be commenced by indictment in the court of common pleas." The penalty for noncompliance ranged up to five hundred dollars, and since a single enterprise could be indicted several times, businesses had either to fall in line or flee the city.[60] The health ordinance of 1865 prepared the city for the anticipated coming of cholera and it now warily awaited the disease's approach.

This ordinance did not change the nature of the municipal health effort; it stood instead as city government's third attempt in less than a decade to create an institution to resolve the problem of public health. Although health boards created by the ordinances of 1858, 1861, and 1865 all sought to achieve the same goal, each broke new ground. The board of 1858 was the first health board in Cincinnati's history required to meet year round, and was empowered to compile mortality returns regularly so as to detect disease before it reached epidemic proportions. The enabling ordinance creating the board of 1861 provided for employment of the city's first fulltime, paid health official, the health officer. He and his assistant operated out of the health office, surveyed the sanitary affairs of the city, investigated suspected nuisances, and suggested legislation to council. Similarly, the board of 1865 also received additional authority. First, it possessed the ability to secure a judgment against a sanitary offender before abating a nuisance. Second, it was given an effective means to fight the noxious trades, for its health officer could now cite a particular establishment several times to get it to desist its harmful practices. Finally, it controlled the city physicians rather than the poor relief department of the city infirmary. This transfer of responsibility indicated that the sick poor had become a health problem, one susceptible to the health board's management rather than that of the infirmary directors.

Council's inability to settle the matter of public health stemmed in part from the newness of the task. It had few clear precedents to turn to and it received little help from the Academy of Medicine. Other factors also hampered formulation of a comprehensive approach to muncipal health matters. Constant wrangling between city and state over who best represented Cincinnati and, therefore, who should administer to and set policy for the muncipality provided one source of discord. Another arose from the battle among physicians' factions for control of Cincinnati's public health institutions. These institutions proved central in the fight to lead the medical community. Neither of the conflicts was resolved by the creation of the health board of 1865. Like the city's quest to develop a new agency to cater to public health, the two disputes persisted beyond the cholera epidemic of 1866.

6   Creating a New Agency:
The Department of Health

Four days after council passed legislation creating the health board of 1865, the board held an organizational meeting and appointed William C. Clendenin health officer.[1] Clendenin, then professor of surgical anatomy at the Miami Medical College, proved an excellent choice and, in anticipation of the arrival of cholera, carried out his duties zealously. During his first two months on the job, Clendenin urged council to construct public urinals, offered the city's mortality returns to the newspapers, complained about the municipal ordinance permitting builders to dump plaster onto the streets, suggested that property owners tap into the city's still-incomplete system of sewerage, and recommended that council pass an ordinance regulating the sale of meats, fish, and produce in the city's markets. At the same time he began a thorough sanitary inspection of the city, prefaced by a public announcement that he hoped to check "all cellars, backyards, and privy vaults." His lack of assistants forced him, though, to concentrate his survey on a single heavily populated city block. There he turned up seventy-nine sanitary ordinance violations, issued a citation for each, and in four days reported great strides in remedying the unhealthful conditions.[2]

While the vigor with which Clendenin prosecuted his tasks stood as tribute to his commitment, his ability to perform these duties reflected the evolution of municipal power. Since the later 1850s, Cincinnatians repeat-

197

edly had clamored for authority necessary to create a
health department staffed by fulltime employees and
operating year round. Indeed, cries for city government
to devise an institutional solution to the public health
problem remained so intense as to withstand the constitutional crisis precipitating the Civil War and to persist
through the war itself. During this ten-year period, both
the city and state had broadened the Cincinnati board of
health's mandate. Though the city still was unable to
form a health department, both the legislature and
council ceded to it new powers to fight disease.

The threat of the cholera epidemic served, then, to
reinforce the health department call. But it was not
enough; formation of a health department awaited the
resolution of two critical issues. These issues proved central because they would determine the nature and form
of a new health department. Put simply, creation of Cincinnati's first health department was an event delayed by
the battle for medical primacy and the contest between
city and state for municipal control. Only when disputants in medicine and public administration resolved
these conflicts (or had the conflicts resolved for them)
could Cincinnatians establish their long-desired institution. That did not occur until 1867, well after cholera's
passage. From that point on, there was no difficulty. The
legislature provided the municipality with the necessary
authority and council formed the city's first department
of health.

The city did not have benefit of this legislation as
it prepared in 1865 for cholera, though it did have
the Academy of Medicine. But, although the academy
turned its attention to the disease and despite the
scourge's imminence, the medical society did little to
help the city ready itself for the expected ordeal. The
academy's insufficiencies prevented it once again from
taking an active policy role. It began deliberations with a

survey of contemporary medical thought about the pestilence's etiology. The survey soon sparked controversy
and academy members took sides on the question of how
cholera spread. Most supported the noncontagiousness
of cholera. They claimed that atmospheric conditions,
operating in conjunction with predisposing causes, produced the disease. This explanation seemed to account
for the disease's apparent tendency to strike certain
groups of the city's population—strangers—whose behavior made them susceptible to disease. A substantial
minority disagreed. They held that cholera constituted
either a contagious or infectious disease, and that it
spread from person to person, or from the dejecta of its
victims through the water supply.[3]

Some members grew impatient with the long etiolog-
ical debate, and when it gave way to another protracted
discussion of the treatment of cholera, they tried to
bring the academy to more practical matters. "Are we,"
asked one member in frustration, "able to tell the authorities how to prevent its coming, or how to meet and
treat it? The cause," he continued, "is interesting to scientific men, but we have little hope of discovering it.
Much attention has been given to this subject, but no
sooner is one theory set up than another knocks it
down." A colleague concurred. "We don't know what
[cholera] is. The whole practical question is how to meet
it and combat it."[4]

The "practical question" proved rhetorical, though,
for given the inability of the academy to agree either on
what caused cholera or how it spread, it could not as an
organization endorse a single policy. Non-contagionists
wanted the society to urge municipal authorities to institute a citywide sanitary campaign that paid particular attention to the condition of the streets, yards, and
tenement houses. Contagionists thought a quarantine
most effective and insisted any sanitary campaign should

focus on disinfecting and cleansing privies, measures that would neutralize human wastes before they reached the water supply. Neither side carried the day.[5]

Meanwhile some city residents concluded that the health board lacked both the staff and authority to prevent the anticipated epidemic from ravaging Cincinnati. Although they noted that council had invested the board with all authority permitted by the legislature, critics now argued that the board's "power was too limited and inadequate to accomplish all that was desired for the protection of the public health." In response, the board ordered Health Officer Clendenin to draw up a bill granting it greater powers and petitioned the legislature for immediate action.[6]

Clendenin constructed a health bill that, not surprisingly, perpetuated the Miami faction's control over the health board, while giving the board a fulltime paid staff and extending its authority over the city's sanitary affairs. Despite pressure from city residents for a health board with more extensive powers, Clendenin's measure ran into trouble in the legislature where the Ohio faction and the infirmary board, still seething from the loss of the health board battle in council, worked to kill his bill. The zeal of the infirmary board's opposition to Clendenin's proposal stemmed from the municipal health ordinance of 1865. The ordinance had given the hospital trustees health board posts previously held by infirmary board members. It also authorized the hospital trustees during epidemics to appoint physicians to care for the sick poor, duties formerly assigned to the infirmary directors. Worse still, the infirmary board had to pay these physicians' salaries and for the medication they dispensed.[7]

The Ohio faction, which had been ousted from the hospital by the creation of a separate board of trustees of the Commercial Hospital in 1861, and stripped of influence over the health board by the Republican-controlled council, found itself in similar dire straits. As a consequence it allied with the infirmary board, its former enemy, and together the two groups not only opposed Clendenin's proposal but also tried to wrest control of the hospital and health board from the Miamians. To cement the alliance, the infirmary board appointed members of the Ohio faction as physicians to the department of outdoor relief.[8] Then, the Ohio–infirmary board combine offered the legislature a proposal to counter Clendenin's health bill.

Though similar in many ways to Clendenin's bill, the infirmary-Ohio proposal differed from his in one important particular. It named the infirmary directors as the board of health and thus placed them in charge of the municipal health effort. Yet the legislature, though dominated by Republicans, could not decide between the two proposals and neither came up for a vote. Instead, it created a special committee composed entirely of the Hamilton County delegation to hammer out a compromise, but the committee too proved unable to achieve a solution satisfying the contenders. Appalled by the deadlock, Mayor Harris lambasted the assembly. If cholera struck the city, he advised Cincinnatians to "place the responsibility . . . in the place where it belongs, and this is with the members of the Legislature who opposed [Clendenin's] Health Bill."[9]

Soon after the legislature adjourned, the dispute over control of the health board erupted once more. This outbreak began in May 1866, when a backer of the Miami faction proposed that council permanently transfer the city physicians from the infirmary board to the health board's jurisdiction. Noting that at present both the health board and the city infirmary employed medical men to attend the sick poor, he cited as justification for his proposal the wastefulness of maintaining two sets

of city physicians. He concluded by urging the city to reduce expenditures by taking power away from the infirmary board and allowing only the health board to
appoint city physicians.[10]

While council considered that suggestion, the infirmary board mounted an offensive to protect its turf. It
not only opposed the motion in council, but also took its
case to the city newspapers to arouse public support.
Members of the infirmary board claimed that their appointees from the Ohio faction did an excellent job as
city physicians, so that the effectiveness of the board's efforts to provide medical care to the poor could not be
questioned. The resolution before council, then, merely
represented another step in the plot of the Miamians.
Through "a perservering and insidious strategy," the infirmary board argued, the Miami faction was using "the
Board of Health to accomplish a change as yet developed only in part, and not for the people who are interested parties." The Miamians' ultimate goal, the
infirmary directors continued, was "that the Infirmary
Board should be abolished, and that the duties of the
Board and the Hospital should be managed by the Doctors." To support their charges, infirmary board members recounted how the Miamians had snatched the
hospital from their control and how that faction had secured the right for itself to supervise the construction of
the new hospital. Those acts, they asserted, constituted
but two parts of the plot, and the infirmary director om-
inously warned readers that "the third is the appointment of City Physicians."

The infirmary directors did not end their assault
there. They also contended that the Miamians' shenani-
gans reflected badly both on the Miamians and on the
city. Instead of demonstrating concern for the quality of
poor relief, the actions of the Miami faction indicated
that it sought to obtain control of the city physicians for

personal gain. If the Miamians, with the aid of council, proved successful in their venture, both the city and its reputation would suffer, for it "would make this great and expensive charity subservient to personal or professional advancement." Despite the infirmary board's appeal, however, council sided with the health board, granting it sole authority to appoint city physicians.[11]

Throughout the battle, the board of health and its health officer continued to prepare the city for the approach of cholera. Clendenin and the city physicians continued tenement house inspections, paying particular attention to the condition of privies and cellars. They also complained about overcrowding, pointing to its unfortunate consequences for the city's health and morality. But Clendenin and the city physicians concentrated their efforts on insuring that the municipality's landlords cleaned up their property, drained their buildings, and either emptied their privies or built new ones. Checking over 130 tenements and 800 privy vaults, inspectors found that fully thirty percent of the cellars contained water, and that nearly half the privies "were either full and emitting noisome odors, or needed repairing and cleaning." Of these foul receptacles, inspectors caused 383 to be cleansed and 22 new privies to be constructed.[12]

Despite the large number of buildings inspected by the health officer and his medical assistants, they felt they had merely scraped the surface. The board concurred, and argued that to pursue more diligently its mandate and to put the city in good sanitary condition, it needed a larger inspection force. Indeed, neither Clendenin nor the city physicians possessed the ability to act as fulltime inspectors because their other duties appeared at least as pressing. And the board felt that to insure the city's preparedness, inspections had to be regular and frequent.

To remedy the situation, the health board advanced a familiar proposal. It asked the councilmen of each ward to convene ward meetings, a standard request since the 1840s when the city first was viewed as a social unit. At these meetings the board wanted citizens elected to check their wards for violations of sanitary law and to report them to the health office. In this manner, any noisome substance or condition would receive the health officer's prompt consideration. Many councilmen complied with the board's request, and soon people were scouring their wards for obvious nuisances. [13]

This method of inspection had its limitations. Citizens of a ward were not municipal employees and therefore enjoyed none of the authority granted the board. Unable to enter private property, their investigations were necessarily confined to readily visible conditions. While this, no doubt, aided the cause, it failed, as the board pointed out, to regulate the internal condition of dwellings.

To overcome the volunteer inspection force's shortcomings, the board in June urged council to establish a municipal sanitary squad and to authorize it to enter, at the direction of the health officer, and in the daytime, "any building, lot or land inclosed." The mayor sent the board's suggestion to council, where a majority agreed with the board on the need for such a squad, and since the ordinance creating the board allowed the board to make this request, council appropriated some of its meager funds to hire ten sanitary inspectors. [14]

The board and its health officer did not limit their efforts to overseeing the cleansing of the city, but also attempted to control the kinds of businesses practiced in Cincinnati. In particular, they lashed out at the noxious trades and undertook the assault themselves. Clendenin and the board members began by touring slaughterhouses, candle factories, and soap, grease, and bone-boiling establishments in the northeastern and northwestern corners of the city, and found there a total of twenty businesses that they thought fell into the "noxious" group. Since the board lacked power to close businesses or even prohibit certain facets of their activities without first obtaining a judgment, Clendenin upon returning to city hall filed suit against the offenders. While some pleaded guilty, a few demanded that the board prove its allegations. In each case the judge upheld the board's claim. He then fined the violators three hundred dollars each and gave them thirty days either to close their factories or to remove their businesses beyond the city limits.[15]

Whatever the effect of this municipal activity, Cincinnati through July developed not a single case of cholera. Yet many Cincinnatians, in light of the devastation the disease could leave in its wake, understood that the board's powers were not commensurate with the moment's immediacy. And regardless of legal constraints on the board, they urged it to do anything, legal or not, that might stop the epidemic from striking the city. They, in short, wanted the board to act as they felt it should, not as it could, and Louis Wright, an early proponent of this approach, offered a concise statement of the position. "Whatever shall be considered necessary to put the whole city in order," he wrote, "must be accepted as right, without regard to cost, precedent or law."[16]

This sentiment gained considerable support after cholera appeared in the city early in August. A special chamber of commerce committee called upon the board, extended the chamber's good offices, and asked the board to enforce more stringent sanitary measures. Even council backed the board, although tacitly. It placed fire equipment for flushing the streets and a boat to dump nuisances at the board's disposal and, more important, appropriated twenty thousand dollars to the board, requiring only that the money be used to fight the pestilence.[17]

The significance of these events was not lost on the board. Its members recognized that they had received virtual carte blanche to pursue the epidemic's abatement. Their first act was to increase the inspection force's size by hiring thirty additional sanitary inspectors. The board's next move was to overstep its legal authority, regulate all sorts of endeavors, and compel citizens to behave in a healthful manner.

Without receiving legal sanction from either council or the state legislature, and in many instances without a judicial ruling, the board and its health officer assumed added authority to put the city in good sanitary shape. They hired inspectors, for example, to prohibit sale of green vegetables at the city's markets, to supervise slaughtering of animals, and to check on the quality of meat, fish, and poultry sold in the municipality. In addition, the board authorized the sanitary force to disinfect all privies in the city, to allow vault cleaners and night cartmen to ply their trades only under the direction of a sanitary official, and to enter into and to halt the operations of all soap, grease, and bone-boiling establishments.

The board did not stop there. It ordered the street cleaning department to disinfect sewers before cleaning them, and detailed a sanitary policeman to make sure the department adhered to the board's new dictate. The city's undertakers likewise received new instructions. The board mandated that they use only airtight coffins in which to bury the dead, and, as in the case of the street cleaners, the board sent an inspector to insure that undertakers complied with the directive.[18]

Perhaps the board's most striking appropriation of power involved the tenement house problem, though it started simply enough. The board first requested councilmen to convene ward meetings at which board members and Clendenin asked for ten volunteers to serve as a "visiting committee." Unlike the board's previous proposal, which focused on election of citizens to police wards for obvious nuisances, these visiting committees were "to visit every family in their respective wards."

Going door to door, visitors entered each abode, discussed the epidemic with their neighbors, and informed them of the measures the board suggested to remain healthy. If visitors noticed any sickness, especially "diarrheal disease," they appointed a "proper person" to stay with the invalid while the others summoned a medical attendant. Board supporters claimed that this procedure would not only allow the committees to "report to the Board many items of interest enabling them [sic] more effectually to carry out measures of reform," but would also lessen the impact of cholera on the community. This followed because in the board's eyes the visiting committee method worked "to induce proper care and circumspection in those with whom they come into contact."

As the next stage of the campaign against tenements, the board authorized the municipal sanitary inspectors to enter and to disinfect every tenement house. Ignoring the legal stricture requiring that each house should first be judged a nuisance and then be treated at the health officer's direction, the board gave its inspectorate complete prerogative to pursue the task. And Clendenin, not satisfied merely with disinfecting tenements, tacked on an additional stipulation. He charged the force "to inspect and measure" each tenement "from cellar to garret." The sanitary squad, in turn, prosecuted its new duties so strenuously that within three weeks it had surveyed and disinfected well over a thousand rooms.[19]

Yet the assault on tenements did not stop there. Appalled by the living conditions uncovered by the visiting committees and the sanitary squad's inspections, the board resolved to move the tenement population into more salubrious surroundings. Seizing some city land and soliciting citizens to donate undeveloped property, the board hastily constructed tents and ordered the city police to place the tenement population in them. Mayor Harris, recognizing the benefit to the city as a whole as well as to those who resided in overcrowded quarters, backed up the board. He even asked the school board to shift control of school buildings to the health board so that it could use the buildings as dormitories for the unfortunates.[20]

At just that moment, however, the epidemic seemed to wane, and the board discontinued many of its extralegal practices. At the same time, it launched a campaign to justify the wisdom and judiciousness of its decisions. Part of the defense consisted of attacking the legislature for not passing Clendenin's bill and for not providing the board with the authority it sought. The other part of the defense consisted of attacking the courts for not supporting the board during the epidemic and for not convicting and penalizing sanitary violators. The board claimed that the courts too frequently accepted from such violators a promise that nuisances would be promptly abated and not allowed to recur. This hurt the city, board members continued, because it not only undermined the board's efforts in particular instances, but also implied to the community that the courts lacked confidence in the board and indirectly encouraged further violation of sanitary law. The crisis in confidence worsened an already dangerous situation, and forced the board for the city's welfare to assume the power of the courts.[21]

The board used other arguments to show the necessity and defend the wisdom of its actions during the epidemic. Arguing that "public opinion [during the cholera epidemic] became strong enough to justify active measures," the board asserted that it therefore possessed *de facto* authority to take all means necessary to enhance the city's sanitary condition. Alluding to the chamber of commerce's support and council's acquiescence, board members claimed that they had executed their offices faithfully and should not be held liable for damages.

The board also suggested measures to protect both future health boards from abuse and the community from disease. Noting that in the epidemic just passed "the wiser course" would have been to provide the board with authority adequate "to prevent the pestilence from finding a lodgement in our city," the board members urged council, the chamber, and the city's other prominent citizens "to use your influence with the lawmaking power of the state . . . as will establish a Health Department, clothed with sufficient power to perform this work. Whatever enhances the comfort and welfare of the whole community," the board contended in its plea, "will equally contribute to the interests and prosperity of her citizens individually."[22]

As the opening shot in the drive for a department of health, the board in October 1866 asked two of its members to draw up another health department bill. Instead of drafting a new measure, however, they merely submitted Clendenin's earlier proposal for the entire board's reconsideration. The board swiftly approved it and forwarded it to Columbus. And in Cincinnati, Clendenin, through his monthly reports and other public announcements, acted as the measure's chief lobbyist. He delineated what seemed necessary to protect the city, thereby providing a justification for the board's past actions. He also looked to the future, taking care to lay out the bill's particulars and to drum up support for its passage in the legislature.

Clendenin's list of particulars was long. He called for creation of a regular, fulltime, paid sanitary squad empowered at all times to abate noisome conditions or substances, establishment of market, milk, and meat inspectors, and permanent transfer of the city physicians to the health board. He requested stiff laws to control the noxious trades and asked for power to regulate construction and cleaning of privies and to place restrictions on the building of "tenement houses, as to size, ventilation, light, etc., so that each occupant shall have the proper amount of air space."

Clendenin did not limit his case to the simple exposition of specific proposals. Instead, he claimed that the health board's health department ought to be a kind of sanitary watchdog, overseeing most facets of community life. Able to prohibit whatever it deemed prejudicial to the public health, the board should not only assume authority during epidemics, but through its department function on a regular, continuing basis. Arguing that the existing "health ordinance provides for the exercise of additional powers [only] when an epidemic disease is prevailing," Clendenin asserted that citizens of Cincinnati "now want laws, the rigid enforcement of which will enable us to prevent disease."[23]

In many ways, Clendenin's campaign was purely demonstrative. Since emergence of the problem of public health in the mid 1850s, many Cincinnatians supported creation of a health department that would possess broad regulatory powers and a fulltime staff. Debate within Cincinnati, as well as the reason for the legislature's failure in 1866 to act on Clendenin's health bill, focused not on a disagreement over the proposed bill's powers, but rather on the new board's control. The issue was not one of party politics, for the rupture was much more complex than party affiliation. Instead, two different sets of disputants, the city and the state on one hand and the factions of the medical community on the other, contended for the privilege of governing the proposed board.

Before the legislature could reconsider the health question, however, the battle for control of the proposed institution flared up in the city once again. This time the infirmary board initiated the fray. At a council meeting early in 1867, it offered a resolution protesting the legislature's consideration of "further legislation on the subject of the Board of Health" and demanding "the repeal of so much of the law as gives control of the Commercial Hospital to the Board of Directors." By this action, the city infirmary board did not seek to stop the legislature from working on a measure to extend the city's public health authority. Rather, the infirmary board hoped to induce the legislature to disband the hospital board, some members of which were appointed by the governor and the Hamilton County common pleas judges, officials who lacked any ties with city government. The objective was to place any new municipal health agency and the Commercial Hospital under the administration of a body which, like the popularly elected infirmary board, was responsible exclusively to the citizens of Cincinnati. In addition to this petition, the board of the city infirmary also asked council to abolish the health board's authority to appoint city physicians and to transfer that authority to the infirmary board. Without debate, council referred both the resolution and the memorial to its committee on special references.[24]

A month later, the committee reported out the resolution and the memorial, giving lukewarm endorsements to both, and entertaining discussion on the propositions. In the discussion supporters of the Miami

faction, not those behind the infirmary board, carried
the day. Although the infirmary's backers argued once
more that some hospital trustees were appointees of officials outside the municipality and that "the people of
Cincinnati . . . ought to govern and control all the affairs
of the city," their words fell on deaf ears. The real reason
for the resolution, asserted one councilman friendly to
the Miamians, was self-interest. The legislature had authorized the city to sell bonds totaling five hundred
thousand dollars for construction of a new hospital, and
"the directors of the City Infirmary wanted to take the
matter out of the hands of those responsible men, and
control the matter themselves." After a short additional
discussion, council voted overwhelmingly to postpone
indefinitely any action on either the resolution or the
memorial.[25]

In the legislature, the infirmary board fared some-
what better. Despite the health board's urging, the
health officer's bill was never reintroduced. A substitute
measure was put forward by a member of the Hamilton
County delegation designed as a compromise to initiate
deliberations on Cincinnati's request for a health department. Creating a four-member board, the compromise proposition differed from that of the health officer
only in that it divided power to appoint board members
equally between council and the superior court justices,
allowing them each to fill two slots. It drew little support
in the legislature, for the compromise satisfied neither
the city nor the state party. Equal division of appointment power would not resolve the tension between the
two jurisdictional units for control of the department,
but would merely perpetuate the conflict. At loggerheads, the legislature once again referred the matter to
the entire Hamilton County delegation.[26]

At first, the Hamilton County delegation could not
work out an amicable settlement of the health question.

While some members argued that it was the city's right to direct its own affairs, others disagreed. They contended that Cincinnati was "too Irish" to govern itself and called on the state to retain exclusive influence over municipal health matters. In a sense, then, while the debate focused on who should control Queen City health institutions, it certainly did not reflect a simple self-interested power struggle. The central consideration in the contest seemed to be the fitness of Cincinnati city government; it was difficult for many in Columbus to conceive of council as composed of responsible citizens when it was selected by and indebted to an electorate, a significant portion of which was apparently unaccustomed to American urban life. Having health policy made and implemented by responsible citizens seemed crucially important because only they seemed to possess the ability of administering it both efficiently and effectively and, therefore, of guaranteeing the public health.

Ironically, movement on the health bill occurred when the delegation decided to join it to another, equally crucial issue. For a number of years, council had attempted to obtain control from the legislature of the city's police board. As it did in the case of health institutions, council claimed that the police was a municipal agency and ought to be governed by officials chosen by either city government or city residents. The legislature repeatedly denied that contention, but in 1867 the Hamilton County delegation suggested that it modify its position as part of a general compromise to cool the city-state battle and that recommendation ultimately paved the way for Cincinnati to form its first health department.

Though framed together, the Hamiltonians reported out two separate bills. Both received the delegation's unanimous endorsement and reflected an optimistic view of council's possibilities. The police board bill

continued the state's domination of the Cincinnati police, but for the first time gave council a minority say in
the board's composition. The prospective health department measure rejected outright the arguments of those
pushing for extramunicipal control and vested appointment power in council. The legislature, now with a Democratic majority, accepted its committee's advice and
passed both bills handily.[27]

The new health law was enacted on March 29, 1867.
It established a health board composed of the mayor and
six other persons selected by council and gave the municipality the right to levy an annual tax on private property to pay the costs of the sanitary effort, a tax "not to
exceed one mill on the dollar of all taxable property" in
the city. It also authorized the board to hire a fulltime,
paid health officer, clerk, and sanitary squad, and as
many city physicians as it needed, who together constituted a year-round department of health. The act also
created a new category of health hazard, the public nuisance, which it defined as "any building, erection, excavation, premises, business pursuit, matter or thing, or
the sewerage, drainage or ventilation thereof" that may
be judged by a member of the department as "dangerous to life or health." Under the law, moreover, the
board could order any public nuisance "to be removed,
abated, suspended, altered or otherwise improved or
purified." If offenders failed to comply with such directives, the board could, through its sanitary squad, take
action itself and "assess the costs and expenses" of the
abatement "upon property as a lien."

In addition to these general powers, the legislature
also gave the new board some particular duties. It obli-
gated the board "to regulate the construction and arrangements of water-closets [and] privy vaults," and to
oversee "the emptying and cleaning of such vaults." It
also required the health board "to create a complete and

accurate system of registration of birth, deaths, and in-
terments . . . to furnish facts for statistical, scientific,
and particularly for sanitary inquiries," and gave the
board the standard powers to institute both an internal
and external quarantine.

Nor was that all. The new act also permitted the
board to order the health department to disinfect the
premises of the poor and to vaccinate unfortunates
gratis. While it could not force Cincinnatians to suffer
the preventative, it could offer inducements, such as a
monetary stipend, to persuade them to be vaccinated.
Most important, though, the board could now "make
and pass all such orders and regulations as it shall . . .
deem necessary and proper for the public health and the
prevention of disease" and compile these orders and
regulations into a single health code, which became law
when sanctioned by council. Then, any violation carried
a possible five hundred dollar fine and up to ninety days
in jail.[28]

While passage of the health legislation of 1867 resolved the city-state conflict in health matters, it did not
terminate the factional fight in medicine. In fact, it
seemed to exacerbate tensions. The new act appeared especially damaging to the Miami faction. While it failed
to give the Ohio faction control of the health board, the
health act had stripped the Miamians of one of their
seats of power. Though they still controlled the hospital,
they had lost the health board and as a consequence denounced the act "as a piece of Council machinery."
Warning that "it is useless to combat poor human nature," the Miamians argued that the new health board
would certainly fail, for "whenever power can be made
tributary to party, it is folly to suppose it will not be so
exerted."[29]

From the Miamians' point of view, things got worse
instead of better. First, council delayed passing an en-

abling ordinance allowing establishment of a new health
board and department because of the imminence of a
council election. Council lacked time to devote proper
attention to the matter, and also deemed it inappropriate for a body to legislate on a subject of such importance so near a time when its members' tenure expired.
Indeed, any action taken by outgoing council might
meet serious objections from the incoming body. It
could necessitate revisions which would create confusion
among the public and engender ill-will among council
members. And to the chagrin of the Miamians, when the
election returns came in, the city had chosen a Democratic council, a council opposed to that faction's aims.

Equally distressing, both to the Miamians and to the
entire medical community, was the call from newspapers
to exclude physicians from the new board. Reacting to
the unseemly, recurring battle between factions for medical superiority, the newspapers demanded a new "executive" health board, one "not converted by zealous
professional theorists into a debating society." Arguing
that "those who observed the workings of the [present]
board . . . will doubtless agree with us," they implored
council, in the interests of the city, to bar physicians from
the board.[30]

Taking the position of the press as an attack on their
group, the factions accommodated their differences and
while the Miamians held on to the hospital, physicians
dropped their factional battles for the new health
board's control. Instead, they chose to work together
and to share whatever power they could wrest from
council. The compromise came to light soon after the recently invested council passed the new health ordinance
and justified the legislature's optimistic judgment of city
government. It appointed six socially prominent and
well-established members of the Queen City business
community to the health board. All members of the new

board belonged to the chamber of commerce, actively
supported benevolent work, and held substantial commercial or manufacturing interests in Cincinnati.[31]

Immediately, the once-factionalized physicians and
their supporters boosted Clendenin for the health officership. They argued that he had distinguished himself
and the medical community generally by his vigorous
prosecution of his duties during the recent cholera epidemic. Even the Academy of Medicine, the society that
claimed to speak for the entire medical community,
threw its support behind Clendenin, commending him
for his service to the city. While "an effort was made to
interest the board in Quacks," Clendenin's broad backing among physicians placed him in the advantage, and
the new board within a week offered him the post.
Board members realized that Clendenin's broad support
among doctors made him a valuable ally, moreover, and
as a consequence, allowed him to participate often in the
board's deliberations and heeded his suggestions.[32]

Board members then moved to flesh out the health
department. Its members selected a clerk, acquired a
sanitary force, and took an office in the basement of city
hall. The board did not select the city physicians, however, but left that chore to Clendenin, who quickly paid
back his supporters. He took care to spread the posts
among each faction of the medical community, offering
positions to members of both the Ohio and Baker's factions. This gesture signaled an unofficial end to the
health board and department as issues in medical
politics.[33]

Upon completing appointment of the new health department, the board established *de facto* bylaws for its
management, carefully setting forth each post's duties
and obligations. These bylaws not only covered the responsibilities of the department's members but also laid
out the conduct the board expected from its appointees.

Members of the sanitary squad, for example, while on duty had to wear the uniform of a regular patrolman, carry special badges signifying that they were part of the sanitary squad, and display these badges whenever they acted as the municipality's representatives. And the sanitary inspectors in dealing with the public were obliged to maintain a courteous and proper demeanor and to remain sober.[34]

Once it had filled all posts in the department and set rules for the conduct of its members, the board next tackled the city's health problems. It began by creating a series of committees, one for each health concern, and each of which sought to develop a system of rules and regulations governing each problem. The board's efforts did not end there. Considering each problem in detail (such as how to clean privies and vaults most efficiently, secure an adequate supply of pure water, alleviate the slaughterhouse nuisance, obtain a wholesome milk supply, and the like) the board hoped to devise measures to control these substances and conditions and, then, to tie them together in the form of a comprehensive municipal health code.[35]

Conceived of as the pinnacle of public health achievement, a single health code would organize the board's pronouncements and dictates in a straightforward fashion and, after council approved it, become law. It would regulate all activities that seemed to menace the public health and provide city government with means to protect its citizens from the deleterious influences of their fellow urban dwellers. It would outlaw practices that seemed to result from ignorance or greed, and could be either expanded or contracted so as to establish a systematic set of health regulations consisting of existing rules as well as any the board members might wish to add.

As the board deliberated the health code, the legislature passed two more acts. Council quickly passed the enabling ordinances and extended the powers of the health board even further. The first act commanded the board to undertake a census of prostitutes in the city and gave its officers authority "to enter all brothels and houses of assignation" to record the name, age, color, and nativity of the inmates. Any female under the age of eighteen was to be returned to her parents immediately or if she refused to go home, sent to the House of Refuge or tried as a vagrant.[36]

The second act empowered the board to expand the influence of the health department by appointing "inspectors of Beef Cattle, Sheep, Hogs, Poultry, Game, Milk, Milk Cows, Fresh Meat, and Fresh Fish." It granted the board great leeway in establishing the inspectors' duties. The sole stipulation mandated in the act was a clear listing in the health code of violations for which the inspectors would check. But the legislation permitted the board to name as inspectors only those persons not "engaged or interested in any branch of business over which they are called upon to exercise official duties," a specification designed to eliminate the possibility of conflict of interest.[37]

Meanwhile, the board continued to consider the health code. Its first effort ran to some one hundred sections, and the document's unwieldiness destroyed the clarity the board sought. The board then pared the proposed code to about thirty articles, and after further debate finally agreed upon a draft containing eighteen sections, which it sent to council.[38]

The code fell under four main headings. Nuisances, the first and broadest division, banned noxious trades from Cincinnati and prohibited any activity that generated "noisome or unwholesome odors, or gaseous

vapors." In addition, it proscribed the dumping of animal carcasses or offal on the streets, said privy vaults
should be disinfected before cleansing in the summer
months, and forbade transportation of diseased persons
through the city without the express permission of the
board or its health officer.

The second division, slaughterhouses, regulated a
number of different activities. It outlawed killing and
sale of pregnant animals, conveyance of bound or tied
animals, and slaughtering of any animal in public view.
But it also regulated dairies, establishing minimum grazing periods for dairy cattle during the summer months
and banning slop feeding.

The third part of the code covered tenements and required landlords to provide at least two exits and "adequate sewerage or drainage, and sewered or vaulted
privies or water closets so situated so as not to be offensive to the inmates or other persons." The fourth section
regulated markets. It authorized meat inspectors to prevent sale of meat or fish "that died of accident or disease" or had been butchered when sick or under four
weeks old. It also stipulated that no green vegetables
with husks or pods, except peas and corn, should be sold
at the markets, and forbade the cleaning of any fish at
the market houses and sale of both "decayed and damaged vegetables or fruits" and "unwholesome, watered,
or adulterated milk . . . [or] any butter or cheese made
from such milk."[39]

Although the health code established rules and regulations to guide both city residents and the health department, the board's various committees continued to
search for more perfect and more comprehensive regulations. The topics they discussed included the merits of
steam cleaning privy vaults, whether certain businesses
constituted violation of the noxious trade clause, and
how to confiscate and dispose of contraband market

products. To handle these committee reports the board met weekly, at which time it adopted measures to upgrade the health code or offered recommendations to protect the public health either to council or the city at large.[40]

The board's health officer also kept busy. In addition to aiding the board in its deliberations, Clendenin supervised the functioning of the health department and reported weekly on the city's sanitary condition and monthly on its mortality statistics. In the latter reports, Clendenin compiled deaths according to sex, color, and age of the deceased and the cause of death, in which he often included as examples accounts of the behavioral patterns that led to death. The health officer also undertook special duties assigned to him by the board. For example, it charged him with devising a procedure for obtaining accurate birth returns. He responded by suggesting that the health department furnish all physicians in the municipality with two identical sets of forms to report each child's date of birth, full name, sex, and color, the number of children in the family, the father's occupation, and the age, address, and nativity of both parents. Clendenin hoped physicians would keep one copy for their own records and return the other to the health office, and to insure this outcome, he urged the board to require the sanitary squad to call on each physician once a week.[41]

The board also asked the health officer to plan the census of prostitutes, a job Clendenin decided city physicians could best accomplish. For this purpose he created another form asking the prostitute's "real name, assumed name, age, complexion, figure, general appearance, place of birth, time of residence in the city, place of last previous residence, [and] present abode." Obtaining such information, Clendenin noted, would both comply with state law and give the board a better idea of who went into prostitution and of the effects of prostitution on the prostitute.[42]

Finally, the board expected Clendenin to establish ways of correcting the dairy nuisance and of improving the quality of the city's milk supply. He tackled the task by setting minimum standards that each milk seller needed to meet to secure a license permitting him to distribute his milk in Cincinnati. Clendenin himself investigated the diaries, checking on the type of feed and the amount of grazing time allotted cows, and issuing permits to sell milk to those dairies that passed muster. He also filed a copy of each dairy survey in a book at the health office. According to Clendenin, this procedure "will enable those who wish to know the condition of the cows and the quality of the milk they are purchasing for family use."[43]

The scope and speed of the actions of the health board, its health officer, and the health department were impressive. In its first ten months, the department's sanitary inspectorate reported 17,134 nuisances, 13,624 of which it ordered abated. Over half of the reported violations dealt with "full, offensive, or unsafe privy vaults, or nuisances resulting from the want of such vaults," while almost a quarter focused on "rubbish, decayed vegetables, or filth in cellars." During the same period, citizens reported to the board only 180 abuses of the sanitary law. The sanitary inspectors' efforts also resulted in the department bringing 136 suits against sanitary violators, 16 of which it dropped for lack of evidence, and 48 of which it withdrew after the offender complied with its directives and paid court costs. All 72 of those convicted received fines and were assessed abatement costs.[44]

The department's meat and market inspectors also pursued their tasks with diligence. They confiscated in ten months over 2,000 live animals, and condemned 29 others as well as 480 pounds of meat, 32 barrels of fish,

200 dressed chickens, and over 600 carcasses of game animals. Inspectors placed the condemned and confiscated material under supervision of the health officer, who would release these tainted goods to their owners only if they posted bond. That requirement virtually insured that condemned and confiscated goods never reached market as food, but reached consumers instead as candles, soap, or in some other fashion.[45]

In all, the department during its first ten months spent over twenty thousand dollars. Battling the municipality's health problems, it seemed an appropriate institution for a city defined as a social unit in which groups of individuals differing only in behavior interacted, and in which heterogeneous behavior on health or health-related questions posed a distinct problem. After its creation, as a consequence, the discourse over public health turned away from an argument over how municipal government could establish "a permanent system of sanitary cleanliness" and then undertake the project "with system and efficiency." Indeed the health department was precisely that kind of agency. Those who continued to consider the public's health urged only that council extend the city's efforts within the framework of the new department system.[46]

That was not necessary, however, because the board and department already possessed authority commensurate to their tasks; they were capable of extending their efforts without seeking additional ordinances. In 1868, for example, the department started periodically to inspect city dairies. Sending the milk inspector armed with a lactometer several times yearly to every dairy within the municipal limits, the board directed him to check both the dairy's surroundings and the cows' health. He was to pay particular attention to the food in use and the milk's butterfat content. If the inspector uncovered health code violations or discovered adulterated milk, he

was authorized to initiate a suit against the offending
dairy. A year earlier, the board had introduced another
new procedure, establishing a regular sanitary survey of
tenement houses. This survey operated citywide but
concentrated on "those districts, which from their situation, the character of the buildings, and which from
other causes, were believed to be most in need of improvement." In a few cases, improvement seemed impossible and, as a consequence, the sanitary policemen's
investigations resulted in the board ordering property
owners to tear down their buildings. This tenement inspection process required oversight by someone on a
fulltime, regular basis and in 1869 a board created a new
position, the office of sanitary superintendent. Heading
the sanitary police, the superintendent took responsibility for directing the survey as well as guiding all sanitary
squad operations.[47]

With the fleshing out of the health department, the
City of Cincinnati then for the first time offered a full
range of municipal social services. Its health department
immediately took its rightful place among the police
department, street cleaning department, board of the
city infirmary, and fire department. With the singular
exception of the fire department, each owed its existence to the articulation of the new distinct concerns of
the mid 1850s; the police department was to resolve
the problem of criminal activity, the street cleaning department the problem of filth, the board of the city infirmary the problem of pauperism, and the health
department the problem of public health. And despite
the fact that each new agency was to come to bear on a
different, discrete set of issues, each was organized similarly and operated in a remarkably similar fashion. Each
was composed of fulltime, paid employees and divided
into a series of squads, each of which specialized in a particular facet of the larger problem. Their duties neatly

circumscribed, these men tackled their special provinces year round in an effort to protect themselves and their fellow urbanites from the nefarious and unthinking actions of others. Working under a codified series of law directed exclusively at their task, these departments were all financed by tax levies and each received not only inspection powers but also enforcement authority; within their spheres, they were designed to function as coherent, complete entities, capable of dealing successfully and systematically with the problem for which they were created.

These service agencies generally were formed in the mid 1850s. Only the health department lagged behind— street cleaning previously had been the board of city improvement's responsibility—and for several reasons. The other agencies' creation required nothing more than an internal reorganization and redirection of municipal administration. Though a significant event, council managed it alone, without state legislative action; the state had neither to cede new authority to city government nor grant it power to levy new taxes. Nor did the other agencies need to contend with a self-declared, organized professional interest group. Cincinnati physicians from the mid 1850s claimed the right to set and implement health policy, but proved unable to do so. As important, the group's factionalism and thirst for power merely exacerbated an already difficult situation as the factions repeatedly played the city off against the state. Finally, no other agency faced active resistance from another municipal body. The competition between the health and infirmary boards over control of city physicians provided the health department movement with a powerful antagonist and slowed the legislative process.

But while the health department's creation was delayed until 1867 by these contests and concerns, its origins rested over a decade earlier. Desire for a fulltime health department first emerged in conjunction with the more general desire for the municipality to provide a full range of social services. And that idea in the mid 1850s was new. Its inception depended upon how city residents conceived of the situations they encountered; midcentury inhabitants of Cincinnati recognized and understood urban conditions in a way fundamentally different than they had earlier. It produced a movement to have city government erect a particular solution to fit each problem that seemed to confront the city; it fueled and provided form and function to the new municipal effort.

 *Coda*

It seemed apparent to mid-nineteenth century Americans that groups of people unfamiliar with, unaccustomed to, or unprepared for living in the United States infested the nation. Whether explained as the consequence of immigration, poor childrearing, lack of attendance at church, or some such thing, these "strangers" to American ways constituted a plague. In most of the country, these strangers caused consternation and emotional distress, but did not seem to pose an immediate physical threat. The routine of agricultural life and practice, combined with the natural salubrity and the relative isolation of the countryside, promised to teach those mal- or ill-tutored persons behavior fit for America. These factors also guaranteed protection for others while the transformation occurred. Only in sites of large or concentrated populations—in big cities—was the presence of peoples exhibiting different behaviors deemed a crisis, which demanded prompt, decisive action. These disparate groups lived in close proximity, and the strange, dangerous, and inappropriate behavior of some seemed in each of these compact, densely populated social units to menace all. The threat was especially intense in particularly dense agglomerations, districts such as New York City's Five Points, Boston's Ann Street, or Cincinnati's Over the Rhine.

Training these groups of strangers in the ways of American living was the work of benevolent organizations, but city residents involved governmental power both to provide an environment suitable for reform and to protect everyone from the noxious habits of a portion of the population. They established broad, general municipal agencies to tackle the single question of a disease of strangers in the 1840s and reconceptualized their effort with the breakdown of that amalgam of conditions in the 1850s and 1860s. In that later period, city inhabitants created functionally specialized bodies of law relating to each of these "new" problems, and formed functionally specialized agencies and redefined established ones to combat each of these "new" issues.

It bears repeating that what made these initiatives necessary, even critical, was places of concentrated population. While groups of strangers blanketed the nation, they generally seemed positioned to provide an immediate physical threat only in cities. In this conceptual framework, an urban place was not a fundamentally different sort of environment, but simply a more densely packed one. That recognition put the onus for erecting mechanisms to deal with the consequences of strangers squarely on each heavily populated locality. Each was left to its own devices. That each developed roughly the same solutions at roughly the same times merely testifies to the similar definitions of the problems they faced.

This notion of a city as not dissimilar to the rest of America waned after the Civil War. Rigid, permanent divisions seemed to separate city and country. Each type of environment—city, rural village, farm, or other unit—appeared to operate according to its own different principles. Not surprisingly, city residents quickly sensed that municipal government had become inadequate. As early as 1876, for example, some Cincinnatians raised objections about the city health department. They did not complain that the department lacked power to act, that its members neglected their work, or that they did not possess the character to perform their duties in an appropriate manner. Instead, the indictment centered on whether department members had the qualifications, the learning, the expertise to do their jobs efficiently. Demands that only physicians be appointed sanitary inspectors became common. Physician-inspectors were deemed necessary because "the inspection of nuisances in general, to be efficiently performed, is a service that requires special qualifications." It was argued that "a sanitary inspector ought to have, at least, a fair knowledge of the subjects of hygiene in general, chemistry, sanitary engineering, and particularly of recognized causes of disease."[1]

The thrust to install physicians as sanitary inspectors was emblematic of a more general effort to convert the health police department into an agency marked by its participants' special knowledge and special abilities.[2] This desire was epitomized by the reaction to A. J. Miles's appointment as health officer in 1880. The health board, which had selected Miles, and council, which had chosen the board, quickly became targets of almost constant verbal abuse. Calling board members "mere ward politicians," one Cincinnatian claimed that council selected these men "without reference whatever to any qualifications for holding the position." That was not true, remarked another. It was just that councilmen "looked to a saloonkeeper and a street contractor and an ex-sign painter as their ideals of sanitary scientists." The board of health, added the *Commercial's* editor, "lacks the nerve and possibly the intelligence to deal with disease," a fact that saddled the city with a "Board of Ill-Health." The onslaught also consumed Miles. While a health officer should know "what is being done in his department in all the great cities of the world," J. A. Thacker, editor of the *Cincinnati Medical News*, complained that Miles did not possess "even a common school education" and, as a consequence, it was folly to think him "versed in medical learning and in the knowledge which a health officer should have." Instead of Miles, concluded Thacker, "a first-class city like Cincinnati should have a gentlemen at the head of the health department thoroughly versed in medicine and the advanced hygiene of the day. He should be an authority in matters of health." The editor of the *Enquirer* went further. He claimed that Miles belonged in "the circus business," but unfortunately "crawled into the Health Office of this city."[3]

Nor was dissatisfaction and criticism limited to health office affairs. Cincinnatians detected in the late 1870s scandalous situations in the comptroller's office, board of city improvements, police department, and board of education. Citizens attributed each of these seemingly separate events to a similar cause: politics and politicians. Those expressing concern urged municipal fathers to right the wrong by appointing only persons specially trained for the respective tasks to these important city posts.

Taken as a whole, the profound objections to the health officer and the various other boards were a forceful condemnation of municipal affairs. Whether these charges were justified, however, is beside the point. What is really striking and what really matters is that they differed dramatically in tone and specifics from those offered by mid-nineteenth century critics. The tenor of these later laments was reminiscent of complaints generally associated with inspiring Progressive Era reforms. Accentuation of special training, learning, and technique and a corresponding disdain of politics and politicians were touchstones of late nineteenth and early twentieth century reformers. Also of note is the classism, or at least occupationism, inherent in the idea of a population in which at least some members have training, learning, or techniques unavailable to all. Quite evident too in these critiques is that cities appear different than other environments, such as rural regions and farms. It was becoming the job of city government through its expert employees to be aware of and to put itself in concert with the newest, most modern lines of urban administration.

These ideas were not unique to Queen City residents, of course. A public, clearly articulated commonality among cities, differentiation from other environments, and established mechanisms to regularize transmission of information among similarly defined environments were phenomena new to post–Civil War America. New Yorkers, for example, expressed these notions in several ways. Most obviously, they railed against William Marcy Tweed as Boss Tweed, a person who lived for—and specialized in—winning elections and controlling municipal offices. Critics portrayed Tweed as representative of the professional politician, a particularly urban blight that owed its allegiance to but one section of city society. Another manifestation was public identification of, and fascination with, urban crime. Edward Crapsey's marvelous series in *Galaxy* in the late 1860s and early 1870s acquainted an entire generation with these "hardened" criminals especially adapted to an urban milieu. This highly developed criminal class, fundamentally different and distinct from other social groups, offered little hope of redemption. It gambled at faro and on the lottery, engaged in murder and thievery, featured the circle swindle, and consorted regularly with fences. Immigrants seemed yet another indelible subset of cities, no longer plastic, moldable persons in transition but a rigidly fixed urban social class. To some in New York, immigrants from each nation formed in cities "large, compact communities of their own, perfectly impervious to American influences . . . in which the prejudices, passions, habits, interests, and vices of the Old World retain all their sway." These enclaves appeared "as distinctive, as essentially foreign, as the population of Dublin or Hamburg."

But perhaps the clearest expression by New Yorkers of these new ideas of the essential distinctiveness of urban settings and the commonality among large cities was the self-conscious exploration of the nature of a municipal government. That examination almost always contained a historical dimension as concerned individuals hunted for city government's ancient and medieval origins and compared what they uncovered with conditions they now recognized as the new distinctly urban environment, of which New York was merely typical. Characteristically, they found the basis of traditional municipal government in "the city . . . [as] a political community," joined together by "bonds of race, religion and corporation" to assert from feudal princes "municipal rights and municipal independence." This homogeneous community of burghers was governed only by those sharing that vision and involved in its enterprises. The present state of affairs appeared quite different. Cities now housed people assumed fundamentally dissimilar from one another, incapable of ever fashioning the unity necessary for communal government. That even residential neighborhoods seemed to be characterized and made distinctive by their inhabitants' class, nationality, race, religion, and/or occupation emphasized social distance and discrepancy and reinforced the utter hopelessness of achieving medieval-styled homogeneity. Late nineteenth century social critics even claimed that many urban dwellers were unable to develop the skills and interests required for successful commercial activity. Commentators repeatedly linked then current municipal ills to the broad provision of the franchise. Only by shucking misplaced democratic tendencies and permitting city administration "to be done by business men, rather than a large mass . . . managed by partisans," could city government again become vital. These individuals did not seek to diminish or outlaw national political parties, of course, as some were quite prominent on the national scene. They simply recognized a radical disjunction between national issues and municipal issues. Cities were an entirely different circumstance, an unique environment requiring nonpartisan, expert administration.[4]

Identification of cities as unique from other political units as well as recognition of commonality among these peculiar environments produced attempts to establish firm intermunicipal links. These efforts were reflected in the mounting of several expert-driven nationwide municipal efforts with various national initiatives. Formation of the American Public Health Association in 1872 and acknowledgment by medical men of the desirability of a municipal division within the organization to tackle big city health questions stemmed from this new milieu as did establishment of the National Municipal League by political scientists and other emerging professional groups in 1894. The Census of 1880—the city census—in which statisticians devoted two entire volumes to the peculiar statistics of cities, reflected the new urban focus, while Judge John F. Dillon's pathbreaking *Treatise on the Law of Municipal Corporations* in 1872 testified to the common problems governing that type of environment. Provision of "model laws" for virtually every urban situation or condition demonstrated the pervasiveness of the gospel throughout the nation's cities.[5]

Recognition of the uniqueness of the urban environment provided the basis for the advent of formal linkages and information pathways among cities. These systematizing institutions and bonds were absent from the mid-nineteenth century because contemporaries lacked a sense of the fundamental peculiarness of cities; no reason existed to erect such extensive paraphernalia.

Mid-nineteenth century America did have a municipal unification of sorts, but that stood as an unrecognized *de facto,* not *de jure,* creation. As each city independently built the new city government of the 1840s and re-vamped its design a decade or so later, a form of nation-wide social regulation in cities was established. And this occurred as well before cities were identified as a dis-crete type of social environment. Simply by attempting to solve the problem of groups of strangers in densely settled parts of America did mid-nineteenth century city residents manufacture a common municipal govern-ment, complete with social service institutions. It re-mained until the late nineteenth and early twenties centuries for this commonality to be acknowledged and formalized.

 *Notes*

Chapter 1

1. The argument about late nineteenth century cities is well known. Some perceptive works include Arthur M. Schlesinger, *The Rise of the City, 1878–1898* (New York: MacMillan, 1933); Samuel P. Hays, *The Response to Industrialism, 1885–1914* (Chicago: University of Chicago Press, 1957); and Robert H. Wiebe, *The Search For Order, 1877–1920* (New York: Hill and Wang, 1967).

2. Maryland, *An Act to Erect Baltimore-Town, in Baltimore County, Into a City and to Incorporate the Inhabitants Thereof, Laws of Maryland* (1786–1800), pp. 361–67.

3. Massachusetts, *An Act Establishing the City of Boston, Statutes* 188 (1822), pp. 734–53.

4. Pennsylvania, *An Act to Incorporate the City of Pittsburg, Statutes* (1815–1816), pp. 160–70; Kentucky, *An Act to Incorporate the City of Louisville, Statutes* (1828), pp. 208–24; Rhode Island, *An Act to Incorporate the City of Providence, Statutes* (October, 1831), pp. 21–30; New York, *An Act to Incorporate the City of Rochester, Passed April 25, 1834, Statutes* 57 (1834), pp. 281–342; and New Jersey, *An Act to Incorporate the City of Newark, Statutes* (1835–1836), pp. 185–203.

5. Blake McKelvey, *Rochester: The Water-Power City 1812–1854* (Cambridge: Harvard University Press, 1945), pp. 179, 252; Constance McLaughlin Green, *Washington: A History of the Capital, 1800–1950* (Princeton: Princeton University Press, 1962), p. 160; Bayrd Still, *Milwaukee, The History of A City* (Madison: State Historical Society of Wisconsin, 1948), p. 97; James F. Richardson, *The New York Police, Colonial Times to 1901*

(New York: Oxford University Press, 1970), pp. 18–22, 32–34; Roger Lane, *Policing the City: Boston, 1822–1885* (Cambridge: Harvard University Press, 1967), pp. 10–12; Eric H. Monkkonen, *Police in Urban America, 1860–1920* (New York: Cambridge University Press, 1981), p. 47; Samuel Walker, *A Critical History of Police Reform: The Emergence of Professionalism* (Lexington, MA: Lexington Books of D. C. Heath and Co., 1977), pp. 5–6; Wilbur R. Miller, *Cops and Bobbies: Police Authority in New York and London, 1830–1870* (Chicago: University of Chicago Press, 1977), pp. 3–4; Ernest S. Griffith and Charles R. Adrian, *A History of American City Government: The Formation of Traditions, 1775–1870* (Washington: University Press of America, 1983), p. 86; David R. Johnson, *Policing the Urban Underworld: The Impact of Crime on the Development of the American Police, 1800–1887* (Philadelphia: Temple University Press, 1979), pp. 7–8; James F. Richardson, *Urban Police in the United States* (Port Washington: Kennikat Press, 1974), pp. 22, 27; and Richard C. Wade, *The Urban Frontier: Pioneer Life in Early Pittsburgh, Cincinnati, Lexington, Louisville, and St. Louis* (Cambridge: Harvard University Press, 1959; Chicago: University of Chicago Press, 1972), p. 88.

6. Richardson, *The New York Police*, pp. 14, 27–30; Lane, *Policing The City*, pp. 26–33; Griffith and Adrian, *A History*, p. 88; Johnson, *Policing the Urban Underworld*, pp. 14–15; Richardson, *Urban Police*, p. 25; John C. Schneider, *Detroit and the Problem of Order: A Geography of Crime, Riot, and Policing* (Lincoln: University of Nebraska Press, 1980), p. 12; and Wade, *The Urban Frontier*, pp. 88–89, 287, 290. Also of interest is David Grimsted, "Rioting in the Jacksonian Setting," *American Historical Review* 67 (1972), pp. 361–67.

7. Green, *Washington*, pp. 94–95; Lane, *Policing The City*, pp. 22–23, 25, 33–34; David R. Goldfield, "Pursuing the American Urban Dream: Cities in the Old South," in Blaine A. Brownell and David R. Goldfield, eds., *The City In Southern History: The Growth of Urban Civilization in the South* (Port Washington: Kennikat Press, 1977), pp. 74–75; Griffith and Adrian, *A History*, pp. 93, 96; and Wade, *The Urban Frontier*, pp. 92–94, 292–93.

8. McKelvey, *Rochester*, p. 218; and Raymond A. Mohl, *Pov-*

erty In New York 1783–1825 (New York: Oxford University Press, 1971), pp. 104–16.

9. Jacqueline K. Corn, "Municipal Organization For Public Health in Pittsburgh, 1851–1895," (Carnegie-Mellon University, D. A. Thesis, 1972), pp. 15–17; Goldfield, "Pursuing the American Urban Dream," p. 69; Griffith and Adrian, *A History*, pp. 68–69; Judith Walzer Leavitt, *The Healthiest City: Milwaukee and the Politics of Health Reform* (Princeton: Princeton University Press, 1982), p. 42; John B. Blake, *Public Health In the Town of Boston, 1660–1822* (Cambridge: Harvard University Press, 1956), pp. 238–41; Thomas N. Bonner, *Medicine in Chicago, 1850–1950: A Chapter in the Social and Scientific Development of A City* (Madison, WI: American Book-Stratford Press, 1957), pp. 176–77; Robert S. Drew, "A History of the Care of the Sick Poor In the City of Detroit (1703–1855)," *Bulletin of the History of Medicine* (1939), pp. 764–66; John Duffy, *The Healers: The Rise of the Medical Establishment* (New York: McGraw-Hill, 1976), pp. 201–2; John Duffy, ed., *The Rudolph Matas History of Medicine In Louisville*, 2 vols. (Baton Rouge: Louisiana State University Press, 1958), vol. 1, p. 397; John Duffy, "The Impact of Asiatic Cholera on Pittsburgh, Wheeling, and Charlestown," *Western Pennsylvania Historical Magazine* 47 (1964), pp. 199–211; John Duffy, *A History of Public Health in New York City 1625–1866* (New York: Russell Sage Foundation, 1968), pp. 152–59; David A Langtry, "The 1832 Epidemic of Asiatic Cholera in New Haven, Connecticut," *Journal of the History of Medicine and Allied Sciences* 25 (1970), pp. 449–56; Nancy D. Baird, "Asiatic Cholera's First Visit to Kentucky: A Study in Panic and Fear," *Filson Club History Quarterly* 48 (1974), pp. 228–40; Stuart Galishoff, "Cholera in Newark, New Jersey," *Journal of the History of Medicine and Allied Sciences* 25 (1970), pp. 438–48; Joseph Ioor Waring, "Asiatic Cholera in South Carolina," *Bulletin of the History of Medicine* 20 (1966), pp. 459–66; and William Travis Howard, Jr., *Public Health Administration And the Natural History of Disease in Baltimore, Maryland 1797–1920* (Washington: Carnegie Institution, 1924), pp. 51–52. Howard points out that the law creating the Baltimore health board also empowered it to collect mortality returns. That is misleading. A close examination

of the Baltimore material shows that in the years in which the city was not threatened by an epidemic its health board either compiled no mortality returns or gathered scattered returns. Also, in the years in which mortality returns were tabulated, they often were compiled only for those months that the city was under siege from pestilential disease. See Commissioner of Health of Baltimore, Maryland, *Baltimore City Health Department: The First Thirty-Five Annual Reports, 1815–1849* (Baltimore: n. p., 1953). For a useful, but not entirely reliable, list of early health boards in American municipalities, see J. M. Toner, "Boards of Health in the United States," *Public Health: Reports and Papers Presented at the Meeting of the American Public Health Association in the Year 1873* (New York: n. p., 1875), pp. 499ff.

    10. See, for example, Jackson Turner Main, *The Sovereign States, 1775–1783* (New York: Franklin Watts, Inc., 1973); Marshall Smelser, *The Democratic Republic, 1801–1815* (New York: Harper and Row, 1968); and George Dangerfield, *The Awakening of American Nationalism, 1815–1828* (New York: Harper and Row, 1965). See also Diane Lindstrom, *Economic Development in the Philadelphia Region, 1810–1850* (New York: Columbia University Press, 1978); and David Montgomery, "The Working Classes of the Pre-Industrial American City, 1780–1830," *Labor History* 9 (1968), pp. 133–58.

    11. Johnson, *Policing the Urban Underworld*, pp. 8, 12, 16; Richardson, *New York Police*, pp. 26–27; Schneider, *Detroit and the Problem of Order*, pp. 54–62; Paul Boyer, *Urban Masses and Moral Order In America, 1820–1920* (Cambridge: Harvard University Press, 1978), pp. 67–75; Charles N. Glaab and A. Theodore Brown, *A History of Urban America* (New York: Macmillan, 1967), pp. 86–87, 95–96; Green, *Washington*, vol. 1, p. 218; and John H. Ellis, "Businessmen and Public Health in the Urban South During the Nineteenth Century: New Orleans, Memphis, and Atlanta," *Bulletin of the History of Medicine* 44 (1970), p. 207. For a description of urban public disorder in the late 1830s and after, see Michael Feldberg, *The Turbulent Era: Riot and Disorder in Jacksonian America* (New York: Oxford University Press, 1980). For the tendency of groups to congregate in the mid-nineteenth century city, see, for example, Stu-

art M. Blumin, *The Urban Threshold: Growth and Change in A Nineteenth-Century American Community* (Chicago: University of Chicago Press, 1976); Peter R. Knights, *The Plain People of Boston, 1830–1860: A Study in City Growth* (New York: Oxford University Press, 1971); Kathleen Neils Conzen, *Immigrant Milwaukee, 1836–1860: Accommodation and Community in A Frontier City* (Cambridge: Harvard University Press, 1976); and Dean R. Esslinger, *Immigrants and the City: Ethnicity and Mobility in A Nineteenth-Century Midwestern City* (Port Washington: Kennikat Press, 1975).

12. Useful on these points are Blake McKelvey, *American Urbanization: A Comparative History* (Glenview: Scott, Foresman and Co., 1973), especially pp. 24 and 37; David Ward, *Cities and Immigrants. A Geography of Change in Nineteenth Century America* (New York: Oxford University Press, 1971); and Adna Ferrin Weber, *The Growth of Cities in the Nineteenth Century* (New York, 1899; Ithaca: Cornell University Press, 1963).

13. For American cities and filth and lawlessness, see Carl Bridenbaugh, *Cities In the Wilderness: The First Century of Urban Life in America, 1625–1742* (New York, 1938; New York: Oxford University Press, 1966), pp. 55–93, 206–48, 364–407; and Wade, *The Urban Frontier*, pp. 72–100, 287–303. For epidemics, see John H. Powell, *Bring Out Your Dead: The Great Plague of Yellow Fever in Philadelphia in 1793* (Philadelphia: University of Pennsylvania Press, 1949); John B. Blake, *Public Health In the Town of Boston, 1630–1822* (Cambridge: Harvard University Press, 1959), pp. 52–98 and *passim*; and John Duffy, *Epidemics In Colonial America* (Baton Rouge: Louisiana State University Press, 1953), pp. 93–103, 138–63. For a list of major economic dislocations, see Richard B. Morris, ed., *Encyclopedia of American History* (New York: Harper and Row, 1970), pp. 536–37. For the Panic of 1819, see Murray N. Rothbard, *The Panic of 1819* (New York: Columbia University Press, 1962).

14. For manifestations of the new benevolent effort, see Ian R. Tyrrell, *Sobering Up: From Temperance to Prohibition in Antebellum America, 1800–1860* (Westport: Greenwood Press, 1979), pp. 159–218; Timothy L. Smith, *Revivalism and Social Reform: American Protestantism on the Eve of the Civil War* (New

York: Abingdon Press, 1957), pp. 34–44; Boyer, *Urban Masses,*
pp. 94–120; Elizabeth M. Geffen, "Philadelphia Protestantism
Reacts to Social Reform Movements Before the Civil War,"
Pennsylvania History 20 (1963), pp. 192–212; Jay P. Dolan, *The
Immigrant Church: New York's Irish and German Catholics, 1815–
1865* (Baltimore: Johns Hopkins University Press, 1975),
especially pp. 121–40; Nathan Kaganoff, "Organized Jewish
Welfare Activity in New York City," *American Jewish Historical
Quarterly* 56 (1966), pp. 27–61; Roy Lubove, "The New York
Association For the Improving of the Condition of the Poor:
The Formative Years," *New York Historical Society Quarterly* 43
(1959), pp. 307–28; and David R. Goldfield, *Urban Growth In
the Age of Sectionalism: Virginia, 1847–1861* (Baton Rouge: Louisiana State University Press, 1977), pp. 160–63. For discussions of midcentury Nativist uprisings directed against blacks
and Roman Catholics and attempts to drive unconventional
religious groups, such as Mormons, from cities, see, for example, Robert F. Flanders, *Nauvoo: Kingdom on the Mississippi*
(Urbana: University of Illinois Press, 1965); Feldberg, *The
Turbulent Era;* Ray Allen Billington, *The Protestant Crusade
1800–1860: A Study of the Origins of American Nativism* (New
York: MacMillan, 1938), pp. 118ff; and Leonard P. Curry, *The
Free Blacks in Urban America 1800–1850: The Shadow of the
Dream* (Chicago: University of Chicago Press, 1981), pp. 81–
111.

   15. Walker, *A Critical History,* pp. 5–6; Monkkonen, *Police,*
p. 42; Johnson, *Policing the Urban Underworld,* pp. 19, 24–26,
35; Richardson, *Urban Police,* p. 27; Richardson, *New York Police,* pp. 39–82; Lane, *Policing the City,* 39–102; Jacob Judd,
"Policing the City of Brooklyn in the 1840s and 1850s," *Journal
of Long Island History* 6 (1966), pp. 13–22; Green, *Washington,*
vol. 1, p. 217; Russell R. Weigley, " 'A Peaceful City': Public
Order in Philadelphia from Consolidation Through the Civil
War," in Allen B. Davis and Mark H. Haller, eds., *The Peoples of
Philadelphia: A History of Ethnic Groups and Lower-Class Life,
1790–1940* (Philadelphia: Temple University Press, 1973), pp.
151–61; Bessie Louise Pierce, *A History of Chicago, 1848–1871*
(Chicago: University of Chicago Press, 1940), pp. 350–52; and
Still, *Milwaukee,* pp. 231–44.

16. Marie George Windell, "Reform In the Roaring Forties and Fifties," *Missouri Historical Review* 39 (1944–1945), pp. 293–94; Goldfield, *Urban Growth*, pp. 157, 164–65; McKelvey, *Rochester: The Water-Power City*, pp. 337–39; David J. Rothman, *The Discovery of the Asylum: Social Order and Disorder In the New Republic* (Boston: Little, Brown, 1971); Jacob Judd, "Brooklyn's Health and Sanitation, 1834–1855," *Journal of Long Island History* 7 (1967), pp. 45–48; and Pierce, *History of Chicago*, p. 337.

17. For the differences between London's police and those in America, see Miller, *Cops and Bobbies*. For discussions of possible modes of communications within America in the early and mid 19th century, see, for instance, Allan R. Pred, "Large-City Interdependence and Pre-Electronic Diffusion of Innovations in the United States," in Leo F. Schnore, ed., *The New Urban History: Quantitative Explorations by American Historians* (Princeton: Princeton University Press, 1975), pp. 51–74; Pred, *Urban Growth and the Circulation of Information: The United States System of Cities, 1790–1840* (Cambridge: Harvard University Press, 1973); Richard B. Du Boff, "Business Demand and the Development of the Telegraph in the United States, 1844–1860," *Business History Review* 54 (1980), pp. 459–79; Alfred D. Chandler, Jr., "The Organization of Manufacturing and Transportation," in David T. Gilchrist and W. David Lewis, eds., *Economic Change In the Civil War Era* (Greenville: Eleutherian Mills-Hagley Foundation, 1965), pp. 137–51; John Hope Franklin, *The Southern Odyssey* (Baton Rouge: Louisiana State University Press, 1967); and Robert G. Albion, *The Rise of New York Port, 1815–1860* (New York: Charles Scribner's Sons, 1939). For transatlantic communications, see Albion, *The Rise*, and Robert Luther Thompson, *Wiring a Continent: The History of the Telegraph Industry in the United States, 1832–1868* (Princeton: Princeton University Press, 1947).

18. For Chadwick's labors, see either S. E. Finer, *The Life and Times of Edwin Chadwick* (London: 1952; New York: Barnes and Noble, 1970), or R. A. Lewis, *Edwin Chadwick and the Public Health Movement, 1832–1854* (London, 1952).

19. For Griscom's New York career, see Duncan R. Jamieson, "Towards a Cleaner New York: John H. Griscom and

New York's Public Health 1830–1870," (Ph.D. dissertation, Michigan State University, 1971); John Duffy, *A History of Public Health in New York City 1625–1866* (New York: Russell Sage Foundation, 1968), pp. 302–8, 312–13; and James H. Cassedy, "The Roots of American Sanitary Reform 1843–1847: Seven Letters from John H. Griscom to Lemuel Shattuck," *Journal of the History of Medicine and Allied Sciences* 30 (1975), pp. 136–47. For Griscom's lone crusade, see Charles E. and Carroll S. Rosenberg, "Pietism and the Origins of the American Public Health Movement: A Note on John H. Griscom and Robert M. Hartley," *Journal of the History of Medicine and Allied Sciences* 23 (1968), pp. 16–17.

20. Still, *Milwaukee*, p. 103; McKelvey, *Rochester: The Water-Power City*, p. 258; Goldfield, *Urban Growth*, pp. 152–58; John Duffy, *Sword of Pestilence: The New Orleans Yellow Fever Epidemic of 1853* (Baton Rouge: Louisiana State University Press, 1966); Stuart Galishoff, "Cholera in Newark, New Jersey," *Journal of the History of Medicine and Allied Sciences* 25 (1970), pp. 444–48; Boston Committee of Internal Health, *Report of the Committee of Internal Health on the Asiatic Cholera* (Boston: J. H. Eastburn, 1849), pp. 3–16, 163–76; Paul W. Brewer, "Voluntarism on Trial: St. Louis' Response to the Cholera Epidemic of 1848," *Bulletin of the History of Medicine* 49 (1975), pp. 102–22; Charles E. Rosenberg, *The Cholera Years: The United States in 1832, 1849, and 1866* (Chicago: University of Chicago Press, 1962), pp. 101–20; and Pennsylvania, *An Act to Establish A Board of Health, And to Secure the City and Port of Pittsburg From the Introduction of Pestilential and Contagious Diseases, and Relative to the Granting of Tavern Licenses In Butler County, Statutes* (1851), pp. 587–89.

21. For complaints about rowdy volunteer fire companies, fire riots, and the creation of fulltime, paid municipal fire departments, see Bruce Laurie, "Fire Companies and Gangs in Southwark: The 1840's," in Davis and Haller, eds., *The Peoples of Philadelphia*, pp. 71–88; Arlen Dykstra, "Rowdyism and Rivalism in the St. Louis Fire Department, 1850–1857," *Missouri Historical Review* 69 (1974/75), pp. 48–64; Stephen F. Ginsberg, "Above the Law: Volunteer Firemen In New York City," *New York History* 50 (1969), pp. 165–86; Bayrd Still, *Urban*

America: A History With Documents (Boston: Little, Brown, 1974), pp. 146–48, 181–82; Jacob Judd, "Brooklyn's Volunteer Fire Department," *Journal of Long Island History* 6 (1966), pp. 29–34; McKelvey, *Rochester: The Water-Power City*, p. 251; McKelvey, *Rochester: The Flower City, 1855–1900* (Cambridge: Harvard University Press, 1949), p. 82; Goldfield, *Urban Growth*, pp. 147–48; Green, *Washington*, vol. 1, pp. 159–60, 256; Walker, *A Critical History*, p. 5; Griffith and Adrian, *A History*, pp. 55, 95–96; and Johnson, *Policing The Urban Underworld*, pp. 30–31, 84–88.

   22. For evidence of the nature of the new calls, see Goldfield, *Urban Growth*, pp. 151–52; Green, *Washington*, vol. 1, p. 212; D. M. Culver, "Tenement House Reform in Boston, 1846–1898" (Ph.D. dissertation, Boston University, 1972); Pierce, *A History of Chicago, 1848–1871*, pp. 327–34, 336–37; Sam Bass Warner, Jr., *The Private City: Philadelphia in Three Periods of its Growth* (Philadelphia: University of Pennsylvania Press, 1968), pp. 106–11; Norman Shaftel, "A History of the Purification of Milk in New York, Or 'How Now, Brown Cow,'" *New York State Journal of Medicine* 58 (1958), pp. 915–21; Still, *Milwaukee*, pp. 241–43; Louis P. Cain, "Raising and Watering A City: Ellis Sylvester Chesbrough and Chicago's First Sanitation System," *Technology and Culture* 13 (1972), pp. 356ff; and Duffy, *A History of Public Health*, pp. 382–86, 415–18, 424–26, 430–37, 527–32.

   23. The literature of the emergence of public health as a distinct public problem in the mid 1850s is voluminous. Much of it is interpreted differently. See, for example, Gert H. Brieger, "Sanitary Reform In New York City: Stephen Smith and the Passage of the Metropolitan Health Bill," *Bulletin of the History of Medicine* 40 (1966), pp. 411ff; Stuart Galishoff, "Public Health in Newark, 1832–1918" (Ph.D. dissertation, New York University, 1969); James H. Cassedy, "Edwin Miller Snow: An Important Public Health Pioneer," *Bulletin of the History of Medicine* 35 (1961), pp. 157–60; Austin Flint, "Editorial Department," *Buffalo Medical Journal* 10 (1855), pp. 377–81; Howard D. Kramer, "The Beginnings of the Public Health Movement in the United States," *Bulletin of the History of Medicine* 27 (1947), pp. 370–76; Wilson G. Smillie, *Public Health Its*

Promise For the Future: A Chronicle of the Development of Public Health in the United States, 1607–1914 (New York: MacMillan Co., 1955), pp. 258–68; and Ellis, "Businesmen and Public Health," pp. 201, 203.

24. *Ibid.;* George Rosen, *A History of Public Health* (New York: MD Publications, 1958), pp. 192–290; Richard H. Shryock, "The Early American Public Health Movement," *Medicine In America: Historical Essays* (Baltimore: Johns Hopkins University Press, 1966), pp. 126–38; and John B. Blake, "The Origins of Public Health in the United States," *Bulletin of the History of Medicine* 21 (1947), pp. 352–76.

25. Monkkonen, *Police*, pp. 42, 45; Walker, *Critical History*, pp. 6–7; Johnson, *Policing the Urban Underworld*, pp. 15, 35, 37–38, 105–6, 133; Richardson, *New York Police*, pp. 46–50, 52, 63, 120–22; and Lane, *Policing the City*, pp. 98–117.

26. See, for example, Thomas N. Bonner, *The Kansas Doctor: A Century of Pioneering* (Lawrence: University of Kansas Press, 1959), pp. 41–43; Bonner, *Medicine In Chicago*, pp. 69–74; Martha Carolyn Mitchell, "Health and the Medical Profession in the Lower South, 1845–1860," *Journal of Southern History* 10 (1944), pp.443–46; Leavitt, *The Healthiest City*, pp. 42–45; and Duffy, *A History of Public Health*, pp. 520–45.

27. Duffy, *A History of Public Health*, pp. 542ff; and Brieger, "Sanitary Reform," pp. 409–26.

28. Harold Cavins, "The National Quarantine and Sanitary Conventions of 1857 to 1860 and the Beginnings of the American Public Health Association," *Bulletin of the History of Medicine* 13 (1939), pp. 404–14; Kramer, "The Beginnings of the Public Health Movement," pp. 370–76; and Smillie, *Public Health*, pp. 258–68. For the sanitary code debates, see *Proceedings and Debates of the Third National Quarantine and Sanitary Convention, Held in the City of New York, April 27, 28, 29, and 30, 1859* (New York: Edmund Jones and Co., 1959), pp. 5–6, 367–674.

29. Griffith and Adrian, *A History*, pp. 36–39, 41–42, 51–62; and Hendrik Hartog, *Public Property and Private Power: The Corporation of the City of New York in American Law, 1730–1870* (Chapel Hill: University of North Carolina Press, 1983), pp. 180–81, 237–39.

30. Monkkonen, *Police In Urban America,* p. 43; Walker, *A Critical History,* p. 27; Richardson, *Urban Police,* pp. 38–40; Richardson, *New York Police,* pp. 79, 82–108; and Leavitt, *The Healthiest City,* p. 45.

31. Cassedy, "Edwin Miller Snow," pp. 156–62. Also of interest is Gordon Gillson, "The Louisiana State Board of Health; the Formative Years," (Ph.D. dissertation, Louisiana State University, 1960).

32. See, for example, Howard, *Public Health Administration,* p. 54; *Proceedings and Debates . . . Third National Quarantine and Sanitary Convention,* pp. 118–21; David R. Goldfield, "The Business of Health Planning: Disease Prevention In the Old South," *Journal of Southern History* 42 (1976); Duffy, *A History of Public Health,* pp. 540ff; Duffy, ed., *Rudolph Matas History,* vol. 2, p. 461; and Pennsylvania, *A Further Supplement to An Act Incorporating the City of Philadelphia, Statutes* (1859), pp. 409–11.

33. See, for example, Charles E. Rosenberg, *The Cholera Years: The United States in 1832, 1849, and 1866* (Chicago: University of Chicago Press, 1962), pp. 202–11; Edwin M. Snow, *Measures Proposed For the Prevention of Asiatic Cholera in the City of Providence* (Providence: Providence Press, 1965), pp. 3–13; Duffy, ed., *Rudolph Matas History,* vol. 2, pp. 461–62; and Pierce, *A History of Chicago,* pp. 334–35.

34. Illinois, *An Act Supplementary to "An Act to Reduce the Charter of the City of Chicago, and the Several Acts Amendatory Thereof, Into One Act, And to Revise the Same," Approved February 13, 1863, and the Several Amendments Thereto, Statutes* (1867), pp. 768–70; New York, *An Act to Create A Metropolitan Sanitary District and Board of Health Therein For the Preservation of Life and Health, and To Prevent the Spread of Disease, Statutes* (1866), pp. 114–44; Missouri, *An Act For the Preservation of the Public Health in the City of St. Louis, Statutes,* pp. 179–83; and Wisconsin, *An Act For the Preservation of Public Health In the City of Milwaukee, Statutes,* pp. 1283–87.

35. For health departments formed in the late 1860s, see, for instance, Joseph Ioor Waring, *A History of Medicine In South Carolina 1825–1900* (Columbia: R. L. Bryan Co., 1967), pp. 161–62; Duffy, *A History of Public Health,* pp. 563–64; Brieger, "Sanitary Reform," pp. 420–24; Still, *Milwaukee,* p. 241;

Leavitt, *Healthiest City*, pp. 46–55; Bonner, *Medicine in Chicago*,
pp. 180–81; John C. Burnham, "Medical Inspection of Prostitutes in America in the Nineteenth Century: The St. Louis Experiment and Its Sequel," *Bulletin of the History of Medicine* 45
(1971), pp. 203–5; Corn, "Municipal Organization" p. 61 and
passim; and Pennsylvania, *An Act to Prevent the Maintenance, or
Location, of Bone Boiling Establishments In the Twenty-Fourth Ward
of the City of Philadelphia, A Supplement to the Several Acts of Assembly of This Commonwealth, In Relation to the Board of Health, In
the City of Philadelphia, A Further Supplement To An Act To Establish A Health Office, And to Secure The City and Port of Philadelphia
From The Introduction of Pestilential and Contagious Diseases,
Passed January Twenty-Ninth, One Thousand Eight Hundred and
Eighteen, and A Further Supplement To An Act To Incorporate The
City of Philadelphia, Approved the Fourth Day of February, Anno Do-
mini One Thousand Eight Hundred and Fifty-Four, and Relative To
the Collection of Debts Due the Department of Health, Statutes*
(1866), pp. 418, 487, 854–55, 946–47, respectively. Sometimes state sanction for health departments was incorporated
within new city charters or municipal codes; it did not always
result in passage of a separate health department law.

36. Stanley M. Elkins, *Slavery: A Problem in American Intel-
lectual and Institutional Life*, 2d. ed. (Chicago: University of
Chicago Press, 1968), pp. 27–34; Bruce Sinclair, *Philadelphia's
Philosopher Mechanics: A History of the Franklin Institute 1824–
1865* (Baltimore: Johns Hopkins University Press, 1974), pp.
241ff; Ian R. Tyrrell, *Sobering Up: From Temperance to Prohibi-
tion in Antebellum America, 1800–1860* (Westport: Greenwood
Press, 1979), pp. 197ff; Frederick Merk and Lois Bannister
Merk, *Manifest Destiny and Mission in American History: A Rein-
terpretation* (New York: Knopf, 1963); Wilfred E. Binkley,
American Political Parties: Their Natural History, 2d. ed. (New
York: Knopf, 1943), pp. 181–234; Richard Hofstadter, *The
Idea of a Party System: The Rise of Legitimate Opposition in the
United States, 1780–1840* (Berkeley: University of California
Press, 1969), pp. 247ff; George H. Daniels, *American Science in
the Age of Jackson* (New York: Columbia University Press, 1968),
pp. 3–33; Sally Gregory Kohlstedt, *The Formation of the Ameri-
can Scientific Community: The American Association For the Ad-*

vancement of Science 1848–1860 (Urbana: University of Illinois Press, 1976); Louis Hartz, *Economic Policy and Democratic Thought, Pennsylvania, 1776–1861* (1948; Chicago: Quandrangle Press, 1968), pp. 181ff; Oscar Handlin and Mary Flugg Handlin, *Commonwealth: A Study of the Role of Government in the American Economy: Massachusetts, 1774–1861*, rev. ed. (Cambridge: Harvard University Press, 1969), pp. 203–44; Alfred D. Chandler, Jr., *The Visible Hand: The Managerial Revolution in American Business* (Cambridge: Harvard University Press, 1977), pp. 79ff; David A. Hounshell, *From The American System to Mass Production 1800–1932: The Development of Manufacturing Technology in the United States* (Baltimore: Johns Hopkins University Press, 1984), pp. 15–66; Timothy L. Smith, *Revivalism and Social Reform: American Protestantism On the Eve of the Civil War* (Nashville: Abingdon Press, 1957), pp. 15–33; and Alan I Marcus, "Am I My Brother's Keeper: Reform Judaism in the American West, Cincinnati, 1840–1870," *Queen City Heritage* 44 (1986), pp. 3–19.

37. For the distinctly American manners and morals, see Nathaniel P. Willis, *Hurry-Graphs: or Sketches of Scenery, Celebrities and Society, Taken From Life*, 2d. ed. (New York: Scribners, 1851), pp. 300, 322; C. M. Sedgwick, *Morals and Manners* (New York: Putnam, 1846); and Peter Pailey, *Manners and Morals of the Principal Nations of the Globe* (Boston: Wilkins, 1845), pp. 20–23. Also of interest and use are Arthur M. Schlesinger, *Learning How to Behave: A Historical Study of American Etiquette Books* (New York: Macmillan; Cooper Square Publishers, 1965), pp. 15–26; and Stow Persons, *The Decline of American Gentility* (New York: Columbia University Press, 1973), pp. 1–71.

38. Ralph Waldo Emerson, "The American Scholar," Phi Beta Kappa Address, delivered in 1837 at Harvard University, reprinted in William H. Gilman, ed., *Selected Writings of Ralph Waldo Emerson* (New York: New American Library, 1965), pp. 223–40.

39. *Cincinnati Daily Times*, November 21, 1846, p. 2. For the national lyceum circuit, see Carl Bode, *The American Lyceum: Town Meeting of the Mind* (1956; Carbondale, IL: Arcturus Books of the Southern Illinois University Press, 1968), pp.

131–82. Donald Scott in "The Popular Lecture and the Creation of a Public in Mid-nineteenth Century America," *Journal of American History* 66 (1980), pp. 791–809, argues that popular lectures created a national culture. It may be that the reverse, in fact, occurred. The notion of an American civilization made the national public lecture circuit a viable form.

Chapter 2

1. Daniel Drake, *Natural and Statistical View, or Picture of Cincinnati and the Miami Country* (Cincinnati: Looker and Wallace, 1815), pp. 61, 137–38, 142–51; Benjamin Drake and Edward Deering Mansfield, *Cincinnati In 1826* (Cincinnati: Morgan, Lodge, and Fisher, 1827), pp. 14–19, 59–66, 72, 74, 78, 84–86; and Charles Cist, *Cincinnati in 1841: Its Early Annals and Future Prospects* (Cincinnati: n.p., 1841), pp. 37, 79–80. See also Richard C. Wade, *The Urban Frontier: Pioneer Life in Early Pittsburgh, Cincinnati, Lexington, Louisville, and St. Louis* (Cambridge, 1959; Chicago: University of Chicago Press, 1972), pp. 53–59, 101, 326–36; Walter Stix Glazer, *Cincinnati In 1840: A Community Profile* (University of Michigan, Unpublished Ph.D. dissertation, 1968), pp. 44–47; Carl W. Condit, *The Railroad and the City: A Technological and Urbanistic History of Cincinnati* (Columbus: Ohio State University Press, 1977), pp. 3–6; Louis C. Hunter, *Steamboats on the Western Rivers: An Economic and Technological History* (Cambridge: Harvard University Press, 1949), pp. 24, 35, 68, 123, 127–28, 326; and Steven J. Ross, *Workers On the Edge: Work, Leisure, and Politics in Industrializing Cincinnati, 1788–1890* (New York: Columbia University Press, 1985), pp. 4–17, 33–40.

2. Wade, *The Urban Frontier*, pp. 270–71.

3. Ohio, *An Act to Amend the Act Entitled, "An Act to Incorporate the Town of Cincinnati,"* Statutes 17 (1819), pp. 175–80; and Ohio, *An Act to Incorporate and Establish the City of Cincinnati, and For Revising and Repealing All Laws and Parts of Laws, Heretofore Enacted on That Subject,* Statutes 25 (1827), pp. 40–56. Cincinnati's Charter of 1819 was cast as an amendment of the

town charter and, as a consequence, did little more than designate Cincinnati a city and establish city courts. (In the nineteenth century, Ohio state statutes were known as Ohio laws. For convenience, I have referred to them throughout as statutes.)

4. The agitation for control of the common schools led the legislature in 1834 to issue the city a new charter. See Ohio, *An Act to Incorporate and Establish the City of Cincinnati, and For Revising and Repealing All Laws and Parts of Laws Heretofore Enacted on That Subject, Statutes* 32 (1834), pp. 244–59. For a discussion of agitation for enforcement of the Black Laws, see Richard C. Wade, "The Negro in Cincinnati," *Journal of Negro History* 39 (1954), pp. 43–57.

5. *Minute Books of the City Council of the City of Cincinnati* (hereafter cited as *City Council Minutes*), April 26, 1821; February 26, 1823; July 23, 1823; November 12, 1823; and November 23, 1823. See also City Council of the City of Cincinnati, "An Ordinance to Prevent Nuisances and To Provide for the Security of the Public Health of the City of Cincinnati"; "An Ordinance Supplementary to an Ordinance to Prevent Nuisances, and For the Security of the Public Health of the City of Cincinnati"; "An Ordinance to Secure the Health of the City, and To Prevent Nuisances"; "An Ordinance Supplementary to An Ordinance Entitled 'An Ordinance to Prevent Nuisances, and To Provide For the Health of the City of Cincinnati' "; and "An Ordinance Further to Secure the Health of the City of Cincinnati," in City Council of the City of Cincinnati, *An Act Incorporating the City of Cincinnati, and Ordinances of Said City, Now in Force* (Cincinnati: Morgan, Fisher and L'Hommedieu, 1828), pp. 58–62, 82–83.

6. City Council, "An Ordinance to Prevent Nuisances and to Provide for the Security of the Public Health of the City of Cincinnati," *Act Incorporating the City of Cincinnati,* p. 59.

7. See, for instance, "Petition from H. Fairbanks to the City Council of the City of Cincinnati, January 20, 1823"; and "Petition of Ernest Dudley to the City Council of the City of Cincinnati Relative to Standing Water on Western Row, August 3, 1824." The newspapers also occasionally complained

about hazardous conditions and urged council to have the marshal investigate. See, for example, *Cincinnati Liberty Hall,* March 27, 1823, p. 2; and December 17, 1823, p. 2.

8. *City Council Minutes,* May 10, 1821; June 14, 1821; August 16, 1821; August 21, 1821; August 28, 1822; September 11, 1822; and April 23, 1823. Often a health officer was employed to kill wild dogs after a rabid animal was sighted in the area.

9. There had been a smallpox scare a month earlier, and the filth accumulated in chimneys was thought to exacerbate the threat. Council investigated the matter, however, and found it "not nysisary [sic] to legislate on that subject at the present time." See "Report of the Committee of City Council on Cleaning Chimneys, January 18, 1826."

10. *National Republican,* February 24, 1826, p. 2; *City Council Minutes,* February 22, 1826; and City Council, "An Ordinance to Prevent the Introduction of the Small Pox Into the City of Cincinnati, and For the Establishment of a Board of Health in Said City," City Council of the City of Cincinnati, *Ordinances Passed by the City Council of the City of Cincinnati Between April, 1825 and February, 1826* (Cincinnati: The Cincinnati Advertiser, 1826), pp. 17–18.

11. *Liberty Hall and Cincinnati Gazette,* March 2, 1826, p. 3. The dual operations of the early nineteenth century boards of health seem to suggest that their creation was not a consequence of a change in theories of the etiology of disease. Rather, the boards simultaneously supervised activities consistent with the miasmatic theory and the theory of contagion.

12. *City Council Minutes,* May 10, 1827. See also City Council, "An Ordinance Providing for the Abatement and Removal of Nuisances; To Keep the Streets, Lanes, Alleys, and Commons of the City of Cincinnati Open and In Repair, and to Regulate the Use of Sidewalks," City Council of the City of Cincinnati, *Act Incorporating the City,* pp. 64–65.

13. *City Council Minutes,* August 7, 1839; and City Council, "An Ordinance to Prevent Nuisances Arising From Grave Yards," William C. Williams, comp., *Laws and General Ordinances of the City of Cincinnati* (Cincinnati: Cincinnati Gazette Co., 1854), pp. 521–22.

14. "Petition of William Wallace to City Council of the City of Cincinnati Applying for the Position of Health Officer, April 12, 1826"; and "Petition of Jesse Churchill to City Council of the City of Cincinnati Asking for Reappointment as Health Officer, April 18, 1826."

15. "Petition of F. Falconer Asking for Appointment as Health Officer for the Lower Part of the City, April 19, 1826"; "Petition of F. Falconer to the City Council of the City of Cincinnati Requesting a Change in Territory and an Increase in his Daily Wage, May 17, 1825"; and *City Council Minutes,* April 12, 1826.

16. Petitions for the investigation of nuisances include: "Petition of Thomas Pierce to the City Council of the City of Cincinnati Relative to the Standing Water in Cellars of Second Street House, March 22, 1826"; "Petition of William Holyoke and Morris Symonds to the City Council of the City of Cincinnati Relative to a Nuisance East of Sycamore Street Between Third and Fourth Streets, May 29, 1826"; "Petition of the Citizens of the Second Ward to the City Council of the City of Cincinnati Complaining of a Lot Filled with Stagnant Water on the South Side of George Street, May 23, 1827"; and "Complaint of Citizens Near Western Row to the City Council of the City of Cincinnati About the Filth Accumulated Between Front and Water Streets, October 18, 1829." Results of nuisance investigations include: "Report of Samuel Ramsay, Health Officer, to City Council of the City of Cincinnati as to the Situation of Columbia Street, April 11, 1826"; "Report of Thomas Henderson, Health Officer, of the Nuisance at Western Row, May 5, 1827"; and "Report of Joseph Ruffner, Health Officer, to the City Council of the City of Cincinnati as to the Standing Water at Race and Second Streets, May 14, 1827." The reports also informed council of the time the health officer devoted to the task.

17. *City Council Minutes,* May 12, 1826; May 16, 1827; January 10, 1829; and June 25, 1832.

18. *City Council Minutes,* August 1, 1827.

19. "Report of the Board of Health to the City Council of the City of Cincinnati, August 3, 1827"; and *City Council Minutes,* August 3, 1827. For a retrospective history of the

epidemics of the 1820s, see E. D. Mansfield, *Personal Memories, Social, Political, and Literary with Sketches of Many Noted People, 1803–1843* (Cincinnati: Robert Clark and Co., 1879), pp. 193–96.

20. *City Council Minutes,* June 25, 1832; City Council, "An Ordinance to Establish a Board of Health for the City of Cincinnati," Williams, *Laws,* pp. 181–82; Petitions include: "Petition of Citizens to the City Council of the City of Cincinnati Relative to the Stagnant Water on Wayne Street, August 29, 1832"; and "A. G. Dodd's Communication to the City Council of the City of Cincinnati Relative to the Water Standing in Her District, September 12, 1832." See also *Cincinnati Daily Gazette,* June 23, 1832, p. 3; June 24, 1832, p. 3; June 28, 1832, p. 3; and July 7, 1832, p. 3.

21. *City Council Minutes,* June 25, 1832. See also *Cincinnati Daily Advertiser and Ohio Phoenix,* October 6, 1832, p. 2; October 9, 1832, p. 2; October 10, 1832, p. 2; and *Cincinnati Daily Gazette,* October 11, 1832, p. 3; October 12, 1832, p. 3; October 14, 1832, p. 3; October 15, 1832, p. 3; and October 18, 1832, p. 3.

22. See, for example, *Cincinnati Daily Gazette,* November 8, 1832, p. 3. In general, council appointed new members to the health board around May 1. In this manner, it could insure that the board had its full compliment as the dangerous summer season approached. See, for example, *City Council Minutes,* May 1, 1834; May 4, 1837.

23. Ohio, *An Act to Amend the Act Entitled, "An Act to Incorporate the Town of Cincinnati,* Statutes 17 (1819), pp. 175–80; and City Council of the City of Cincinnati, "An Ordinance to Amend an Ordinance Entitled 'An Ordinance to Establish a Nightly Watch in the City of Cincinnati, Passed 9th of July, 1834,'" *Digest of Laws and Ordinances of Cincinnati; of a General Nature, Now in Force, 1842* (Cincinnati: E. Morgan and Co., 1842), pp. 201–2. The 1834 ordinance merely provided for the temporary deployment of an unpaid watch. See *City Council Minutes,* April 4, 1834.

24. Ohio Anti-Slavery Society, Executive Committee, *Narrative of the Late Riotous Proceedings Against Liberty of the Press in Cincinnati* (Cincinnati: n. p., 1836), pp. 40–41.

25. City Council of the City of Cincinnati, "An Ordinance to Form the Fire Wardens of This City Into a Fire Company," *Cincinnati Ordinances . . . April, 1825 and February, 1826,* pp. 16–17; and "An Ordinance for Preventing and Extinguishing Fires, to Regulate the Keeping of Gun Powder; Also, to Prevent the Erection of Wooden Buildings With Certain Limits," *Digest of Laws . . . 1842,* pp. 69–76.

26. See, for example, *Cincinnati Daily Gazette,* November 26, 1832, p. 2; March 3, 1833, pp. 1, 2.

27. Ibid.

28. *Cincinnati Daily Gazette,* June 28, 1831, p. 2; June 29, 1831, p. 2; June 30, 1831, p. 3; and July 4, 1831. For a discussion of the situation in Kentucky, see Wade, *The Urban Frontier,* pp. 183–84.

29. *Cincinnati Daily Gazette,* February 14, 1832, p. 2; February 15, 1832, p. 2; March 1, 1832, p. 3; March 6, 1832, p. 3; and *City Council Minutes,* February 22, 1832. See also Wade, *The Urban Frontier,* pp. 294–95.

30. Ohio, *An Act to Incorporate and Establish the City of Cincinnati, and For Revising and Repealing All Laws and Parts of Laws Heretofore Enacted on That Subject, Statutes* 32 (1834), pp. 144–259.

31. Drake, *Natural and Statistical View,* pp. 61–62, 137–38, 161–65, 171–72; Drake and Mansfield, *Cincinnati in 1826,* pp. 33–36, 57; and Cist, *Cincinnati In 1841,* pp. 20, 79–80. See also Wade, *The Urban Frontier,* pp. 22–24, 54–59, 106–7, 109, 133, 207, 213–16, 221, 224–29, 264; Glazer, pp. 48–51, 102–4, 114, 120–26, 134–35; Condit, pp. 5–11; and Henry L. Taylor, "On Slavery's Fringe: City-Building and Black Community Development in Cincinnati, 1800–1850," *Ohio History* 95 (1986), pp. 8–23.

32. Historians have noted the early nineteenth century emphasis on opportunity. They generally link it to a political party—Jacksonian Democracy—or social group, but some identify it as part of the revolutionary tradition—republican ideology. See, for example, Rush Welter, *The Mind of America, 1820–1860* (New York: Columbia University Press, 1975), pp. 142–57; John R. Bodo, *The Protestant Clergy and Public Issues, 1812–1848* (Princeton: Princeton University Press, 1954), pp.

254 *Notes to Chapter 2*

152–91; Daniel Walker Howe, *The Political Culture of the American Whigs* (Chicago: University of Chicago Press, 1959); Rowland Berthoff, "Independence and Attachment, Virtue and Interest: From Republican Citizen to Free Enterprise, 1787–1837," in Richard Bushman, ed., *Uprooted Americans: Essays to Honor Oscar Handlin* (Boston: Little, Brown, 1979), pp. 104–14; Lynn L. Marshall, "The Strange Stillbirth of the Whig Party," *American Historical Review* 72 (1967), pp. 445–68; and John F. Kasson, *Civilizing the Machine: Technology and Republican Values in America, 1776–1900* (New York: Penguin Books, 1977), pp. 1–106.

33. Drake, *Natural and Statistical View*, pp. 166–67; and Drake and Mansfield, *Cincinnati In 1826*, pp. 88–91.

34. For Cincinnati's response to rabies, see *Cincinnati Daily Gazette*, July 16, 1831, p. 2; August 2, 1831, p. 3.

35. *Cincinnati Daily Commercial*, July 15, 1844, p. 2; August 26, 1845, p. 2; *Daily Cincinnati Chronicle*, May 5, 1846, p. 2; and *Cincinnati Daily Gazette*, May 25, 1848, p. 2.

36. *Cincinnati Daily Enquirer*, September 2, 1847, p. 2; and William H. Channing, ed., *The Memoir and Writings of James Handasyd Perkins*, 2 vols. (Cincinnati: Trueman and Spofford, 1851), vol. 1, pp. 116–17.

37. Rev. Horace Bushnell, *Seventh Annual Report to the Ladies' City Missionary Association of Cincinnati* (Cincinnati: Office of the Great West, 1850), pp. 6–7.

38. *Cincinnati Daily Gazette*, February 15, 1855, p. 2; and *Cincinnati Daily Enquirer*, September 2, 1847, p. 2; December 16, 1852, p. 2.

39. John L. Vattier, M.D., "Health of the City," *Journal of Health* (published by the members of the Cincinnati Dispensary and Vaccine Institution), 1 (June, 1845), p. 201; Starbuck's comments were reprinted in the *Cincinnati Daily Commercial*, March 4, 1844, p. 2; March 7, 1844, p. 2.

40. Cincinnati Ladies' Home Missionary Society of the Methodist Episcopal Church, *Annual Report of the Cincinnati Ladies' Home Missionary Society of the Methodist Episcopal Church For 1852* (Cincinnati: Ben Franklin Steam Printing Co., 1853), pp. 9–11.

41. *Daily Cincinnati Chronicle*, February 3, 1846, p. 2.

42. Cist, *Cincinnati In 1841*, p. 261.

43. *Cincinnati Daily Enquirer*, April 14, 1852, p. 2.

44. Thomas C. Carroll, M.D., "Observations on the Asiatic Cholera, As It Appeared in Cincinnati During the Years 1849 and 1850," *Western Lancet* 15 (1854), pp. 325–27.

45. *Cincinnati Daily Gazette*, July 4, 1849, p. 2.

46. *Cincinnati Daily Gazette*, May 5, 1852, p. 2.

47. For the piestistic awakening argument, see, for example, Charles E. Rosenberg and Carroll Smith Rosenberg, "Pietism and the Origins of the American Public Health Movement," *Bulletin of the History of Medicine* 35 (1961), pp. 245–59; and Carroll Smith Rosenberg, *Religion and the Rise of the American City: The New York City Mission Movement, 1812–1870* (Ithaca: Cornell University Press, 1971). For social control, see, for instance, David J. Rothman, *The Discovery of the Asylum: Social Order and Disorder in the New Republic* (Boston: Little, Brown and Co., 1971); Ross, p. 68 and *passim;* and Clifford S. Griffin, "Religious Benevolence as Social Control, 1815–1860," *Mississippi Valley Historical Review* 44 (1957), pp. 423–44.

48. *Daily Cincinnati Chronicle*, November 17, 1846, p. 2.

49. *Cincinnati Daily Nonpareil*, July 7, 1852, p. 2; *Cincinnati Daily Gazette*, January 23, 1851, p. 1; May 25, 1852, p. 2; and Channing, ed., *The Memoir and Writings of James Handasyd Perkins*, vol. 1, p. 116.

50. Cist, *Cincinnati In 1841*, pp. 42–43, 50, 52–58, 79, 80, 96–99; and Cist, *Sketches and Statistics of Cincinnati In 1851* (Cincinnati: Wm. H. Moore and Co., 1851), pp. 44–51, 88–102, 130–31, 134–37, 164–67, 268–70, 279. See also Zane L. Miller, *Boss Cox's Cincinnati: Urban Politics in the Progressive Era* (New York: Oxford University Press, 1968), pp. 3–5; Henry D. Shapiro and Zane L. Miller, *Clifton: Neighborhood and Community in An Urban Setting. A Brief History* (Cincinnati: n. p., 1976), pp. 2–13; Glazer, *Cincinnati In 1840;* Henry L. Taylor, "Spatial Organization and the Residential Experience: Black Cincinnati in 1850," *Social Science History* 10 (1986), pp. 47–64; Taylor, "On Slavery's Fringe," pp. 8–23; Condit, pp. 7–11; Hunter, pp. 30–31, 37, 55–56, 106, 327, 331–33; and Ross, pp. 71–93.

/

51. Glazer, *Cincinnati In 1840,* pp. 140–41; Cist, *Cincinnati In 1841,* pp. 32–43; and Cist, *Sketches and Statistics,* pp. 47–48.

52. See, for example, Bushnell, *Fifth Annual Report;* Ladies' Benevolent Society of Christ Church, *Report of the Ladies' Benevolent Society of Christ Church Rev. Richard Gray, City Missionary* (Cincinnati: Cincinnati Gazette Co., 1852), p. 3; Ladies' Benevolent Society of St. John's Church, *General Report, with Constitution, By-Laws, List of Officers and Members of the Ladies' Benevolent Society of St. John's Church* (Cincinnati: C. F. Bradley and Co., 1859), pp. 4–5; Baptist City Missionary Society, *Annual Report of the Baptist City Mission, of Cincinnati* (Cincinnati: Ellis and Hart, 1854), pp. 6, 13–14; Cincinnati: Ladies' Home Missionary Society of the Methodist Episcopal Church, *Annual Report of the Cincinnati Ladies' Home Missionary Society of the Methodist Episcopal Church For 1852* (Cincinnati: Ben Franklin Steam Printing Co., 1853), pp. 9–11; *The Occident* 4 (1846), pp. 406–7, 556, 607, 683; St. Peter's Benevolent Society, *Constitution and By-Laws of the St. Peter's Benevolent Society and the St. Xavier's Auxiliary of Cincinnati* (Cincinnati: Wright, Ferris and Co., 1851), pp. 3–5; Ohio, *An Act to Incorporate the 'Emigrants' Friend Society of Cincinnati, Statutes* 36 (1838), pp. 208–9; Hermann Borkum, *First Report of the Mission Among the German Population of the City of Cincinnati* (Cincinnati: Morgan and Overend, 1850), pp. 3–6; Ohio, *An Act to Incorporate the New England Society of Cincinnati, Statutes* 43 (1845), p. 187; Ohio, *An Act to Incorporate the Stone Masons' Benevolent Society of Cincinnati, Statutes* 43 (1844), p. 31; and Cincinnati Relief Union, *Constitution and By-Laws of the Cincinnati Relief Union* (Cincinnati: Collins and Van Wagner, 1848), pp. 2–3.

53. *Cincinnati Daily Gazette,* September 28, 1848, p. 2.

Chapter 3

1. City of Cincinnati, "An Ordinance Authorizing the Establishment of a Patrole" (passed August 5, 1839), *Digest of Laws and Ordinances of Cincinnati, of a General Nature, Now in Force, 1842* (Cincinnati: E. Morgan and Co., 1842), pp. 199–202, and *City Council Minutes,* August 5, 1842.

2. City of Cincinnati, "An Ordinance Creating a City Watch," *Digest of Laws . . . 1842*, p. 203.

3. *City Council Minutes*, January 22, 1842; and City of Cincinnati, "An Ordinance to Secure More Effectually the City, and the Inhabitants Thereof, Against Injuries by Thieves, Robbers, Burglars, and Other Persons Violating the Public Peace, and for the Suppression of Riots, and Other Disorderly Conduct," *Digest of Laws . . . 1842*, pp. 203–5.

4. *City Council Minutes*, May 27, 1842; and City of Cincinnati, "An Ordinance to Establish a Day Watch," *Digest of Laws . . . 1842*, pp. 205–6.

5. *City Council Minutes*, February 24, 1843; and City of Cincinnati, "An Ordinance Licensing and Regulating Taverns, Coffee Houses, and Restaurats [sic], in the City of Cincinnati," *Digest of Laws and Ordinances of Cincinnati, of a General Nature, Now in Force, 1842–1846* (Cincinnati: E. Morgan and Co., 1846), pp. 25–27.

6. Ibid.

7. *City Council Minutes*, October 23, 1843; and City of Cincinnati, "An Ordinance for the Prevention of Certain Immoral Practices," *Digest of Laws . . . 1842–1846*, p. 73.

8. *City Council Minutes*, November 20, 1844; and City of Cincinnati, "An Ordinance to Increase the Police Force of the City of Cincinnati," *Digest of Laws. . . 1842–1846*, p. 72.

9. *City Council Minutes*, November 20, 1844; and City of Cincinnati, "An Ordinance to Provide for Cleaning the Streets, Lanes, Alleys, etc., and for the Appointment of a Superintendent of Pavements in the City of Cincinnati," *Digest of Laws . . . 1842–1846*, pp. 73–75.

10. *Cincinnati Daily Gazette*, December 7, 1844, p. 2; and *City Council Minutes*, December 15, 1844.

11. Ohio, *An Act for the More Effectual Relief of the Poor in the City of Cincinnati, Statutes* 43 (1845), p. 162; *An Act to Provide for the Election of the Watch in the City of Cincinnati and Other Purposes, Statutes* 43 (1845), pp. 384–87; and *An Act to Authorize the City of Cincinnati to Erect a House of Corrections, Statutes* 43 (1845), pp. 393–95.

12. *City Council Minutes*, March 19, 1845; and City of Cincinnati, "An Ordinance to Prevent the Spread of the Small

Pox Within the City of Cincinnati, *Digest of Laws . . . 1842–1846*, pp. 79–80.

13. *City Council Minutes*, April 9, 1845; and City of Cincinnati, "An Ordinance to Organize, Prescribe the Duties, Define the Powers, and Fix the Compensation of the City Night Watch," *Digest of Laws . . . 1842–1846*, pp. 84–88.

14. Ohio, *An Act to Authorize the City of Cincinnati to Erect a House of Corrections*, Statutes 43 (1845), pp. 393–95.

15. *Cincinnati Daily Commercial*, April 3, 1845, p. 2.

16. *City Council Minutes*, May 14, 1845; June 11, 1845; and City of Cincinnati, "An Ordinance for the Appointment of Directors of the House or Houses of Correction and Reformation"; and "An Ordinance to Carry into Effect an Act of the Legislature of Ohio, for Building and Support of Houses of Correction and Reformation," *Digest of Laws . . . 1842–1846*, pp. 90–91.

17. *Daily Cincinnati Chronicle*, November 10, 1845, p. 2; *City Council Minutes*, November 7, 1845; January 2, 1846; February 18, 1846; and City of Cincinnati, "An Ordinance to Amend an Ordinance entitled 'An Ordinance Licensing and Regulating Taverns, Coffee Houses and Restaurants, in the City of Cincinnati' "; and "An Ordinance to Provide for Dividing the City of Cincinnati into Two Districts for Cleaning the Streets, the Appointment of Street Contractors, Their Duty, ETC.," *Digest of Laws . . . 1842–1846*, pp. 28–29, 47–49.

18. *Daily Cincinnati Chronicle*, June 10, 1846, p. 2; June 17, 1846, p. 2; June 24, 1846, p. 2; and June 30, 1846, p. 2.

19. *City Council Minutes*, October 4, 1846; February 24, 1847; and City of Cincinnati, "An Ordinance Supplementary to the Several Ordinances Preventing the Obstruction of Sidewalks in the City of Cincinnati"; and "An Ordinance Further to Prevent and Restrain Immorality," *Digest of Laws and Ordinances of Cincinnati, of a General Nature, Now in Force, 1847* (Cincinnati: E. Morgan and Co, 1847), pp. 16, 18.

20. Ohio, *An Act to Amend the Act to Authorize the City Council of Cincinnati to Erect a House of Corrections*, Statutes 45 (1847), pp. 112–13.

21. *Daily Cincinnati Chronicle*, November 22, 1846, p. 2.

22. Horace Bushnell, *Fifth Annual Report to the Ladies' City Missionary Association* (Cincinnati: Collins and Van Wagner, 1847), pp. 6, 10.

23. *City Council Minutes,* June 7, 1848; September 16, 1848; October 3, 1848; City of Cincinnati, "An Ordinance Levying a Tax Upon the Grand Levy for the Different Purposes Authorized by Law for the Year 1848," *Digest of Laws and Ordinances of Cincinnati, of a General Nature, Now in Force, 1849* (Cincinnati: E. Morgan and Co., 1849), pp. 61–62; and *Cincinnati Daily Gazette,* July 28, 1848, p. 2; September 18, 1848, p. 2; October 6, 1848, p. 2.

24. Ohio, *An Act to Authorize the City of Cincinnati to Erect a Poor House, and for Other Purposes,* Statutes 47 (1849), pp. 148–50.

25. Ibid.

26. *Cincinnati Daily Gazette,* September 13, 1848, p. 2. See also, for example, *Cincinnati Daily Gazette,* September 25, 1848, p. 2; and October 12, 1848, p. 2.

27. *City Council Minutes,* June 11, 1849; and City of Cincinnati, "An Ordinance Further to Provide for the Abatement and Removal of Nuisances," printed in City Council of the City of Cincinnati, *Charter, Amendments, and General Ordinances, of the City of Cincinnati, Revised, A.D. 1850* (Cincinnati: Day and Co., 1850), pp. 321–22.

28. *City Council Minutes,* September 21, 1848; December 2, 1848; and *Cincinnati Daily Gazette,* September 23, 1848, p. 2; December 4, 1848, p. 2.

29. *City Council Minutes,* December 27, 1848; and City of Cincinnati, "An Ordinance to Amend 'An Ordinance to Establish a Board of Health for the City of Cincinnati,' " William G. Williams, comp., *Laws and General Ordinances of the City of Cincinnati* (Cincinnati: Cincinnati Gazette, 1854), pp. 183–86.

30. *City Council Minutes,* December 28, 1848; January 2, 1849; and *Cincinnati Daily Gazette,* December 29, 1848, p. 2; January 3, 1849, p. 2.

31. *Cincinnati Daily Gazette,* January 4, 1849, p. 2; January 9, 1849, p. 2; January 10, 1849, p. 2; January 12, 1849, p. 2; January 24, 1849, p. 2; and February 26, 1849, p. 2.

32. *Cincinnati Daily Gazette,* May 7, 1849, p. 2; May 9, 1849, p. 2; May 16, 1849, p. 2; May 23, 1849, p. 2; and June 26, 1849, p. 2.

33. *City Council Minutes,* May 16, 1849; June 13, 1849; June 22, 1849; June 27, 1849; *Cincinnati Daily Gazette,* June 25, 1849, p. 2; June 29, 1849, p. 1; and City of Cincinnati, "An Ordinance to Provide for the Removal of House Offal, and for Other Purposes"; and "An Ordinance Levying a Tax Upon the Grand Levy, for the Different Purposes Authorized by Law, for the Year 1849," *Digest of Laws . . . 1849,* pp. 36, 62–63.

34. *Cincinnati Daily Atlas,* May 29, 1849, p. 2; June 1, 1849, p. 2.

35. *Cincinnati Daily Gazette,* June 27, 1849, p. 2; June 28, 1849, p. 2.

36. Ibid.

37. *Cincinnati Daily Gazette,* June 30, 1849, p. 2; July 12, 1849, p. 2.

38. *Cincinnati Daily Gazette,* July 2, 1849, p. 2; July 6, 1849, p. 2.

39. *Cincinnati Daily Gazette,* August 2, 1849, p. 2; August 8, 1849, p. 2. See also *Cincinnati Daily Gazette,* July 16, 1849, p. 2; July 17, 1849, p. 2; July 24, 1849, p. 2.

40. *City Council Minutes,* November 19, 1849.

41. Ohio, *An Act to Amend the Act Entitled An "Act to Authorize the City of Cincinnati to Erect a Poor House, and for Other Purposes," Passed March 19, 1849,* printed in *Charter, Amendments, and General Ordinances . . . 1850,* pp. 98–99.

42. *City Council Minutes,* April 22, 1850; and City of Cincinnati, "An Ordinance to Create Officers of the Watch, and to Define the Duties of Said Officers, and of the Watchmen," *Charter, Amendments, and General Ordinances . . . 1850,* pp. 401–3.

43. For the proceedings of the convention, see J. V. Smith, *Report of the Debates and Proceedings of the Convention For the Revision of the Constitution of the State of Ohio, 1850–51,* 2 vols. (Columbus: S. Medary, 1851). For an analysis of the convention with respect to municipalities, see Judith Spraul-Schmidt, "The Municipal Corporation and the State, 1840–1880," (Ph.D. dissertation, University of Cincinnati, in progress).

44. Ohio, *Constitution of the State of Ohio* (1850), Article

XIII, Sec. 6; and *Cincinnati Daily Gazette,* February 26, 1850, p. 2.

45. *Cincinnati Daily Nonpareil,* June 18, 1850, p. 2; *Cincinnati Daily Gazette,* July 31, 1850, p. 2; August 17, 1850, p. 2; December 2, 1850, p. 2; *Daily Cincinnati Chronicle,* August 12, 1846, p. 2; and *Cincinnati Daily Commercial,* August 20, 1851, p. 2.

46. Albert Bushnell, "Report of the Agent," *Third Annual Report of the Cincinnati Relief Union* (Cincinnati: Ben Franklin Printing Co., 1851), pp. 6, 8.

47. Ibid.; *Cincinnati Daily Commercial,* May 1, 1851, p. 2; and *Cincinnati Daily Enquirer,* November 12, 1851, p. 2.

48. It is quite likely that ship and California fever were less virulent forms of cholera.

49. *Cincinnati Daily Gazette,* August 14, 1850, p. 2; November 25, 1850, p. 2; and *Cincinnati Daily Commercial,* June 16, 1851, p. 2; June 17, 1851, pp. 1, 2; June 19, 1851, p. 2; July 2, 1851, p. 2; July 4, 1851, p. 2; October 9, 1851, p. 2.

50. *Cincinnati Daily Gazette,* August 19, 1850, p. 2.

51. *Cincinnati Daily Commercial,* July 2, 1851, p. 2; July 16, 1851, p. 2.

52. *Cincinnati Daily Gazette,* June 26, 1850, p. 2; March 14, 1851, p. 2; March 31, 1851, p. 2; April 2, 1851, p. 2.

53. *Cincinnati Daily Enquirer,* March 27, 1852, p. 2; and Ohio, *An Act to Provide for the Organization of Cities and Incorporated Villages, Statutes* 50 (1852), pp. 223–59.

54. Ibid.; *Cincinnati Daily Gazette,* April 8, 1853, p. 2; and Ohio, *An Act to Amend the Act Entitled "An Act to Provide for the Organization of Cities and Incorporated Villages," Statutes* 51 (1853), pp. 360–74.

55. *Cincinnati Daily Enquirer,* December 15, 1852, pp. 1, 2; *City Council Minutes,* March 10, 1853; and City of Cincinnati, "An Ordinance to Regulate the Management of the City Infirmary, Commercial Hospital, Pest House, Burying Ground, and the Granting of Outdoor Relief to the Poor," Williams, *Laws,* pp. 228–53.

56. *Daily Cincinnati Chronicle,* July 9, 1846, p. 2; July 11, 1846, p. 2; and *City Council Minutes,* July 8, 1846; July 10, 1846.

57. J. H. Walker, William P. Stratton, J. W. Piatt, Charles F. Wilstach, and D. T. Hoke, Special Committee of Council, *Report on the Re-Organization of the Fire Department* (Cincinnati: n. p., 1853); *City Council Minutes,* March 16, 1853; and City Council of the City of Cincinnati, "An Ordinance to Establish a Fire Department, and for Preventing and Extinguishing Fires," Williams, *Laws,* pp. 350–64. The committee report included a concise history of the problems attributed to volunteer fire companies. For other historical reflections on the voluntary fire companies, see Charles Cist, *Cincinnati In 1841: Its Early Annals and Future Prospects* (Cincinnati: n. p., 1841), p. 143; and Cist, *Sketches and Statistics of Cincinnati in 1859* (Cincinnati: n. p., 1859), pp. 355–56. In reality, volunteer fire companies provided a potent threat to established political parties. Political alliances were cemented in voluntary fire companies and these agencies often challenged the more conventional party machinery. Whether Whig, Democrat, Republican, or Know-Nothing, virtually every Cincinnati politician who achieved political maturity between 1830–1850 was for some part of the time a member of a volunteer fire company.

Chapter 4

1. *Cincinnati Daily Gazette,* July 21, 1854, p. 2; August 10, 1854, p. 2; May 29, 1858, p. 2.

2. *Cincinnati Daily Times,* January 27, 1858, p. 3. Faran also noticed the filthy state of the city and worried that city officials lacked an understanding of the problem. See *Cincinnati Daily Enquirer,* May 3, 1854, p. 2; May 27, 1854, p. 3. The emergence of the condition of the city's thoroughfares as a distinct public health question is interesting. Indeed, the city's streets were almost certainly cleaner than they had been just a decade earlier. The reason for the improvement rested in the introduction of a new paving material, bowlderized rock. Until about 1840, Cincinnati had used limestone exclusively as its road pavement. This friable material would "soon break into inequalities" under the weight of daily traffic and produce a mess both in wet and dry weather. During heavy rains, water

would seep underneath and between the fractured rocks, "increasing and extending the irregularity of the surface," and permit mud to ooze between stones. The water would not only erode the road, but would also become trapped and stagnant. In the dry summer, the situation was far worse. The pulverized rocks would generate "clouds of dust," blocking out even the sun. To most Cincinnatians during these years, the dust clouds "constitute our greatest street nuisance." Only after 1840 did the city substitute igneous rock for the limestone. Introducing the material first on new thoroughfares and then replacing older streets, the new paving substance produced a road that was "nearly indestructable" and "relatively smooth." It neither crumbled to yield dust clouds nor fissured to admit water. And the substitution process occurred so rapidly that by the early 1850s it was virtually complete. For a brief history of this event, see Charles Cist, *Sketches and Statistics of Cincinnati in 1851* (Cincinnati: William H. Moore and Co., 1851), p. 340.

3. *City Council Minutes,* July 9, 1856; and City of Cincinnati, "An Ordinance to Define the Powers and Duties of the Mayor of the City of Cincinnati; and to Repeal Ordinances Therein Named," *Ordinances and By-Laws of the City of Cincinnati; As Prepared and Revised By A Committee of City Council. Published by Order of the City Council, February, 1857* (Cincinnati: Enquirer Co., 1857), pp. 160–63.

4. For pre-1855 compilations of city laws, see either City of Cincinnati, *Digest of Laws and Ordinances of Cincinnati, of A General Nature, Now In Force, 1842* (Cincinnati: E. Morgan and Co., 1842); or City Council of the City of Cincinnati, *Charter, Amendments, and General Ordinances, of the City of Cincinnati. Revised, A.D. 1850* (Cincinnati: Day and Co., 1850). For the misdemeanor code, see *City Council Minutes,* September 3, 1856; and City of Cincinnati, "An Ordinance For the Punishment of Misdemeanors, and to Repeal Ordinances Therein Named," *Laws and Ordinances of the City of Cincinnati; Published By Order of City Council, May, 1859* (Cincinnati: Gazette Steam Print, 1859), pp. 255–61.

5. City of Cincinnati, "An Ordinance Defining the Spaces of and Regulating the Markets Within the City of Cincinnati;

and to Repeal Ordinances Therein Named," *Laws and Ordinances of the City of Cincinnati*, pp. 227–40.

6. City of Cincinnati, "An Ordinance to Regulate the Management of the City Infirmary, Commercial Hospital, Pesthouse, City Burying-ground, and the Granting of Out-door Relief to the Poor," *Ordinances and By-Laws . . . 1857*, pp. 36–54; and "An Ordinance to Define the Duties of the Board of City Improvements, and the Several Members Thereof; To Repeal 'An Ordinance to Create the Board of City Improvements, And to Prescribe The Duties of The City Commissioners,' Passed May 13, 1853; and the Second Section of the Ordinance to Create the Office of Civil Engineer, Passed March 17, 1846," *Laws and Ordinances . . . 1859*, pp. 76–81. The latter ordinance was enacted April 4, 1855.

7. *Cincinnati Daily Enquirer*, November 2, 1864, p. 3; December 13, 1864, p. 3; November 14, 1865, p. 1; *Cincinnati Daily Times*, October 5, 1865, p. 2; January 27, 1866, p. 2; and *Cincinnati Daily Gazette*, April 18, 1866, p. 2.

8. See, for example, *Cincinnati Daily Times*, February 8, 1860, p. 3; April 14, 1866, p. 2; April 21, 1866, p. 2; *Cincinnati Daily Gazette*, December 30, 1865, p. 1; April 13, 1866, pp. 1, 2; April 17, 1866, p. 1; *City Council Minutes*, November 10, 1865; and the Cincinnati Relief Union, *Sixteenth Annual Report of the Cincinnati Relief Union* (Cincinnati: n. p., 1866), pp. 57–63; and *Eighteenth Annual Report of the Cincinnati Relief Union* (Cincinnati: n. p., 1867), pp. 58–86.

9. Ibid., except *Minutes;* see also *Cincinnati Daily Times*, February 9, 1860, p. 2; March 23, 1860, p. 2.

10. For confirmation of the existence of the noxious trades in Cincinnati at about 1830, see *The Cincinnati Directory, for the Year 1831: Containing the Names of the Inhabitants, the Occupations, Places of Business and Dwelling-Houses* (Cincinnati: Robinson and Fairbanks, 1831). During that year, over two hundred Cincinnatians made their livings by slaughtering animals, making sausage, tanning hides, or as tallow chandlers. The first reference I could find decrying the noxious trades as a menace to morals was *Cincinnati Daily Gazette*, July 19, 1849, p. 3.

11. *Cincinnati Daily Times*, June 14, 1856, p. 3; June 20,

1856, p. 3; August 14, 1856, p. 3; August 31, 1856, p. 3; November 30, 1865, p. 3; February 16, 1866, p. 2; *Cincinnati Daily Press,* May 10, 1859, p. 3; *Cincinnati Daily Gazette,* January 31, 1862, p. 2; *Cincinnati Daily Enquirer,* February 19, 1862, p. 2; March 4, 1862, p. 2; September 16, 1863, p. 3; September 1, 1865, p. 2; April 20, 1866, p. 2; April 27, 1866, p. 2; December 19, 1866, p. 2; December 31, 1866, p. 2; and *City Council Minutes,* September 18, 1863.

12. *Cincinnati Daily Enquirer,* September 5, 1865, p. 2. The discussion about water in the decade before 1855 revolved only around the municipality's ability and responsibility to obtain sufficient quantities of the liquid. The municipality's duty to insure its purity emerged as an issue only after this date. See, for example, *Report of the Trustees of the City Water Works For the Year Ending 1st January, 1848* (bound at the Cincinnati Historical Society as *Cincinnati Water Works Reports, 1848–1856*), pp. 1–3; *Annual Report of the Trustees of the City Water Works For the Year Ending 31st December, 1850* (Cincinnati: Daily Times Company, 1851), pp. 3–10; and Faran, *Second Annual Report of the Mayor,* p. 9.

13. *Cincinnati Daily Press,* October 28, 1860, p. 2; November 1, 1860, p. 2.

14. *Cincinnati Daily Enquirer,* December 19, 1863, p. 3.

15. *Cincinnati Daily Enquirer,* August 20, 1859, p. 2; August 20, 1866, p. 2; November 22, 1866, p. 2; and *Cincinnati Daily Gazette,* January 14, 1867, p. 2; February 1, 1867, p. 2.

16. *Cincinnati Daily Enquirer,* August 20, 1859, p. 2; August 21, 1859, p. 2; August 20, 1866, p. 2; *City Council Minutes,* December 18, 1863; and L. A. Harris, Mayor, "Second Annual Message of the Mayor of Cincinnati to City Council, April 25, 1864," *Annual Reports of the City of Cincinnati For the Year Ending February 28, 1864* (Cincinnati: Gazette Steam Print, 1864), pp. 21–22. The first chemical analysis of Cincinnati's water and the only one prior to 1859 was John Locke and Joseph Morris Locke, *Analysis of the Waters in the Vicinity of Cincinnati Reported to the Trustees of the City Water Works* (Cincinnati: Enquirer Job Print, 1853). The Lockes determined that the Ohio River contained the least amount of organic matter.

17. *Cincinnati Daily Gazette,* October 21, 1864, p. 2; January

14, 1867, p. 2; April 26, 1867, p. 1; and *Cincinnati Daily Enquirer,* September 5, 1865, p. 2. See also Trustees of the City Water Works, "Annual Report of the Trustees of the City Water Works for the Year Ending December 31, 1863," *Annual Reports of the City Departments of the City of Cincinnati for the Year Ending February 28, 1864* (Cincinnati: Gazette Steam Print, 1864), pp. 243–44, 250–51.

18. *Cincinnati Daily Gazette,* May 29, 1858, p. 2; June 15, 1858, p. 1; June 17, 1858, p. 1; *Cincinnati Daily Enquirer,* September 7, 1858, p. 3; and *Cincinnati Daily Times,* August 31, 1865, p. 3.

19. *Cincinnati Daily Enquirer,* August 23, 1859, p. 2; August 24, 1859, p. 2; August 25, 1859, p. 2; *Cincinnati Daily Times,* September 22, 1862, p. 1; and *Cincinnati Daily Commercial,* April 1, 1866, p. 4.

20. *The Cincinnati Directory for the Year 1831* shows seven milk dealers in Cincinnati, four of whom had some connection with a brewery. For a brief overview of the history of urban dairies, see Harold B. Stoner, "The Dairy Industry" (M. A. thesis, University of Cincinnati, 1929), pp. 5–6, 15–17.

21. *Cincinnati Daily Times,* January 15, 1858, p. 2.

22. Ibid; *Cincinnati Daily Enquirer,* September 7, 1858, p. 3; *Cincinnati Daily Commercial,* April 1, 1866, p. 4; and *Cincinnati Daily Gazette,* June 4, 1858, p. 2.

23. *Cincinnati Daily Gazette,* May 24, 1852, p. 2; March 23, 1853, p. 2; March 24, 1853, p. 2.

24. *Cincinnati Daily Gazette,* October 20, 1866, p. 2; November 14, 1866, p. 2.

25. Ibid.

26. *Cincinnati Daily Times,* June 28, 1856, p. 2; April 7, 1856, p. 3.

27. *Cincinnati Daily Gazette,* March 28, 1857, p. 2; August 15, 1864, p. 4; *Cincinnati Daily Press,* September 10, 1859, p. 2; September 24, 1859, p. 2; *Cincinnati Daily Enquirer,* July 13, 1860, p. 2; January 23, 1862, p. 2; October 22, 1864, p. 2; *City Council Minutes,* January 22, 1858; and Thomas C. Peters, *First Annual Report of the City Civil Engineer to the Honorable City Council, February 2, 1859* (Cincinnati: Gazette Steam Print, 1859), pp. 3–12. For an excellent history of governmental pol-

icy and the Cincinnati sewer system, see Geoffrey Giglierano, "The City and the System: Developing a Municipal Service 1800–1915," *Cincinnati Historical Society Bulletin* 35 (1977), pp. 223–47.

28. *Cincinnati Daily Gazette,* May 14, 1858, p. 2; May 10, 1860, p. 2.

29. *City Council Minutes,* August 29, 1855; December 1, 1855; February 13, 1856; *Cincinnati Daily Enquirer,* August 24, 1855, p. 3; *Cincinnati Daily Gazette,* December 1, 1855, p. 2; and City of Cincinnati, "An Ordinance to Provide for the Abatement of Nuisances, and to Repeal Ordinances Therein Named," *Ordinances and By-Laws . . . 1857,* pp. 172–77.

30. *City Council Minutes,* January 13, 1857; May 18, 1859; and City of Cincinnati, "An Ordinance Supplementary to an Ordinance to Provide for the Abatement of Nuisances, and to Repeat Ordinances Therein Named," passed February 13, 1856, *Ordinances and By-Laws . . . 1857,* pp. 178–79. I have not found a printing of the other ordinance.

31. The new sanitary code held practical implications. Each city patrolman received a copy of the code and, therefore, apparently knew its terms when called upon to act. The code also seemed likely to increase public compliance, for it made the legal particulars simpler to understand and simpler to follow.

32. Ohio, *An Act to Amend the Sixty-First and Seventy-Seventh Sections of the Act Entitled "An Act to Provide for the Organization of Cities and Incorporated Villages" and the Thirteenth Section of the Act Entitled "An Act to Amend the Act Entitled 'An Act to Provide for the Organization of Cities and Incorporated Villages,'"* Statutes 52 (1854), pp. 125–26. This Act provided for Cincinnati to establish a police force of about 110 men, a force much too small to protect the city from criminal activity and to devote much time to the regular enforcement of public health law.

33. Ohio, *An Act to Provide for the Registration of Births, Marriages, and Deaths, in Ohio,* Statutes 53 (1856), pp. 73–75. See also George Mendenhall, M.D., "Sanitary Reform"; "Registration Law—Sanitary Survey and Reform"; and "Registration Law," *Cincinnati Medical Observer* 1 (1856), pp. 128–29, 237–38, 376.

34. *City Council Minutes,* February 3, 1858; June 2, 1858.

35. *City Council Minutes,* June 2, 1858; August 3, 1858; *Cincinnati Daily Gazette,* June 4, 1858, p. 2; and *Cincinnati Daily Enquirer,* August 5, 1858, p. 3.

36. *Cincinnati Daily Enquirer,* August 24, 1859, p. 2; August 25, 1859, p. 2.

37. Shortly after the onset of the Civil War, it appeared as if Cincinnati might be the object of a Confederate onslaught. Council immediately declared martial law and rushed volunteers to the nearby hills of Northern Kentucky. The Confederate threat is aptly described by Chester F. Gleason, *Our Moment of Glory in the Civil War: When Cincinnati was Defended from the Hills of Northern Kentucky* (Newport, KY: Otto Publishing Co., 1972), pp. 13–66.

38. *City Council Minutes,* January 20, 1862; *Cincinnati Daily Enquirer,* October 22, 1864, p. 2. See also Select Committee of City Council, *Report on Sewers and Drainage, Presented to the City Council, July 11, 1860* (Cincinnati: Gazette Steam Print, 1860), pp. 3–8; and Ohio, *An Act Supplementary to an Act Relating to Cities of the First Class, Having a Population Exceeding Eighty Thousand Inhabitants, Passed May 5, 1860, Statutes* 58 (1861), pp. 86–88.

39. *City Council Minutes,* September 18, 1863; December 19, 1863; December 7, 1864; and Ohio, *An Act Prescribing the Rates of Taxation for State, County, Township, City, and Other Purposes, Statutes* 65 (1868), p. 195.

40. See, for example, *City Council Minutes,* July 8, 1856; July 13, 1859; *Cincinnati Daily Times,* April 10, 1856, p. 3; *Cincinnati Daily Gazette,* July 14, 1857, p. 2; January 20, 1860, p. 2; *Cincinnati Daily Enquirer,* September 1, 1860, p. 3; August 20, 1863, p. 3; and James J. Faran, *Second Annual Report of the Mayor of the City of Cincinnati, April, 1856* (Cincinnati: Daily Enquirer Steam Print, 1856), pp. 6–7.

41. See, for example, *City Council Minutes,* October 26, 1859; February 8, 1860; December 12, 1860; July 15, 1864; August 4, 1864; and December 12, 1864. See also *Cincinnati Daily Times,* July 4, 1856, p. 3; January 27, 1858, p. 3; February 10, 1860, p. 2; July 25, 1861, p. 3; February 24, 1864, p. 3;

Cincinnati Daily Gazette, April 1, 1857, p. 2; May 29, 1858, p. 2; November 26, 1860, p. 2; *Cincinnati Daily Enquirer,* November 3, 1859, p. 2; September 8, 1860, p. 2; November 4, 1863, p. 3; and *Cincinnati Daily Commercial,* August 10, 1864, p. 2.

42. *City Council Minutes,* June 2, 1856; *Cincinnati Daily Enquirer,* February 16, 1865, p. 3; March 26, 1865, p. 3; June 3, 1865, p. 2; June 18, 1865, p. 2; August 27, 1865, p. 2; *Cincinnati Daily Gazette,* February 22, 1865, p. 2; and *Cincinnati Daily Times,* July 2, 1865, p. 3; September 15, 1865, p. 3; October 4, 1865, p. 2; October 17, 1865, p. 2.

43. *Cincinnati Daily Times,* November 8, 1865, p. 3; November 13, 1865, p. 3; and *Cincinnati Daily Enquirer,* December 16, 1865, p. 2.

44. *City Council Minutes,* November 17, 1865; December 1, 1865; and *Cincinnati Daily Enquirer,* December 16, 1865, p. 2.

45. *City Council Minutes,* December 15, 1865; *Cincinnati Daily Enquirer,* December 16, 1865, p. 1.

46. *Cincinnati Daily Gazette,* December 29, 1865, p. 1.

47. *City Council Minutes,* February 9, 1866.

48. City Council of the City of Cincinnati, "An Ordinance to Establish a Street Cleaning Department and to Regulate the Same, and to Repeal Certain Parts of Ordinances Hereafter Mentioned," printed in Cincinnati Board of Health, *State Law, City Ordinances, and Code of Health Laws and Rules and Regulations of the Cincinnati Board of Health* (Cincinnati: n. p., 1867), pp. 26–30; *Cincinnati Daily Enquirer,* March 7, 1866, p. 2; March 8, 1866, p. 2; and *Cincinnati Daily Gazette,* May 18, 1866, p. 1.

49. *State Law,* pp. 26–30; *Cincinnati Daily Commercial,* April 8, 1866, p. 4; *Cincinnati Daily Enquirer,* April 27, 1866, p. 2; and *Cincinnati Daily Gazette,* May 18, 1866, p. 1.

Chapter 5

1. C. B. Hughes, "Academy of Medicine, of Cincinnati. Abstract of Proceedings and Papers. Regular Meeting May 4th, 1857," *Cincinnati Medical Observer* 2 (1857), pp. 457–58.

2. C. B. Hughes, "Academy of Medicine, of Cincinnati. Abstract of Proceedings and Papers. June 1, 1857," *Cincinnati Medical Observer* 2 (1857), p. 459.

3. Ibid., p. 460.

4. Ibid.; A. M. Johnson, "Proceedings of the Cincinnati Academy of Medicine, August 9, 1858," *Cincinnati Lancet and Observer* 1 (1858), pp. 556–62; W. T. Brown, "Milk and Its Adulterations," *Cincinnati Lancet and Observer* 1 (1858), pp. 577–87; *Cincinnati Daily Enquirer,* September 7, 1858, p. 3; and J. A. Thacker, "Proceedings of the Cincinnati Academy of Medicine, September 5, 1859," *Cincinnati Lancet and Observer* 2 (1859), pp. 597–607.

5. City of Cincinnati, "An Ordinance to Establish a Board of Health For the City of Cincinnati, and To Repeal Certain Ordinances Therein Named (passed April 2, 1858)," *Laws and Ordinances of the City of Cincinnati: Containing All Laws and Ordinances Relating to the Government of the City, Passed Since December, 1854 and Still in Force* (Cincinnati: Cincinnati Gazette Steam Print, 1859), pp. 86–92; *City Council Minutes,* March 17, 1858; April 2, 1858; and *Cincinnati Daily Times,* March 18, 1858, p. 3.

6. *Cincinnati Daily Times,* April 6, 1858, p. 3.

7. *City Council Minutes,* May 6, 1858; May 5, 1859; and May 3, 1860.

8. *City Council Minutes,* September 1, 1858; September 15, 1858; and *Cincinnati Daily Enquirer,* September 2, 1858, p. 3.

9. *Cincinnati Daily Enquirer,* November 6, 1859, p. 2. Beginning around 1860, the editor of the *Cincinnati Gazette* contacted the city's undertakers and compiled and published his own mortality statistics. See, for example, *Cincinnati Daily Gazette,* May 5, 1860, p. 2.

10. *Cincinnati Daily Times,* March 23, 1860, p. 2; R. M. Bishop, "Mayor's Annual Message," *Organization of the City Council and Annual Message of Hon. R. M. Bishop, Mayor, April 11, 1860* (Cincinnati: Gazette Steam Print, 1860), pp. 14–15.

11. See, for example, John Keith Moore, "Academy of Medicine, November 19, 1860," *Cincinnati Medical and Surgical News* 2 (1861), pp. 12-14; A. H. Baker, "Academy of Medicine, February 11, 1861 and February 18, 1861," " *Cincinnati Medi-*

cal and Surgical News 2 (1861), pp. 80–86; Baker, "Academy of Medicine, March 25, 1861," *Cincinnati Medical and Surgical News* 2 (1861), p. 124; E. B. Stevens, "Proceedings of the Cincinnati Academy of Medicine, September 9, 1861 and September 16, 1861," *Cincinnati Lancet and Observer* 4 (1861), pp. 683–97, 721–33; W. T. Brown, "Proceedings of the Cincinnati Academy of Medicine, September 23, 1861," *Cincinnati Lancet and Observer* 5 (1862), pp. 23–24; Brown, "Proceedings of the Cincinnati Academy of Medicine, March 17, 1863," *Cincinnati Lancet and Observer* 6 (1863), pp. 279–92; Brown, "Proceedings of the Cincinnati Academy of Medicine, March 23, 1863," *Cincinnati Lancet and Observer* 6 (1863), pp. 301–8; and C. P. Wilson, "Proceedings of the Cincinnati Academy of Medicine, June 24, 1864," 7 (1864), pp. 728–29.

12. W. T. Brown, "Proceedings of the Cincinnati Academy of Medicine, December 7, 1863," *Cincinnati Lancet and Observer* 7 (1864), pp. 224–25.

13. W. T. Brown, "Report of the Committee of the Cincinnati Academy of Medicine on Diarrhea and Dysentery, Dr. Carson, Chairman and Proceedings of the Society, January 11, 1864," *Cincinnati Lancet and Observer* 7 (1864), pp. 225–27.

14. Ibid.; *Cincinnati Daily Commercial*, October 4, 1864, p. 1.

15. C. P. Wilson, "Proceedings of the Cincinnati Academy of Medicine, October 10, 1864," *Cincinnati Lancet and Observer* 7 (1864), pp. 599–602; Reginald C. McGrane, *The Cincinnati Doctors' Forum* (Cincinnati: The Academy of Medicine of Cincinnati, 1957), pp. 92–93.

16. Wilson, "Proceedings," pp. 599–602.

17. *Minute Books of the Board of Trustees of the Medical College of Ohio* (housed in the University of Cincinnati, Special Collections Department, Medical History Division), July 6, 1857; *Minute Books of the Miami Medical College of Cincinnati*, July 12, 1857; and *Minute Books of the Faculty of the Medical College of Ohio*, July 17, 1857; July 24, 1857.

18. *Minute Books of the Faculty of the Medical College of Ohio*, June 24, 1857; June 26, 1857; and *Minute Books of the Board of Trustees of the Medical College of Ohio*, July 7, 1857.

19. *Minute Books of the Faculty of the Medical College of Ohio*, March 9, 1858; March 31, 1858.

20. *City Council Minutes,* June 23, 1858; *Cincinnati Medical News,* August 15, 1858, p. 1; E. B. Stevens, "A New Hospital Building," *Cincinnati Lancet and Observer* 2 (1859), pp. 741–45; and *Cincinnati Daily Times,* August 9, 1858, p. 3; August 18, 1858, p. 3.

21. *City Council Minutes,* June 23, 1858; *Cincinnati Medical News,* August 15, 1858, p. 1. This had not always been the case. Until the 1850s, the hospital provided care for the lunatics of southwestern Ohio, contracted with the United States government to treat its sick boatmen, and often housed the nonresident poor—those poor people from parts of Ohio outside the township.

22. *City Council Minutes,* November 19, 1858; and *Cincinnati Medical News,* December 11, 1858, p. 1; February 1, 1859, p. 1.

23. "Majority Report of the Standing Committee on Medical Colleges and Societies," *Appendix to the Journal of the House—Ohio General Assembly* 55 (1859), pp. 106–8; "Minority Report of the Select Committee on House Bill No. 223," *Appendix to the Journal of the House—Ohio General Assembly* 55 (1859), pp. 111–14; and *Journal of the House—Ohio General Assembly* 22 (1859), pp. 364, 479, 499.

24. *Minute Books of the Faculty of the Medical College of Ohio,* August 12, 1858; August 18, 1859; and August 28, 1859.

25. Unfortunately, the records of the Superior Court of Cincinnati no longer exist. The case, Carey *v.* the Directors of the City Infirmary of Cincinnati, is cited in a letter from M. B. Wright, Dean of the Medical College of Ohio, to Samuel Hirst, Chairman of the Special Committee of Council on the Petition of the Students of the Cincinnati College of Medicine and Surgery to Witness Hospital Practice in the Commercial Hospital, dated December 24, 1860 (housed in the City of Cincinnati—Clerk of Council Office).

26. *Minute Books of the Faculty of the Medical College of Ohio,* April 9, 1860; April 10, 1860; April 11, 1860; April 13, 1860; and April 16, 1860.

27. *Minutes Books of the Trustees of the Medical College of Ohio,* May 5, 1860; May 11, 1860; July 6, 1860; and E. B. Stevens, "The Medical College of Ohio," *Cincinnati Lancet and Observer* 3 (1860), pp. 597–600.

28. Stevens, "Medical College of Ohio," p. 600.

29. E. B. Stevens, "Summer Medical Instruction," *Cincinnati Lancet and Observer* 3 (1860), pp. 453–54.

30. The case Alexander *v.* the Directors of the City Infirmary of the City of Cincinnati is cited in M. B. Wright to S. Hirst, December 24, 1860.

31. *Minute Books of the Faculty of the Medical College of Ohio,* October 31, 1860.

32. *Minute Books of the Faculty of the Medical College of Ohio,* November 4, 1860; November 10, 1860; and November 12, 1860.

33. Ibid.; November 20, 1860; and November 21, 1860.

34. *City Council Minutes,* November 14, 1860; *Cincinnati Daily Gazette,* November 15, 1860, p. 2.

35. Ibid.; M. B. Wright to S. Hirst, December 24, 1860.

36. Samuel Hirst, Chairman, "Report of the Special Committee of Council on the Petition of the Students of the Cincinnati College of Medicine and Surgery to Witness Hospital Practice in the Commercial Hospital, January 2, 1861"; and "Communication from the Directors of the City Infirmary in Relation to the Management of the Commercial Hospital to Samuel Hirst, Chairman of the Special Committee of Council on the Petition of the Students of the Cincinnati College of Medicine and Surgery to Witness Hospital Practice in the Commercial Hospital January 2, 1861" (both housed in the City of Cincinnati—Clerk of Council Office).

37. *City Council Minutes,* January 2, 1861; *Cincinnati Daily Gazette,* January 3, 1861.

38. *Cincinnati Daily Commercial,* January 18, 1861, p. 2.

39. Ibid.; J. A. Murphy, "The Commercial Hospital of Cincinnati," *Cincinnati Lancet and Observer* 4 (1861), pp. 119–22.

40. Ohio, *An Act Regulating the Commercial Hospital of Cincinnati, Statutes* 58 (1861), pp. 151–52; J. A. Murphy, "The Commercial Hospital of Cincinnati," *Cincinnati Lancet and Observer* 4 (1861), pp. 241–42; and A. H. Baker, "Commercial Hospital," *Cincinnati Medical and Surgical News* 2 (1861), pp. 94–95.

41. *Journal of the Senate—Ohio General Assembly* 57 (1861), pp. 124, 130, 140, 166; *Journal of the House—Ohio General Assembly* 57 (1861), pp. 230, 256, 261, 288, 303.

42. *Cincinnati Daily Enquirer,* July 21, 1861, p. 2; J. A. Murphy, "City Hospital of Cincinnati," *Cincinnati Lancet and Observer* 4 (1861), pp. 555–57. The board seemed to divide up the hospital appointments so that each trustee got to place three men on the clinical staff. As a consequence, the Miamians never held all the clinical positions at the hospital. Instead, they only held about 15 of the possible 21 spots. The others were filled by graduates—not faculty members—of the Medical College of Ohio or Baker's college.

43. *City Council Minutes,* February 18, 1861; March 8, 1861; March 27, 1861; *Cincinnati Daily Commercial,* February 19, 1861, p. 2; March 12, 1861, p. 2; and *Cincinnati Daily Times,* March 13, 1861, p. 1; March 29, 1861, p. 3. The only published version of the ordinance appeared in the *Cincinnati Daily Gazette,* March 28, 1861, p. 2.

44. *City Council Minutes,* March 27, 1861; *Cincinnati Daily Gazette,* March 28, 1861; *Cincinnati Daily Commercial,* April 5, 1861, p. 2; and *Cincinnati Daily Enquirer,* June 6, 1861, p. 2.

45. *City Council Minutes,* July 17, 1861.

46. Ibid.; and *Cincinnati Daily Times,* July 15, 1861, p. 3; July 18, 1861, p. 3.

47. *City Council Minutes,* July 31, 1861; *Cincinnati Daily Enquirer,* August 1, 1861, p. 3; and *Cincinnati Daily Times,* August 1, 1861, p. 3; August 2, 1861, p. 2; August 5, 1861, p. 2.

48. *Cincinnati Daily Gazette,* August 7, 1861, p. 2; August 8, 1861, p. 1; and October 26, 1861, p. 2.

49. *Cincinnati Daily Gazette,* November 4, 1861, p. 2.

50. J. A. Murphy, "The Board of Health and Health Officer of Cincinnati," *Cincinnati Lancet and Observer* 4 (1861), p. 498.

51. *Cincinnati Daily Enquirer,* August 9, 1861, p. 2.

52. *City Council Minutes,* November 7, 1861; December 11, 1861. Much of the attention Cincinnatians paid to public health rested in their participation in the United States Sanitary Commission and the Western Sanitary Fair. See William Quentin Maxwell, *Lincoln's Fifth Wheel: The Political History of the United States Sanitary Commission* (New York: Longmans, Green 1956); *Scrapbook of the Cincinnati Great Western Sanitary Fair,* housed in the manuscript division of the Cincinnati His-

torical Society; and Charles Brandon Boynton, *History of the Great Western Sanitary Fair* (Cincinnati: C. F. Vent, 1864). For the activities of Cincinnati's doctors during the war, see Mc-Grane, *The Cincinnati Doctors' Forum.*

53. *Minute Books of the Faculty of the Medical College of Ohio,* May 30, 1865. At first, Wright received no response from the trustees. After several months, the request was issued again and, after a delay, the trustees gave their approval. See *Minute Books of the Faculty of the Medical College of Ohio,* October 13, 1865; and *Minute Books of the Board of Trustees of the Medical College of Ohio,* December 6, 1865. I have no evidence that a suit was ever filed.

54. *City Council Minutes,* July 21, 1865.

55. *City Council Minutes,* September 1, 1865; *Cincinnati Daily Enquirer,* September 2, 1865, p. 2.

56. Ibid.

57. *City Council Minutes,* November 3, 1865.

58. Ibid.; City of Cincinnati, "An Ordinance to Establish a Board of Health for the City of Cincinnati, and to Repeal Ordinances Inconsistent Herewith," William Disney, comp., *Laws and General Ordinances of the City of Cincinnati: Containing the Laws of the State, Relating to the Government of the City; All General Ordinances in Force, September 15, 1865* (Cincinnati: Robert Clark and Co., 1865), pp. 979–83. The ordinance appears in the appendix, added after the closing date.

59. Disney, *Laws,* pp. 979–83.

60. Ibid.

Chapter 6

1. *Cincinnati Daily Enquirer,* November 7, 1865, p. 2. Unfortunately, the official minutes of the health board no longer exist. The newspapers, however, closely followed the board, detailing a reporter to cover the meetings. The *Gazette* and the *Enquirer* were particularly diligent and provided the most complete coverage.

2. *Cincinnati Daily Enquirer,* November 15, 1865, p. 2; De-

cember 20, 1865, p. 1; February 7, 1866, p. 2; and *Cincinnati Daily Times,* November 22, 1865, p. 3.

3. C. P. Wilson, "Proceedings of the Cincinnati Academy of Medicine, October 30, 1865," *Cincinnati Lancet and Observer* 8 (1865), pp. 745–46; Wilson, "Proceedings of the Cincinnati Academy of Medicine, November 7, 1865," *Cincinnati Lancet and Observer* 8 (1865), pp. 749–50; W. H. McReynolds, "Proceedings of the Cincinnati Academy of Medicine, November 13, 1865," *Cincinnati Lancet and Observer* 9 (1866), pp. 77–79; McReynolds, "Proceedings of the Cincinnati Academy of Medicine, December 4, 1865," *Cincinnati Lancet and Observer* 9 (1866), pp. 230–37; and M. B. Graff, "Proceedings of the Academy of Medicine," *Cincinnati Lancet and Observer* 9 (1866), pp. 362–72. Predisposition to disease also figured prominently in the contagionist position. It seemed to explain why some exposed persons contracted disease while others did not. The notion of liability, or perhaps susceptibility, to disease provided the crucial link between these two apparently distinct theories of disease transmission. Indeed, the dependence on susceptibility as explanation reduced the problem of disease transmission and therefore of public health to preventing the citizenry from becoming liable to disease.

4. Wilson, "Proceedings . . . October 30, 1865," p. 747; McReynolds, "Proceedings . . . December 4, 1865," p. 238.

5. Wilson, "Proceedings . . . October 30, 1865," pp. 747–48, 751–52; McReynolds, "Proceedings . . . November 13, 1865," p. 97; "Proceedings . . . December 4, 1854," pp. 239–43; and "Proceedings . . . January 3, 1866," p. 304.

6. *Cincinnati Daily Gazette,* March 7, 1866, p. 1; *Cincinnati Daily Enquirer,* March 8, 1866, p. 2.

7. City of Cincinnati, "An Ordinance to Establish a Board of Health for the City of Cincinnati, and to Repeal Ordinances Inconsistent Herewith," William Disney, comp., *Laws and General Ordinances of the City of Cincinnati: Containing the Laws of the State, Relating to the Government of the City; All General Ordinances in Force, September 15, 1865* (Cincinnati: Robert Clarke and Co., 1865), pp. 979–83.

8. Directors of the City Infirmary of the City of Cincinnati, *Fourteenth Annual Report of the Directors of the City Infirmary*

of the City of Cincinnati for the Fiscal Year from March 1, 1865 to March 1, 1866 (Cincinnati: Times Steam Book and Job Print, 1866), p. 20.

9. *Cincinnati Daily Gazette,* March 7, 1866, p. 1; *Cincinnati Daily Enquirer,* March 8, 1866, p. 2; L. A. Harris, "Fourth Annual Message of the Mayor of Cincinnati to City Council," *Annual Reports of the City Departments of the City of Cincinnati for the Year Ending February 28, 1866* (Cincinnati: Times Steam Book and Job Print, 1866), pp. 15–16; and *Journal of the House—Ohio General Assembly* 62 (1866), pp. 348–49.

10. *City Council Minutes,* May 4, 1866; and *Cincinnati Daily Enquirer,* May 5, 1866, p. 2; May 6, 1866, p. 2.

11. *City Council Minutes,* May 4, 1866; *Cincinnati Daily Enquirer,* May 11, 1866, p. 2.

12. *Cincinnati Daily Gazette,* April 13, 1866, p. 2; April 17, 1866, p. 1; and April 30, 1866, p. 1.

13. *Cincinnati Daily Enquirer,* May 3, 1866, p. 2.

14. *City Council Minutes,* June 15, 1866; *Cincinnati Daily Gazette,* June 23, 1866, p. 1. The sanitary inspectors possessed all the powers of the regular policemen.

15. *Cincinnati Daily Gazette,* March 12, 1866, p. 2; April 4, 1866, p. 3; July 23, 1866, p. 1; July 24, 1866, p. 1; *Cincinnati Daily Enquirer,* April 20, 1866, p. 2; April 24, 1866, p. 2; April 27, 1866, p. 2; May 3, 1866, p. 2; July 24, 1866, p. 2; *Cincinnati Daily Commercial,* May 4, 1866, p. 5; and *Cincinnati Daily Times,* May 4, 1866, p. 3.

16. *Cincinnati Daily Gazette,* July 26, 1866, p. 2.

17. *Minute Books of the Cincinnati Chamber of Commerce and Merchant's Exchange,* August 13, 1866; August 15, 1866; *Cincinnati Daily Gazette,* August 15, 1866, p. 1; and *City Council Minutes,* August 10, 1866; August 15, 1866.

18. *Cincinnati Daily Gazette,* August 13, 1866, p. 2; August 15, 1866, p. 1.

19. *Cincinnati Daily Gazette,* August 15, 1866, p. 2; *Cincinnati Daily Enquirer,* August 17, 1866, p. 2; and *City Council Minutes,* August 15, 1866.

20. *Cincinnati Daily Enquirer,* August 18, 1866, p. 2.

21. *Cincinnati Daily Enquirer,* August 23, 1866, p. 2; August 29, 1866, p. 2.

22. The board outlined its position in an open letter to the public. See *Cincinnati Daily Enquirer,* September 4, 1866, p. 2.

23. *Cincinnati Daily Gazette,* October 3, 1866, p. 1; and *Cincinnati Daily Enquirer,* November 7, 1866, p. 2; December 5, 1866, p. 2; March 7, 1867, p. 1.

24. *City Council Minutes,* January 18, 1867.

25. *City Council Minutes,* February 15, 1867; *Cincinnati Daily Gazette,* February 16, 1867, p. 1; and Ohio, *An Act to Amend an Act Entitled "An Act Regulating the Commercial Hospital of Cincinnati," Passed March 11, 1861, Statutes* 61 (1864), p. 142.

26. *Journal of the House—Ohio General Assembly* 63 (1867), pp. 46, 143; *Cincinnati Daily Times,* March 9, 1867, p. 2; and *Cincinnati Daily Gazette,* February 18, 1867, p. 3; March 13, 1867, p. 3.

27. *Cincinnati Daily Times,* March 13, 1867, p. 2; *Cincinnati Daily Gazette,* March 14, 1867, p. 2; *Journal of the House—Ohio General Assembly* 63 (1867), pp. 207, 302, 341, 383, 406, 483; and *Journal of the Senate—Ohio General Assembly* 63 (1867), pp. 347–48, 383–84, 391, 419–20, 424.

28. Ohio, *An Act to Create a Board of Health in Any City, and to Prevent the Spread of Diseases Therein, Statutes* 64 (1867), pp. 67–68.

29. J. A. Murphy, "Health Bill," *Cincinnati Lancet and Observer* 10 (1867), pp. 243–44.

30. *Cincinnati Daily Gazette,* March 29, 1867, p. 2; *Cincinnati Daily Commercial,* April 3, 1867, p. 4.

31. *City Council Minutes,* April 8, 1867; April 19, 1867.

32. J. A. Murphy, "Health of Cincinnati," *Cincinnati Lancet and Observer* 10 (1867), pp. 287–88; and "The Board of Health," pp. 288–90; and *Cincinnati Daily Gazette,* April 23, 1867, p. 2.

33. *Cincinnati Daily Gazette,* April 23, 1867, p. 2; April 24, 1867, p. 1; and *Cincinnati Daily Commercial,* April 26, 1867, p. 8.

34. *Cincinnati Daily Gazette,* April 24, 1867, p. 1. See also Cincinnati Board of Health, *State Law, City Ordinances, and Code of Health Laws and Rules and Regulations of the Cincinnati Board of Health* (Cincinnati: n. p., 1867), pp. 10–14; and *Cincinnati Daily Enquirer,* May 29, 1867, p. 2.

35. *Cincinnati Daily Gazette,* April 24, 1867, p. 1; April 26, 1867, p. 1; May 1, 1867, p. 1; and *Cincinnati Daily Enquirer,* May 18, 1867, p. 2.

36. Ohio, *An Act to Arrest the Social Evils in Cities of the First Class, Having Over One Hundred Thousand Inhabitants, Statutes* 64 (1867), pp. 32–34.

37. Ohio, *An Act to Authorize the City Councils to Appoint Inspectors of Beef Cattle, Sheep, Hogs, Poultry, Game, Milk, Milk Cows, Fresh Meat, and Fresh Fish, Statutes* 64 (1867), pp. 46–47; *City Council Minutes,* April 19, 1867; May 17, 1867; City of Cincinnati, "An Ordinance to Establish a Board of Health for the City of Cincinnati and to Repeal Certain Other Ordinances," (passed April 19, 1867); City of Cincinnati, "An Ordinance Authorizing the Appointment of Inspectors of Beef Cattle, Sheep, Hogs, Poultry, Game, Milk, Milk Cows, Fresh Meat and Fresh Fish," (passed May 17, 1867), William Disney, comp., *Supplement, Containing the Laws and General Ordinances of the City of Cincinnati, Passed Since September 15, 1865, and in Force January 1, 1869* (Cincinnati: Gazette Book and Job Print, 1869), pp. 49–53, 127–28; and *Cincinnati Daily Commercial,* April 20, 1867, p. 4.

38. *Cincinnati Daily Gazette,* May 1, 1867, p. 1; June 12, 1867, p. 1; June 13, 1867, p. 2; and *Cincinnati Daily Enquirer,* May 11, 1867, p. 1; May 14, 1867, p. 1.

39. *Cincinnati Daily Gazette,* June 12, 1867, p. 1.

40. See, for example, *Cincinnati Daily Gazette,* June 15, 1867, p. 1; June 26, 1867, p. 1; July 8, 1867, p. 1; July 17, 1867, p. 1; July 31, 1867, p. 1; August 21, 1867, p. 1; September 11, 1867, p. 2; September 18, 1867, p. 1; and October 16, 1867, p. 1.

41. See, for example, *Cincinnati Daily Gazette,* July 3, 1867, p. 2; August 7, 1867, p. 1; October 2, 1867, p. 1; and *Cincinnati Daily Enquirer,* May 29, 1867, p. 2; June 5, 1867, p. 2.

42. *Cincinnati Daily Gazette,* August 7, 1867, p. 1; September 11, 1867, p. 1.

43. *Cincinnati Daily Gazette,* July 3, 1867, p. 1; July 24, 1867, p. 1; and William C. Clendenin, M.D., "First Annual Report of the Health Officer," *Annual Reports of the City Departments of the City of Cincinnati for the Year Ending February*

28, 1868 (Cincinnati: Gazette Steam and Job Print, 1868), pp. 454–55.

44. Clendenin, "First Annual Report," p. 452. The sanitary squad was required to file a written report with the health officer for each nuisance they uncovered.

45. *Cincinnati Daily Gazette,* October 16, 1867, p. 1; October 23, 1867, p. 1; and Clendenin, "First Annual Report," pp. 461–62.

46. *Cincinnati Daily Gazette,* April 13, 1867, p. 2.

47. Cincinnati Board of Health, "Milk Inspector's Report," *Third Annual Report of the Cincinnati Board of Health For the Year Ending February 28, 1870,* (Cincinnati: Daily Enquirer Steam Print, 1870), pp. 15–19; Cincinnati Board of Health, "General Review of the Proceedings of the Board from March 1, 1868 to February 28, 1869—Second Annual Report," *Annual Reports of the City Departments of the City of Cincinnati For the Year Ending February 28, 1869* (Cincinnati: Daily Enquirer Steam Print, 1869), p. 461; and Cincinnati Board of Health, "General Review of the Proceedings of the Board From March 1, 1869 to February 28, 1870," *Third Annual Report,* pp. 6–7.

Coda

1. Cincinnati Department of Health, "Health Officer's Report," City of Cincinnati, *Annual Reports of the City Departments of the City of Cincinnati For the Year Ending December 31, 1877* (Cincinnati: Cincinnati Gazette Co., 1878), p. 969.

2. *Cincinnati Daily Gazette,* March 3, 1876, p. 2; March 19, 1876, p. 4; *Cincinnati Daily Enquirer,* January 24, 1880, p. 4; January 27, 1880, p. 4; February 13, 1880, p. 4; and Ohio, *An Act to Provide For the Establishment of a Board of Health In Cities and Incorporated Villages, Statutes* 78 (1880), pp. 116–19.

3. J. A. Thacker, M.D., "Cincinnati Board of Health," and "Cholera Bugaboo," *Cincinnati Medical News* 9, (1880), pp. 421–22, 499; *Cincinnati Daily Commercial,* April 23, 1880, p. 4; May 4, 1882, pp. 4–5; and *Cincinnati Daily Enquirer,* July 27, 1880, p. 8; July 25, 1880, p. 8; January 5, 1881, p. 7; August

22, 1881, p. 8; August 22, 1881, p. 8; August 24, 1881, p. 5; November 21, 1881, p. 4; December 14, 1881, p. 4.

4. For Tweed, see, for instance, James Parton, "The Government of New York," *North American Review* (October 1866), pp. 413–65; "Classes in Politics," *Nation* 4 (1867), pp. 519–20; Charles Nordhoff, "The Misgovernment of New York,—A Remedy Suggested," *North American Review* (October 1871), pp. 321–43; and "Municipal Politics," *Nation* 19 (1874), pp. 21–22. For Crapsey's pieces, see "The Nether Side of New York," *Galaxy* 7 (1869), pp. 383–94; 8 (1869), pp. 344–54, 519–27; 10 (1870), pp. 536–45; 11 (1871), pp. 188–97, 355–63, 401–9, 494–502, 559–67, 652–60, 827–35; 12 (1871), pp. 57–65, 171–78; and 13 (1872), pp. 315–23, 489–97. Also of interest are "Germany in New York," *Atlantic Monthly* 19 (1867), pp. 555–64; "The Bowery at Night," *Atlantic Monthly* 20 (1867), pp. 602–8; and "The Street-Cries of New York," *Atlantic Monthly* 25 (1870), pp. 199–204. For the explorations of municipal government's nature, see "The Government of Our Great Cities," *Nation* 3 (1866), pp. 312–13; "The Bottom of the Great City Difficulty," and "Municipal Government," *Nation* 13 (1871), pp. 157–59, 188–90; "Politics," *Atlantic Monthly* 29 (1872), pp. 126–28; Isaac Butts, "The Management of Cities," *Galaxy* 13 (1872), pp. 173–80; "Table-Talk," *Appleton's Journal* 7 (1872), p. 498; Dorman B. Eaton, "Municipal Government," *Journal of Social Science* 5 (1873), pp. 1–35; and Elisha Harris, "The Public Health," *North American Review* 127 (1878), pp. 444–55.

5. See, for example, John Stockton-Hough, "On the Relative Influence of City and Country Life on Morality, Health, Fecundity, Longevity, and Mortality"; C. A. Leas, "A Report Upon the Sanitary Care and Utilization of the Refuse of Cities"; and Ezra M. Hunt, "The Need of Sanitary Organization in Villages and Rural Districts," *Public Health, Reports and Papers Presented At the Meetings of the American Public Health Association in the Year 1873* (New York: Hurd and Houghton, 1875): ix–xii, 115–38, 454–58, 491–98; Kenneth Fox, *Better City Government: Innovation in American Urban Politics* (Philadelphia: Temple University Press, 1977); National Municipal League, *Proceedings of the Conference For Good City Government and the*

Annual Meeting of the National Municipal League 1 (1894), pp. 2–6 and *passim*; Department of the Interior, Census Office, *Report on the Social Statistics of Cities. Part I, The New England and Middle States* (Washington: Government Printing Office, 1886), and *Report on the Social Statistics of Cities. Part II, The Southern and Western States* (Washington: Government Printing Office, 1887); and John F. Dillon, *Treatise on the Law of Municipal Corporations* (Chicago: James Cockcroft and Co., 1872). Also of great utility is Zane L. Miller, "The Rise of the City," *Hayes Historical Journal* 3 (Spring/Fall 1980), pp. 73–84.

 *Index*